T0121189

Peasant-Citizen and Slave

Peasant-Citizen and Slave

The Foundations of Athenian Democracy

ELLEN MEIKSINS WOOD

VERSO

London · New York

First published by Verso 1988
Corrected paperback edition published 1989
© 1988 Ellen Meiksins Wood
All rights reserved

Verso
UK: 6 Meard Street, London W1V 3HR
USA: 29 West 35th Street, New York, NY 10001-2291

Verso is the imprint of New Left Books

British Library Cataloguing in Publication Data
Wood, Ellen Meiksins
  Peasant-citizen and slave: the
  foundations of Athenian democracy.
  1. Ancient Greece. Athens. Society
  I. Title
  938'.5

  ISBN 0-86091-911-0
  ISBN 13: 978-0-86091-911-7
US Library of Congress Cataloging in Publication Data
Wood, Ellen Meiksins
  Peasant-citizen and slave : the foundations of Athenian democracy
  / Ellen Meiksins Wood
  Includes index
  ISBN 0-86091-911-0
  1. Athens (Greece) politics and government.   2. Peasantry-
  Greece–Athens–Political activity–History.
  3. Slavery–Greece–Athens–History.   I. Title.
  JC79.A8W66 1989
  3233.'3'224'0938

Typeset by Leaper & Gard Ltd, Bristol, England
Printed in Finland by Werner Söderström Oy

For Neal

Contents

Preface

Acknowledgements have become so much a matter of routine that it seems necessary to insist that these expressions of thanks are more than just a ritual. I owe a continuing debt to Neal Wood, not simply for his support and advice on this single piece of work but for the years of discussion, joint teaching and co-authorship which have been absorbed in it. Perry Anderson deserves my very particular gratitude for the characteristic generosity with which he has subjected my work to painstaking and constructive criticism, in an effort to strengthen arguments with which he often profoundly disagrees. My thanks also to Professor Ernst Badian, whom I have never met but who, as editor of the *American Journal of Ancient History* – which published the article ('Agricultural Slavery in Classical Athens'; *AJAH* 8:1 [1983], 1986) that forms the basis of Chapter II – was unfailingly courteous and generous in his editorial and scholarly help. Since he has been so kind in his encouragement of my incursions into the field of ancient history, I very much hope that this book will not outrage or disappoint him. To my colleague at Glendon College, Walter Beringer, my thanks both for his own suggestive work on early Greece and for our brief but fruitful exchange of letters – in which he did the giving and I the receiving – on the concept of freedom. I also owe thanks to the two publisher's readers, neither of whom I have met but from whose work I have gained a great deal and whose reports proved exceedingly useful to me – though the results may not seem to them commensurate with their efforts. Robin Osborne was especially helpful in his criticisms and suggestions, and if any gaffes have escaped his careful reading, they are undoubtedly the result of my stubborn refusal to take good advice. The other reader, Professor S.C. Humphreys, raised a few objections to my argument, at least some of which I hope I have now met; but if I have failed, neither she nor any of my other advisers and critics can be held responsible. Finally, I wish to express my gratitude to the staff at Verso, especially for tolerating my anxieties; and to Glendon College, York University, for the faculty fellowship which helped me to complete work on this book.

Unavoidably, there have been additions to the relevant literature since work on this book was completed, and I shall simply have to live with the regrets occasioned by my failure to get them in time. There is one book, however, which I really must mention, the one major scholarly study of Athenian democracy to reach me in this dangerous period between completion and publication: Martin Ostwald's *From Popular Sovereignty to the Sovereignty of Law: Law, Society and Politics in Fifth-Century Athens* (Berkeley and Los Angeles: University of California Press, 1986). The easiest thing to say is that this book (to my enormous relief) neither renders mine redundant – since it examines the democracy in a very different aspect – nor does it conflict with my own account; but I very much wish that it had been ready to hand as I was writing my book. Although I did not set out to trace the institutional development of Athenian democracy (just as Ostwald did not intend to explore its social foundations), my understanding of popular power in Athens would have been greatly enriched by his analysis of the process by which popular sovereignty was established, from the first stages of legislative control, to 'the most far-reaching popular control of the administration of justice the world has ever known' (p. 69), and finally the subordination of popular sovereignty to the sovereignty of law when the democracy was restored after the oligarchic coup of 404/3. Certainly my remarks concerning the effects of the democracy on Greek culture would have gained much from Ostwald's discussion of popular sovereignty and social thought: for example, he elaborates his earlier study of *nomos*, demonstrating how changes in that concept – and its increasing association with a notion of *enactment*, a beginning in time brought about by human intervention – expressed a 'general trend in the fifth century to assign mortals a higher degree of control over their world … reflected in the specific attribution to human initiative not only of the laws by which society is governed politically but also of its customs, behavioral norms, and, to a more limited extent, religious practices. Norms, which before Cleisthenes were thought of as having existed from time immemorial, now came to be regarded as having been enacted and as being enforceable in a way similar to that in which statutes are decided by a legislative agency' (p. 93). I wish I had said that.

E.M.W.

Introduction

This book represents, among other things, an attack on conventional wisdom, but it is a conventional wisdom whose logic permeates scholarly studies. Just the other day, I came across a statement in the *Guardian* which illustrates to perfection the kind of misconception I have in mind and its wide-ranging effects. In an article on 'anti-racist' maths ('The Unknown Quantity', Tuesday, 3 November 1987) a senior lecturer at a London polytechnic was explaining the proposition that 'maths is as much a social invention as any other form of knowledge'. So far so good. The interviewer raised the inevitable objection. Isn't the Pythagorean theorem (for example) value-free and culturally neutral? 'The difference between Greek and Babylonian maths', came the reply, 'is that the Greeks brought in abstractions because they were a slave society, work was beneath them whereas the Babylonians did work and their maths were related to their working, practical lives. The great advance in Greek maths was because of certain social values.'

Now I have no objection in principle to the notion that maths, like other forms of knowledge, is a cultural artifact (a proposition which, it apparently needs to be said, does not imply that mathematical theorems are false, whatever their provenance). But this interpretation of Greek maths is simply nonsense. It is, however, a nonsense which itself represents a significant cultural artifact, constructed out of historical misconceptions that have become part of Western Culture.

Greece was certainly a 'slave society' (though to what extent that description already applied to the time of Pythagoras in the sixth century BC is another question), but it is equally true that chattel slavery in Greece had as its corollary a citizen population of working peasants and craftsmen. Poleis whose citizens were most completely spared the necessity, even the right, of working for a living tended to be

1

those in which other forms of dependent labour predominated over chattel slavery – the helots of Sparta, the 'serfs' of the Cretan cities or Thessaly. In the most notable 'slave society' of ancient Greece, classical Athens, the majority of citizens laboured for a livelihood. The difference between these particular Greeks and the Babylonians was certainly not that Athenians regarded labour as 'beneath them' while Babylonians worked, but, on the contrary, that labouring Athenians were full citizens while Babylonian workers were not.

The unique status accorded by Greek democracy to people who worked for a living was the culmination of a historical process which also produced a distinctive cultural legacy – the kind of pride in the 'practical arts' which even before the democracy encouraged Greek craftsmen to sign their work (in sharp contrast to the anonymity of their counterparts in the ancient Near East) and which inspired dramatists like Aeschylus and Sophocles to glorify the practical arts as the foundation of civilized life. (It is, incidentally, worth noting that mathematics was lumped together among these arts with very practical activities like farming, carpentry and navigation.)

But these developments also produced an oppositional culture. In fact, some of the most notable achievements of Greek civilization – such as the philosophy of Plato – belong to this reaction, the reaction of people who did indeed regard labour with contempt, against the political status of labouring citizens. These developments, of course, came to fruition long after Pythagoras produced his famous theorem, but he lived at a time when conservatives – like the poet Theognis – were already expressing their unease at social and political pressures from below. If the Pythagorean theorem reflects 'certain social values', it may belong to this conservative tradition. At least, Pythagorean principles, the essence of which is the concept of 'proportionate equality' and the harmonious unity of unequal parts, whether expressed in the proportions of the right-angled triangle or in the ratios of a musical scale, were later consciously deployed in theory and practice by disciples of Pythagoras (like Archytas of Tarentum) as defences of inequality against democratic egalitarianism. Similar abstractions expressing the principle of order in inequality were adopted by Plato to challenge the Athenian democracy.

It might be very tempting, then, to argue almost the reverse of the view expressed by the *Guardian*'s expert: that (some) Greeks 'brought in abstractions' because their compatriots showed *too much* respect for work. At least this explanation accords better with the known facts of Greek history. But whatever the explanation for this particular cultural product, it needs to be said that the attempt to associate Pythagorean mathematics with slavery is symptomatic of a much more general tendency to attribute the patterns of Greek culture to the institution of slavery and to a disdain for labour which is supposed to have been associated with it.

Curiously, this tendency is not confined to non-specialists who proceed from a faulty conventional wisdom. While disputes still rage about the extent and function of slavery, scholarly opinion is all but unanimous in the view that many Greek citizens, and more particularly the majority in the most culturally vigorous polis, Athens, worked for a living as peasants, craftsmen, and even casual labourers. Yet this labouring citizenry, which has no known precedent and arguably no later parallel, has somehow never achieved quite the same status as a 'distinctive', 'essential', or 'determinative' feature which has so often been accorded to slavery in the explanation of Greek culture. To some extent, this has been true simply by default, since probably the most common alternative to the association of Greek culture with the ideology of slavery has been a detachment of Greek political and intellectual history from *any* social roots. At any rate, it seems to me that there remains an imbalance between the growing body of knowledge about Greek economic and social history and the accounts that have been given of Greek political and cultural development. My object is to offer some suggestions as to how this imbalance may have occurred, and, above all, to make a contribution toward its correction – first, in Chapter I, by tracing the myth of the idle Athenian citizenry to its ideological roots in the historiography of the late eighteenth and nineteenth centuries; and then in subsequent chapters, by reconsidering the roles of slaves and labouring citizens, especially peasant-farmers, in the evolution of Athenian democracy and its culture.

The book is, then, intended for more than one audience. It ought to be possible to address several audiences without cheating any one of them, and I have tried to write the book in such a way that it has something worth the attention of specialists while capable of capturing the interest of the 'intelligent general reader'. Inevitably, there will be some imbalances. I am aware, for example, that there is a difference in tone and style between Chapter II which began as an article for a 'refereed' journal and is more replete with scholarly apparatus and reference to primary sources, and other chapters which proceed in a more interpretative vein. It seemed to me appropriate to leave that chapter as it was, and even to expand it along similar lines, because it deals with some of the more highly contentious issues around which much of my argument revolves. I hope – and believe – that this will not detract from its appeal to the general reader. At the same time, the interpretative character of other chapters, if I have succeeded in what I set out to do, ought not to disqualify them from the specialist's respect.

I hope – and believe – that I have made something new of old evidence.

So this is neither a specialist monograph nor a general textbook. Nor does it pretend to an exhaustive coverage of Athenian democracy, its narrative history or its political procedures. Specialists will know more than enough about all that, as will many non-specialists; and others can refer to the many excellent general studies, some of which I cite. This study should stand on its own as an exploration of some distinctive features of Athenian democracy – and especially the 'peasant-citizen' – whose distinctiveness explains much else.

I am very conscious that in my effort to give due weight to the unique position of the labouring citizen in Athens I have a tendency to lapse into rhapsody. I have tried to stave this off by keeping in mind the less attractive features of Athenian life which are every bit as integral to it – slavery (about which I have quite a lot to say), the position of women, or the simple fact that life for the ordinary Athenian citizen was surely always hard and for many pretty miserable. But in case I have sometimes failed to keep my enthusiasm in check, perhaps it needs to be said explicitly that, while I make no apology for being impressed by much that is good in Athenian democracy, I have no intention of downplaying the evils of slavery (even if I think there are some things about this institution that must be reassessed, as I have tried to do) or the subordination of women and their exclusion from citizenship (even if Greece is regrettably far from distinctive in this respect, and even if what I have to add to the growing literature on this subject is very modest indeed).

One more thing. Perceptions of ancient Greek history have, as I argue in Chapter I, been deeply coloured by political commitments and controversies which have had as much to do with the historian's contemporary world as with the history of ancient Greece. I do not regard such political motivations as unavoidably disabling; they need not, though they can, distort the picture. Nor is there anything rigidly predictable about the outcomes of such commitments. For example, the tendency to neglect or underestimate those aspects of Greek history which seem to me so important has been motivated by commitments from both ends of the political spectrum – from the right, because there is a resistance to 'history from below' or to placing the labouring poor in the vanguard of history; and from the left (indeed from political locations very close to my own) because slavery, and increasingly also the subordination of women, seem to overshadow everything else. In any case, I freely acknowledge that my own enthusiasm for the subject of this book is inseparably both political and scholarly. Readers will have to judge for themselves, as I have judged other historians, whether my extra-scholarly commitments have distorted my historical perceptions.

The Myth of the Idle Mob

Before the Myth: Athens, the Industrious 'Mechanic Commonwealth'

In *The Spirit of the Laws*, published in 1748, Montesquieu wrote a brief analysis of slavery which was to become perhaps 'the most influential intellectual attack on slavery written in the eighteenth century'.[1] In his discussion there is much about ancient Rome, but, curiously, Athenian slavery recedes into the background. He even tells us that slavery is contrary to the spirit of the democratic constitution.[2] Montesquieu was certainly aware that slavery existed on a massive scale in Athens – indeed, like many others, he seems to have grossly overestimated the number of Athenian slaves; but for him the essence of Athenian democracy was that Athenian citizens laboured for their livelihood, in contrast to Sparta, whose citizens were 'obliged to be idle'.[3] When he outlines the institutions of ancient Greece and maintains that the Greeks in general held labour in contempt, regarding both industry and agriculture as servile occupations to be practised only by people excluded from the rights and freedoms of citizenship, he exempts the democracies – or at least some of them – from these generalizations. 'It was only by the corruption of some democracies that artisans became freemen,' he writes, and 'True it is that agriculture was not everywhere exercised by slaves: on the contrary, Aristotle observes the best republics were those in which citizens themselves tilled the land: but this was brought about by the corruption of the ancient governments which had become democratic: for in earlier times the cities of Greece were subject to aristocratic government.'[4] Montesquieu's principal examples of servile labour in Greece are drawn not from Athenian slavery, but from the helotage of Sparta or the serfdoms of Crete and Thessaly. Athenian democracy, however much

5

admired, is treated as *exceptional*, a 'corruption' of the Greek ideal type, to the extent that citizens engaged in the daily labour of craftsmanship and agriculture instead of leaving such tasks to a servile population. It was precisely the love of industry and labour – which, according to Montesquieu, the laws of Solon were intended to instill in the citizen body – that made Athens a model of the 'well-regulated democracy'.[5]

Some decades later, there appeared a very different assessment of the relation between democracy and slavery in ancient Greece, by a great admirer of Montesquieu and one whose account of classical antiquity is otherwise profoundly influenced by *The Spirit of the Laws*. In *The Philosophy of History*, a compilation of lectures delivered between 1822 and 1831, Hegel cites with approval Montesquieu's contention that '*virtue* is the basis of Democracy'.[6] He nevertheless goes on to observe that slavery

> was a necessary condition of an aesthetic democracy, where it was the right and duty of every citizen to deliver or to listen to orations respecting the management of the State in the place of public assembly, to take part in the exercises of the Gymnasia, and to join in the celebration of festivals. It was a necessary condition of such occupations, that the citizens should be freed from handicraft occupations; consequently, that what among us is performed by free citizens – the work of daily life – should be done by slaves.[7]

Neither Montesquieu nor Hegel was a historian whose primary concern was with fact or detail. In their different ways both were interested in penetrating to the essence or 'spirit' of various social and cultural types. It is, therefore, difficult to tell whether their very divergent evaluations of Athenian democracy were based on disagreements of fact or disparities of historical knowledge, or whether they were simply extracting different essences from the same set of facts. Still, the contrast is striking, and the transition from a view of the democracy as grounded in the labour of its citizens to one in which the essential condition of the democracy's existence is a citizenry not engaged in 'the work of daily life' is something that requires explanation. An explanation seems all the more necessary when one considers that, although Montesquieu's version was more nearly right, if not in its relegation of slavery to the periphery of Athenian life, certainly in its insistence on a labouring citizenry, it is nevertheless Hegel's view which more closely approximates what was long to be the conventional wisdom: that Athenian democracy, for better or worse, was characterized by a leisured citizen body which depended for the material conditions of its daily life on the labour of slaves.

It is not often that the accessibility of historical information, or even its availability to conventional wisdom, regresses instead of advancing. If, as no ancient historian today is likely to deny, the majority of Athenian citizens laboured for a livelihood, in craft production as well as in agriculture, and if this fact was not so obscure as to be invisible to an educated amateur like Montesquieu in the first half of the eighteenth century, how did it happen that an equally or better educated amateur like Hegel, several decades later, could neglect this simple historical truth (or, at least, this overwhelming historical probability)? How did the myth of the idle mob not only find its way into conventional wisdom but even (as will be argued in what follows) establish the framework of debate among scholars and specialists?

It must be emphasized that the issue here is not whether and how views on the magnitude of Athenian slavery were transformed. Those who bothered to mention slavery at all in eighteenth-century accounts of classical antiquity were not inclined to underestimate the size of the slave population in Athens or the prominence of slavery in Athenian social life. If anything, the quantitative significance of slavery was likely to be exaggerated, as in the case of Montesquieu. And even when Athens, or democracy in principle, was treated as an exception to the general rule concerning the exclusion of citizens from 'servile' occupations, the extent of Athenian slavery was taken for granted and its role in social life even overestimated. The critical development occurred in the evaluation of the part played by *citizens* in the democracy.

Before the late eighteenth century, characterizations of Athenian democracy, if they made reference to the status of labour at all, would have stressed the predominance of the 'banausic' classes within the citizen body, as against aristocracies or oligarchies in which 'base mechanics' were excluded from citizenship and even farming was likely to be reserved for helots or other servile elements. So, for example, James Harrington, writing in the seventeenth century, classifies Athens among 'such commonwealths as are or come nearest to mechanic', in contrast to Sparta, where the ruling population 'neither exercised any trade nor laboured their lands or lots, which was done by their helots'.[8] The Spartan citizenry as a whole constituted a nobility, according to the definition borrowed by Harrington from Machiavelli: 'that they are such as live upon their own revenues in plenty, without engagement either unto the tilling of their lands or other work for their livelihood', while in Athens the nobility was subordinated to the people, the 'mechanic' multitude.

Similarly, in 1767 Adam Ferguson numbered Athens among those Greek states in which, though slavery existed, the benefits derived by the free from this cruel institution 'were not conferred equally on all the citizens. Wealth being unequally divided, the rich alone were exempted from labour; the poor were reduced to work for their own subsistence.'[9] As a critic of the democracy, Ferguson located one of its chief disadvantages in the fact that 'mechanics' were admitted to the public councils; for 'How can he who has confined his views to his own subsistence or preservation, be intrusted with the conduct of nations? Such men, when admitted to deliberate on matters of state, bring to its councils confusion and tumult, or servility and corruption; and seldom suffer it to repose from ruinous factions, or the effect of resolutions ill formed or ill conducted.'[10] In this respect, Ferguson follows ancient critics like Plato, Xenophon, and Aristotle in their characterization of Athenian democracy.

At first glance, Adam Smith, both in the *Lectures on Jurisprudence* and in *The Wealth of Nations* may seem to depart from these characterizations of Athenian society when he suggests that 'the great body of the people were in effect excluded from all trades which are now commonly exercised by the lower sorts of the inhabitants of towns. Such trades were, at Athens and Rome, all occupied by the slaves of the rich ...'[11] Smith argues that poor free men could not compete with slaves in the market for labour, and also that the relegation of these trades to slaves impeded technical innovation, since slaves 'are very seldom inventive'. All these arguments were to be taken up later by writers heavily influenced by the myth of the idle mob, and especially Marxists, beginning with Friedrich Engels. Nevertheless, it is not clear that Smith's account is intended to diverge from the facts as presented by his friend, Adam Ferguson. Smith does not take issue with the proposition that the majority of Athenian citizens laboured for a livelihood. He simply assumes that, since the ancients honoured agriculture more than manufacture or trade, even in those states where there was no prohibition against the practice of dishonourable trades by citizens (as there was in Sparta, and Thebes, but not in Athens), these activities were generally discouraged, and to the extent that they existed, tended to be taken over by slaves.

It is also perhaps important that Smith is here simply concerned with the distinction between agriculture and trade or manufacture, while Ferguson is dealing with the distinction between 'liberal' and 'mechanical' employments. The critical difference for Ferguson does not lie in the nature of the activities themselves so much as in whether they are conducted for the purpose of 'mere subsistence'. In this respect, farm labour, no less than manufacture or trade, as labour for a livelihood, may be 'sordid' and driven by necessity or 'interest'. In 'polished society, [man's] desire to avoid the character of sordid, makes him conceal his regard for what relates merely to his preservation or his livelihood. In his estimation, the beggar, who depends upon charity; the labourer, who toils that he may eat; the mechanic, whose art requires no exertion of genius, are degraded by the object they pursue, and by the means they employ to attain it.' In the ancient republics, citizens strove to attain the position of freedom, the essence of which was to rise above mere subsistence, necessity, and interest, and 'to take that part in society, to which they are led by the sentiments of the heart, or by the calls of the public'.[12] In some states, however, since the benefits of slavery 'were not conferred equally' and 'the poor were reduced to work for their subsistence', this aspiration to freedom could not be realized by the majority of citizens. There is nothing in Smith's analysis that contradicts this account of the facts, nothing to suggest that Athenian citizens lived a life of leisure and politics while slaves carried on 'the work of daily life'.

In the ensuing century, there developed a tendency to overestimate the importance of manufacture and trade in classical Athens – a tendency very visible in Engels – and to read back into Greek history a kind of bourgeoisie in embryo, despite the fact that Athens remained a fundamentally agrarian society throughout our period. This view of 'bourgeois Athens', when coupled with the conviction that the Athenians held artisanal labour in contempt and in practice relegated it to slaves, might have the effect of exaggerating the importance of slavery in production by placing 'manufactories', owned by the Athenian 'bourgeoisie' and manned by slaves, at the centre of the Athenian economy. How this perception evolved, in the face of all the evidence which suggests that there were very few large 'manufactories', and how Athens came to be thought of as a 'bourgeois' trading nation when the evidence suggests that production for exchange was limited even at the height of Athenian prosperity, remains obscure; but the explanation probably lies in a more general disposition, not uncommon in the nineteenth century, to read the 'bourgeois' experience into all history and even into nature itself.

Until the late eighteenth century, then, there is a significant continuity from Plato or Aristotle's hostile view of Athens' 'mechanic' democracy to the later, sometimes more favourable, assessments of the democracy and its foundation in the 'labour and industry' of its citizens – a continuity which is visibly broken in Hegel's account. The change cannot, of course, be attributed simply to a new awareness of slavery, since, as we have seen in the case of Montesquieu, the 'labouring and industrious' multitude was not incompatible with even the most inflated estimate of slave numbers – and certainly a Greek commentator like Aristotle cannot be accused of failing to notice the dimensions of Athenian slavery. On the contrary, it can be argued that the myth of the idle mob came first, that indeed it was only much later that scholars began to take a systematic interest in slavery[13] (when they did, the tendency was rather to revise the estimates of slave numbers downward), and above all, that – leaving aside the question of numbers – the interpretation of slavery's role in the democracy tended to be coloured, directly or indirectly, by the myth of the idle mob. This myth is arguably at the root of at least one major tradition, the view that slavery constituted the productive base of Athenian democracy, or, in a familiar Marxist formulation, that Athens exemplifies the 'slave mode of production'. But even among scholars who reject such propositions, the myth of the idle mob has set the agenda of debate concerning slavery.

The Turning-Point: Mitford and the Idle, Turbulent Multitude

The history of British scholarship in the late eighteenth and early nineteenth centuries illustrates the point most sharply. Although Britain was not – with one or two notable exceptions, such as Richard Bentley – in the forefront of classical scholarship in eighteenth-century Europe, it did produce the first major modern narrative and political histories of ancient Greece, while Continental scholars – and particularly the Germans – were preoccupied with literary and philological studies. It is in these British political histories that Athenian democracy, and the status of labour within it, become a central issue of intellectual debate. The particular way in which the issue of Athenian democracy captured the attention of British intellectuals tells us a great deal about how the myth of the idle mob emerged. The immediate and explicit motivation for these first political histories of Greece was not disinterested scholarship but partisan politics. John Gillies' *The History of Ancient Greece*, published in 1786, and William Mitford's *The History of Greece*, the first volume of which appeared in 1784 and the last in 1810 – the first major works of their kind – were intended as interventions in a contemporary political debate. The critical point is that these interventions were unequivocally on the side of conservative forces against democracy and against even milder forms of parliamentary reform. The direction taken thereafter by historiography on ancient Greece cannot be adequately understood without a recognition of its roots in anti-democratic politics.

That democracy should become a live and pressing issue at just this moment is hardly an accident. While for Montesquieu the question of democracy could remain a matter of abstract speculation with no immediate prospect of practical consequences, the events of the late eighteenth century had put the question much more urgently on the political agenda. The new interest in the politics of ancient Athens coincided with the revolutionary outbreaks of the age and inspired particularly those who were most horrified by these revolutionary developments. As Frank Turner has written in his admirable study of *The Greek Heritage in Victorian Britain*,

> during the last quarter of the century the American Revolution, the radical movement for reform in Parliament, and later the French Revolution awakened a new interest in the Athenian experience on the part of defenders of the political status quo. During those years *democracy* or genuine *republicanism* could denote no existing European polity. Consequently, when the American colonies began to form a government without a monarch, it was not unnatural for some writers to look to the classical Greek republics for indications of what the future might hold for the Americans. In 1778 John Gillies warned that if any people should ignore the unhappy history of Greece and, 'disdaining to continue happy subjects of the country under whose protection they have so long flourished, would set on foot a republican confederacy, let them tremble at the prospect of those calamities, which, should their designs be carried into execution, they must both inflict and suffer'. Three years later Josiah Tucker, the irascible dean of Bristol, with both the Americans and their British supporters in mind, attacked the Lockean concept of government by compact and consent in hope of rousing in 'every true Friend to Liberty an Abhorrence of the Idea of an Athenian Common-Wealth'. In 1797 Gillies voiced a similar warning against government based on consent in his introduction to Aristotle's *Politics*. In this manner there emerged a conservative polemical strategy of portraying the ends of the American revolt and of the Yorkshire Association reform movement as democratic in character and then decrying democracy through enumeration of the disasters and crimes of Athens. This conservative response to the revolutions of the later eighteenth century provided the occasion for the first major English narrative history of Greece.[14]

This milestone was the work of William Mitford, not a scholar but a Tory country gentleman whose history, for all its defects of scholarship and style, was nevertheless destined to exercise a tremendous influence on historiography for many years to come. Although Gillies published a history of Greece two years after Mitford's first volume appeared (as royal historiographer for Scotland, Gillies told his royal patron in the dedication that his purpose was to reveal the evils of democracy and the benefits of monarchy), it was Mitford's history which 'held the field essentially unchallenged for almost half a century'; and as a result, his 'concept of the Greek political experience directly or indirectly influenced every history of Greece written in English for over one hundred years'.[15] It may be supposed that, since the political and social history of Greece continued for a long time to be generally neglected by Continental scholars, the influence of Mitford's history probably extended beyond the shores of Britain, if only by default and perhaps through the indirect medium of the more distinguished British writers on whom he had left his mark.[16]

Mitford's *History of Greece* provides a striking illustration of the back-handed way in which an interest in slavery established itself among historians of ancient Greece. There is in his study no systematic or extended consideration of that institution, nor is it in any way a central concern of his work. Nonetheless, he regards slavery as necessary to the democracy: the productive labour of slaves was an essential condition for the leisure which permitted citizens to engage in political activities. Yet this association of democracy with slavery is not unambiguous and is distorted by his undisguised hatred of democracy.

Mitford's *History* abounds in denunciations of the 'avarice', 'licentiousness', 'ambition', and 'tyranny', the constant desire for 'amusement' and 'gratification' which were, according to him, the principal motivations of the Athenian people in their public dealings. In his eyes, democratic institutions become simply a matter of 'flattery', 'bribery', 'gratification' of the mob; public payments to allow the poor to participate in meetings of the assembly are interpreted as the use of public funds for private purposes, the satisfaction of personal greed. The following typical passage is especially striking because it refers to an episode which even Plato, otherwise such a stringent critic of the democracy, singles out for praise. Mitford's judgment contrasts sharply with Plato's (at least in the *Seventh Epistle* which is usually attributed to him) on the moderation of the democrats in their dealings with oligarchic conspirators after the two oligarchic coups of the late fifth century BC and after the Thirty Tyrants' reign of terror:

> But, since the restoration of democracy, the people, frantic with the wild joy of recovered power, and not less mad with jealousy of superior men, were more than ever dupes to the arts of designing orators; and, like a weak and fickle tyrant, whose passion is his only law, tho no single tyrant can really be so lawless, were led as the flattery, or the stimulation, mostly in consonance with the passion of the moment, pointed the way.[17]

The primary lesson that Mitford expects his readers to learn from the 'political institute' of Greek history is 'that democracy, with the pretence of an establishment proposing nothing but the equal welfare of the people, is, beyond all others, a constitution for profligate adventurers, in various ways, to profit from, at the people's expense'.[18] He makes no attempt to disguise that this lesson is intended to have very immediate and local political implications; and when the French

Revolution intervenes, as if to confirm his worst fears and substantiate his dire warnings, he interrupts his narrative to comment on recent events and on the differences between the French and English constitutions, explicating them in the light of Greek history:

But while, under the security of our own admirable constitution, we wonder at the defective polity of a people whom we find so many causes to admire, it is not a little advantageous, for the writer of a Grecian history, that circumstances have been occurring, in a nation calling itself the most polished of the most polished age of the world, which not only render all the atrocious, and therefore scarcely credible, violence of faction among the Greeks, probable, but almost make them appear moderate. At the same time it may not be digressing improperly to remark that, as what has been passing in France may tend to illustrate Grecian history, and to exculpate the Grecian character from any innate atrocity, beyond what is common among other nations, there occurs also, in Grecian history, what may inable to form a juster estimate of the French character, than a view of the late enormities, compared only with what has at any time passed in our own country, might lead us to conceive ...

For, so many men of the brightest talents and highest acquirements, as in Greece turned their thoughts, with the closest attention, to a subject so universally and deeply interesting, not one seems to have been able to imagine a form of government which might, in a great nation reconcile the jarring pretensions arising from that variety of rank among men, without which even small societies cannot subsist. Our own writers ... have very much overlooked what, in importance, is perhaps not inferior to any one circumstance in the singular constitution of our government ... that nowhere else in the world, such harmony subsists, between the several ranks of citizenry, as in England.

This harmony is indeed the foundation, the firm foundation, on which the proud superstructure of the British constitution rests. Ranks vary, as much, or perhaps more than elsewhere. But no rank has that gigantic preeminence, which can inable it to trample upon its next inferior. In the scale of subordination, the distance from top to bottom is great; but the gradation is scarcely perceptible, and the connection intimate. Each rank, moreover, is interested in the support of its next superior: none are excluded from the hope of rising: and, of all the various ranks, the highest is most interested in the support of all. We cannot consider without wonder, that an order of things, apparently the most natural, as well as the most beneficial, never subsisted in any country but our own ...

Montesquieu has undertaken to foretell the fall of the English Constitution. ... Montesquieu evidently, had not duly adverted to that peculiar amalgamation of ranks in England, through which all coalesce. ... Through this advantageous constitution, England has always avoided, and it may well be hoped will continue to avoid, that violence of internal fermentation, which continually disordered, and at length destroyed the governments of Athens and Rome, and hence she has been inabled to resist the contagion of French politics.... A Grecian history, and indeed any history perfectly written (these volumes pretend to no such merit) but especially a Grecian history perfectly written should be a political institute for all.[19]

The principal failing of Athenian democracy, then, was that it lacked any such mechanism for 'harmonizing the various ranks of men':

> the Greeks were unfortunately deficient in the more important science of framing that great machine we call a government; harmonizing the various ranks of men of which a nation must consist; providing, at the same time, security for property, and equal justice for those who have no property; establishing, for the well-disposed of every rank, an interest in the preservation of the constitution, and, for the unprincipled and turbulent, strong coercion to secure it against disturbance; reconciling the protection of private rights with the maintenance of public force, and making a general private interest in the support of the existing order of things the basis of patriotism, and the source of general concord and public spirit.[20]

It is in Mitford's elaboration of this fatal flaw in Athenian democracy that we begin to see how slavery figures in his interpretation of the democracy.

> Under circumstances then such as those of the Athenian republic, the rich and the poor evidently could not live in any harmony.... In fact, the balances of Solon's constitution were no sooner overthrown, and sovereign power become so absolute in the hands of those without property, or rather in the hands of any demagogue who could, for the moment, lead them, than the interests of all who had property placed them necessarily in the situation of conspirators against the existing government. Indeed, throughout Greece, the noble and wealthy, served by their slaves, not only as domestics, but as husbandmen and manufacturers, had little connection with the poorer Many, but to command them in oligarchical states, and in the democratical, to fear, flatter, solicit, and either deceive, or be commanded by them. No common interest, or scarcely any, united the two descriptions of men; so that, for maintaining civil order and holding the state together, flattery and bribes alone could persuade the multitude, and the only alternative was violence. Hence that impossibility of lasting harmony, and that readiness for extreme discord which the Grecian republics so strikingly exhibit.[21]

The Greek 'republics', then, and more particularly the democracies, were in constant turmoil because the 'poorer Many' were free of the need to serve the propertied few. In the absence of a relationship in which the one 'rank' laboured for the other, there could be no 'common interest' between them. It was slavery that made possible this lack of mutual dependence between the two classes. Furthermore, in Athenian democracy the poor who lacked property which would bind them to the public good and who therefore could have no 'interest' in the commonwealth, 'citizens without property, without industry, and perhaps without objects for industry', were enabled to enter the public domain and pervert the body politic because they were maintained in their 'idleness' by payment for public service.[22] Mitford's principal objections to Athenian democracy – that it lacked a mechanism for social harmony among classes and that it permitted the corrupting influence of the poor to invade the body politic – thus appear to have a common source: the 'idleness' of the 'poorer Many', sustained on the one hand by slavery and on the other by public payments.

This characterization of the democracy and the role of slavery within it seems straightforward enough; but on closer inspection, it proves to be somewhat ambiguous. Mitford is not primarily concerned with slavery but with the political status of the 'multitude', and his account of the former is shaped to the requirements of the message he wishes to convey concerning the dangers of admitting the multitude into the public councils. His account of the multitude contains a contradiction which in turn distorts the image of slavery. On the one hand, he complains of the multitude's lack of 'industry', the idleness which permits their participation in civic affairs. On the other hand, and apparently without being conscious of any contradiction, he writes of the 'imperious "crowd of fullers, shoomakers [sic], carpenters, braziers"' (quoting Xenophon) whose control of the democracy and whose oppression of men of rank and property was so intolerable that it justified the latter's 'antipathy toward the body of the lower people from whom they suffered such oppression' and even excused the crimes of the Thirty Tyrants.[23] In other words, the mass of Athenian citizens whose control of government corrupted the city was at one and the same time a mob of idle paupers and a class of labourers and craftsmen; and the democracy's corruption was at once the consequence of government by a mass of idlers and government by 'base mechanics', the 'banausic' Many who could not live on their own property and were forced to live by their own labour.

This contradiction is not uncommon among critics of the democracy, and it is perhaps not too much to say that it lies at the heart of the myth of the idle mob. It should be noted, first, that when Mitford speaks of the noble and wealthy who were served by their slaves, he makes no reference to the *idleness* of the 'poorer Many' or to the lack of industry of which he complains elsewhere. His concern here is with their *independence*. The problem is apparently not that they did not *labour*, but that they did not labour for the noble and wealthy, that they did not *serve.* And when he does speak of 'idleness' and lack of 'industry' or even 'objects of industry' among the poorer Many – who are also apparently an imperious crowd of fullers, shoemakers, carpenters, and braziers, that is, people who labour for a livelihood – he seems to have in mind a *relative* idleness, a freedom from constant toil which leaves time for political participation. In this case, then, the 'idle mob' stands for a group of people who do, indeed must, labour for their livelihood but who, partly because they are supported by public funds when they lose a day's work in the performance of public services, but perhaps even more because their time is not occupied in producing the wealth of the noble and rich, are not so driven by the exigencies and discipline of constant labour that they cannot attend juries and assemblies.

It is worth noting that Mitford does not attack democracy on the simple grounds that it was directly parasitic on slavery, in the sense that the masses of citizens lived on the labour of slaves. His principal objection to slavery in the case of ancient Greece seems to be rather that slaves, instead of free labourers, were used to produce the wealth of the few, so that a considerable number of free labourers existed who were not dependent on 'men of rank and property' and who were able to play a significant role in Athenian politics. And yet, he depicts for us an Athenian demos whose central characteristics are idleness and freedom from the discipline of necessary labour. In the end, he leaves his readers with a strong impression that the democracy rested on a leisured citizen body, differentiated not so much into a class of producers and a class of appropriators as simply into rich and poor, the latter living on public payments and both sustained by the labour of slaves. Without fundamentally changing the facts that informed the perceptions of Harrington, Montesquieu or Ferguson, Mitford has given us the idle mob; and with the idle mob necessarily comes a new evaluation of slavery and its function in sustaining the democracy. In short, we have been offered an interpretation of slavery which is dictated by the need to demonstrate that democracy cannot exist without, indeed has as its necessary conditions, evils like slavery, an idle multitude, and constant civil strife.

After Mitford

Mitford's case would be instructive even if his work had not been so influential. However other historians may have come by their conceptions of the relation between democracy and slavery, Mitford was not alone in using the idle Athenian mob as a weapon against democracy in his own time and place; and he is, if nothing else, an exemplary case in this respect. Nevertheless, although histories of classical scholarship often neglect him, no doubt on the grounds that he was not a serious or even competent scholar, it would be a mistake to underestimate his influence. As Turner has shown, that influence extended well into the nineteenth century and had its effects not only on other anti-democrats disturbed by events like the French Revolution, but also on less conservative figures like James Mill, who in the absence of an alternative prescribed Mitford's *History* to his son John Stuart.[24] Mitford's judgments of Athens were absorbed into textbooks and even into the seventh and eighth editions of the *Encyclopaedia Britannica*.[25] But the most significant effect of Mitford's work, argues Turner, was more subtle:

> So complete had been his condemnation of the character of the Athenian state and so widespread was the acceptance of his views that he had in effect also established the grounds on which the reputation of Athens would have to be restored. The civic virtues that Mitford denied Athens possessed and, by implication, that a democratic polity could possess were features of government prized by Englishmen of various political persuasions. Later liberal historians consequently had to prove that Athens and, by implication, democracy had actually achieved those virtues. Only with difficulty would the debate over the Athenian constitution escape the parameters that Mitford had set.[26]

A major casualty of this framework of debate was an adequate understanding of slavery. The distortion of this question took several forms. One particularly striking consequence was that some commentators who were concerned to defend the democracy on behalf of political reform in their own day felt obliged virtually to ignore Athenian slavery. The most notable example is George Grote, a friend of John Stuart Mill, an activist on behalf of the Reform Bill, and leader of the philosophic radicals in the House of Commons. Grote's *History of Greece* (1846–56) was, and still is, highly respected, not only in Britain but throughout Europe – so much so, for example, that, according to at least one scholar, 'All the German studies on Greek history of the last fifty years of the nineteenth century are either for or against Grote.'[27] Although Grote's history is without doubt a more serious work of scholarship than Mitford's, he was quite open about its polemical intent; and it is clearly directed against Mitford's political message. There is certainly much to admire in Grote's work, and unlike Mitford's, it can, used with care, still serve as a scholarly resource. In the present context, however, what is most remarkable about his *History* is that slavery figures in it hardly at all. Grote makes passing mention of dependent labour in Greece, though more in the context of states like Thessaly or Sparta than Athens, and leaves the thorny questions raised by Mitford concerning the relation between democracy and slavery conspicuously unexamined.

Others of Grote's political persuasion, like J.S. Mill, were unable to accept this silence but found various ways of rationalizing Athenian slavery, though without ever subjecting that institution to systematic study or seeking an alternative to Mitford's account of the association between democracy and slavery. Excuses and rationalizations became less acceptable, especially in the latter part of the nineteenth century, as the political role of the working class in British politics grew; and some liberals felt compelled to deny that Greek democracy deserved the name at all because of its dependence on slavery. But even then, such judgments were so imbued with the image created by historians like Mitford that ancient democracy could be contrasted to the modern case, which was more entitled to the name, on the grounds that the latter, unlike the former, entailed 'the dignifying of labour by the entry of labourers into the circle of citizenship'.[28] So completely had the myth of the idle mob taken hold that the 'industrious' citizen so prominently visible to Montesquieu, or Ferguson's 'mechanic' citizen, and even Mitford's 'imperious crowd' of craftsmen and labourers, not to mention Plato, Aristotle, and Xenophon's banausic citizenry, seem to have disappeared from view.

And so the history of modern British scholarship on slavery began with a paradox: an interest in, and even some condemnation of, slavery was evinced by anti-democratic historians whose main concern was to keep the poor and labouring multitude out of politics, at a time when those of more liberal inclinations were tempted to ignore or make excuses for that institution. Perhaps a certain vagueness about production in Athens had a special utility for liberals at a time when they were transforming the conception of 'democracy' itself – away from the ancient meaning of popular rule or rule by the poor, toward the 'liberal democratic' emphasis on representative institutions and civil liberties, often associated with little enthusiasm for government by and for the demos (the common people). Those who invoked Athenian democracy in support of parliamentary reform were usually less inclined to dwell on the role of the mechanic multitude in the democracy than on the individualism and variety of Athenian life, in contrast to the hidebound Toryism of Sparta. This was certainly the inclination of J.S. Mill, who in his reviews of Grote's history of Greece for the *Edinburgh Review* actually refers to the Spartans as 'those hereditary Tories and Conservatives of Greece'; and Grote himself, in his famous – certainly splendid – defence of Cleon, the 'demagogic' leader of the post-Periclean democracy, presents him less as a leader of the banausic demos than as an English liberal parliamentarian playing the combative role of a loyal Opposition.

At any rate, when, belatedly, an interest in Athenian slavery was finally sparked in those who might have been expected to lead the way, their perceptions were already deeply coloured by the views of their adversaries. It had become very difficult to dissociate the question of slavery from the myth of the idle mob – and therefore difficult to look for the significance of slavery anywhere but in the *productive base* of Athenian democracy. The easiest alternative, once the labouring citizenry had been acknowledged, was simply to deny or ignore the magnitude of slavery without relocating its function in the democracy.

Boeckh and the Political Economy of Indolence

The association of democracy and slavery as seen through the prism of contemporary politics by historians fearful of democracy in their own time and place was not peculiar to Britain. After British historians had pioneered the political history of Greece, the next major milestone in the development of Greek historiography was the first, and for a long time the only, economic history of Greece: August Boeckh's *Public Economy of Athens*. This ground-breaking work (whose author had read Mitford and Gillies), first published in 1817 and translated into English in 1842, as the only major study of its kind not only in Germany but elsewhere undoubtedly had an enormous influence and is still cited today as a classic in its genre. What is striking about this study as it concerns the question of slavery is that, despite the painstaking compilation of facts and figures which often run counter to his own conclusions, Boeckh remains wedded to the image of Athenian democracy as sustained by an idle citizenry supported by the productive labour of slaves. His book ends on the following note:

> But though they executed the most splendid works which have ever been conceived by the mind of man, their resources could not be altogether applied to such noble objects: the craving wants of the lower order of citizens also required to be satisfied: who by salaries and donatives in time of peace had become accustomed to indolence, and to the idea that the state was bound to maintain them; and as by these means the lowest persons were placed sufficiently at their ease to attend the administration of the state, the influence of the democracy was insensibly extended. Their statesmen were always endeavouring to discover some method by which the mass of the people might be enriched and supported out of the public revenues, rather than by individual industry and prudence; as the commonwealth was considered as a private possession to be enjoyed in common, the proceeds of

which were to be distributed among the members who composed the state. And yet it would appear that donatives and salaries are nowhere less necessary than for states in which slavery is established. The degradation of the greater part of the inhabitants enables those who are free to obtain their subsistence by the labour of the slaves; and it is thus that they have sufficient leisure to attend to affairs of state; whereas in countries in which slavery does not exist, the citizens having to labour for their subsistence are less able to employ themselves in the business of governments. . . .

The power of confiscating property was in the hands of wild and thoughtless demagogues, a dreadful scourge upon the rich and great; particularly if the proceeds were distributed among the people. . . . Even in the noblest races of Greece, among which the Athenians must without doubt be reckoned, depravity and moral corruption were prevalent throughout the whole people.[29]

The political message to his contemporaries is unmistakable, and is stated explicitly earlier in the work:

unless the governing power is to fall into the hands of the mob, the people should receive no pecuniary compensation for their share in government, an expense which it is impossible to defray by revenues justly raised; it is a condition requisite for good government, that all who wish to partake in the ruling power should support themselves upon their own property.[30]

For this reason, Boeckh is even more critical of public payments than of slavery in Athens. Such payments, which are consistently described as merely a means of self-enrichment and self-gratification for the masses, demonstrate that democracy is itself nothing but a scheme for self-enrichment by the greedy and selfish multitude. Thus, the democratic leaders and reformers were simply flattering and bribing the masses, while the latter supported them out of greed and indolence. Democracy was, and presumably must always be, in essence a conspiracy between avarice and power-lust.

Boeckh singles out Pericles for special condemnation:

For this statesman, finding himself unable by reason of the scantiness of his fortune to vie with other public leaders and demagogues in liberality, thought of supplying his private incapacity ... by a distribution of the public revenue, and bribed the multitude partly with the theorica, partly with the payment of dicasts, and salaries of other descriptions. . . .

The admirers of Lacedaemonian customs, who, like Plato and his master, formed a correct judgment in a moral point of view, perceived that Pericles had made his countrymen covetous and indolent, loquacious and effeminate, extravagant, vicious and unruly, by maintaining them at the public expense with donatives, salaries, and cleruchiae, and by flattering their sensuality and love of enjoyment with sumptuous festivals.[31]

Boeckh's remarks about slavery, then, occur in the context of a denunciation of democracy in principle; and it is worth noting that his misgivings about the degradation of slaves have more to do with the political opportunities afforded by slavery to the lower classes than with any general objection to the creation of leisure at the expense of another's labour. Public payments are apparently even more pernicious than slavery, in that they enable the 'lowest persons' to engage in public affairs; while those who 'support themselves upon their own property' generally do so by appropriating the labour of others who cannot – in Athens, this would mean the labour of both free men and slaves. It is, after all, the 'lower orders', and not the idle rich, who are being castigated for their leisure and dependence upon the labour of slaves.

What makes these conclusions particularly remarkable is that, notwithstanding Boeckh's stress on the indolence of the 'lower orders', much of his book, dealing with such matters as the wages of labour and the cost of living, clearly demonstrates that the 'inferior' classes of citizens were compelled to labour for their livelihood. By his own account, public payments for attendance at assemblies and jury-trials, even when they reached their highest rate, 'only served as a contribution to the support of citizens', and, when measured against the cost of living, were not sufficient to support the average citizen in idleness[32] (the more so, it must be added, as these payments were irregular and unpredictable, since only a portion of the citizenry could attend at any one time). Boeckh also spends a great deal of time discussing the wages of labour, for slaves (who could be contracted out by their masters to work for wages) and free labourers alike, even going so far as to suggest that after the Peloponnesian War – that is, during the period of worst corruption and idleness according to this own testimony – large numbers of citizens who had not been accustomed to work 'were compelled to maintain themselves by working for daily wages at any manual labour....'[33] In fact, he suggests that throughout the history of democratic Athens, 'The inferior citizens were as much reduced to the necessity of manual labour as the poor aliens and slaves.'[34] There is little here to sustain the proposition that 'the lower orders' of citizens 'obtain[ed] their subsistence by the labour of slaves' or that they were 'supported out of the public revenues, rather than by individual industry and prudence'.

We are, then, back where we were with Mitford: in the idiom of these critics of democracy, the 'indolence' or lack of industry of Athenian citizens, their dependence on the productive labour of slaves for their daily subsistence, must be read as referring simply to the fact that somehow the 'lower orders' were not so consumed by the need to labour that they were unable to participate in politics. Indeed, the myth of the idle mob has to do not with the *idleness* of the multitude but, on the contrary, with the fact that 'citizens having to labour for a livelihood' were *nevertheless* 'able to employ themselves in the business of governments'. It will be argued in subsequent chapters that there may be another explanation for the relative freedom of the labouring citizenry which does not require us to treat slavery as the productive base of Athenian democracy, or else to neglect the importance of slavery and/or underestimate its magnitude. For the moment, it is enough to say that the framework of analysis created by the opposition to democracy in general seems to have foreclosed any account of slavery which did not depend upon equating it with an idle mob. The pervasive influence of this equation – which seems to have left a far deeper impression than the historical details that contradict it – is nowhere more strikingly evident than in conventional Marxist interpretations of ancient Greek history. Despite a very different ideological standpoint and a very different evaluation of democracy in general, they appear to echo not only Boeckh's account of a citizenry living on the material production of slaves, but also his assessment of the polis as a 'private possession' treated by citizens as a means of appropriation.

Burckhardt and the Greek 'Contempt' for Labour

A common corollary of the 'idle mob' is the proposition that 'the Greeks' held labour in contempt. The Athenian attitude toward labour will be considered in greater detail in Chapter IV. All that needs to be noted now is that little, if any, evidence exists to support the claim that the Athenian population in general, including the multitude who were obliged to work for a living at various 'contemptible' occupations, felt any such contempt. What is clear is that an unmistakable disdain for 'menial' labour and for those obliged to engage in it can be found among opponents of the democracy, the gentleman-philosophers on whose writings historians have so often depended for their view of Athenian democracy. Reliance on these one-sided texts may be enough to account for the generalization that Athenian culture was characterized by a contempt for labour; but perhaps there is more to the story. The close association of this generalization with the myth of the idle mob should encourage us to look more closely at the question, especially since one of the axioms most commonly encountered in analyses of Athenian culture is that a disdain for labour was inspired by the association of labour with slavery.

There is one great historian whose interpretation of Athenian culture and its decline rests on the central proposition that the fatal flaw in Athenian society was a widespread contempt for labour, and here we may find a clue to the origin and meaning of this view. Jacob Burckhardt, in his *Griechische Kulturgeschichte*, writes that 'The chief evil was that democracy had been pervaded by the strong antibanausic attitude, and equality of right was associated with an aversion to work, as a result of which idlers used the right to vote and judicial proceedings as a permanent threat to the propertied.'[35] The demos, the common people, 'shirking labour with all their might', lacked the discipline of constant labour; and the polis declined because 'the citizens were obviously unsettled by the many popular assemblies and court sessions ... because most of them lacked the calming effect of daily work'.[36] When during the democracy the demos exploited the propertied class by means of the courts, always overestimating the wealth of their propertied compatriots which they magnified through the prism of their own greed,

> The reason ... why the demos permitted this kind of behaviour is not far to seek. Namely, that these people, who had turned away from honest labour and had become accustomed only to popular assemblies and court sessions, suffered from a completely warped and greedy imagination, like an idler who thinks always of food; their conception of the property of the victim, the possible booty, was determined by their greed.[37]

This is how Burckhardt sums up his judgment of Athenian democracy:

> The whole difference between Rome and the cities of Greece lay in the fact that in the former, the propertied classes had developed a completely different power of resistance than in the latter. In Greece, however, when equality had been achieved and it was no longer necessary to fight for principles and rights, the war between rich and poor began, in some cities already with the introduction of democracy, elsewhere after a short interval of moderation.
> In the old days of aristocratic rule, this misery was, of course, hardly known. It was equality of rights which first made inequality of condition really felt. An adjustment by means of labour (which the wealthy needed done and the poor could have done for pay) was impossible because of the general anti-banausic attitude. Now the poor man discovered that as master of the vote he could also become the master of property. In Athens and elsewhere he first had himself paid for attending assemblies and law courts, then he sold his vote, especially as judge, imposed all kinds of liturgies on the rich and decreed confiscations (with exile) completely arbitrarily.... Property had lost all sanctity, and everyone measured his rights only according to his so-called needs (that is, his desires).[38]

The repetition of familiar themes is striking, though Burckhardt if anything goes beyond Boeckh or even Mitford – and well beyond what is justified by historical evidence – in his indictment of Athenian democracy, characterizing it as a regime not only of expediency and vice, but of persecution and mass murder. His solution to the social disorder created by the greed and idleness of the demos is, as the passage quoted above suggests, very much like that of his anti-democratic predecessors: a solution could have been found in 'work which the wealthy needed done and the poor could have done for pay'. This work would have had to be so all-consuming that the demos could not be 'unsettled' by participation in self-government. The people would have had to be too occupied in maintaining their existence and in performing labour that 'the wealthy needed done' to have time for assemblies; and, of course, there could be no payment for public duties. This solution was, however, unavailable to the Greek democracies according to Burckhardt because of their general contempt for labour.

Here we come to an interesting point. Burckhardt does not attribute the contempt for labour simply to the existence of slavery (if anything, the reverse would be true). Instead, the general 'anti-banausic' attitude was the result of a cultural legacy inherited from the aristocratic age and transmitted by the education of the Greeks through poetry and drama depicting the lives and the ethos of royal and noble houses. Unlike modern Europe, whose world-view was shaped by the mediaeval bourgeoisie, argues Burckhardt, the Greek world-view was that of its 'heroic' age, a 'world without utility' (*eine Welt ohne Nützen*), a world of action without utilitarian purpose. Such a world-view was appropriate to an aristocracy and was eminently desirable in itself but disastrous when adopted by the lower classes. Greece, Burckhardt maintains, was unique in this respect. In the ancient Orient, the status of various activities was clearly established at the outset: a ruling caste of priests and warriors reserved for itself the functions of ruling, war and hunting, as well as the privilege of luxurious living. All other activities were left to the rest of the population, sometimes distributed in a caste system, sometimes not; but always the productive activities of industry and agriculture were socially degraded, and the distinction between those engaged in such activities and those who were above them was clearly delineated. In mediaeval Europe, he continues, the nobility developed an outlook that similarly despised labour as well as bourgeois acquisition; but at the same time, there gradually arose a bourgeoisie which not only engaged in these despised activities but held them in high esteem. Only in Greece was the line between rulers and producers blurred while the middle and lower classes themselves despised the very activities on which their existence depended.

Burckhardt divides the history of Greece before the Macedonian conquest into four stages, four cultural configurations characterized by four distinct types of man or human ideals: the heroic age, the agonal and colonial age, the fifth century or perhaps the political age, and the final decline in the fourth century. The agonal age is for Burckhardt the golden one; the fifth century, when the democracy reached its peak of success and prosperity, is for him the 'century which, after the brightest morning, brought to the Hellenes the gloomiest night'.[39]

The heroic ideal of early Greece, explains Burckhardt, was in direct opposition to the 'banausic', though it was still not entirely 'agonal'. The heroic adventures of the Homeric lords still had a purpose beyond the desire to excel before one's peers; they were the actions of warriors seeking victory in battle. It remained for the post-Homeric aristocracy of the colonial age to develop fully the ideal of truly 'useless', 'purposeless' action and competition in non-utilitarian excellence among equals. It was the aristocrats of more peaceful times – who, for example, exercised their military skills not only in battle but in tournaments and athletic contests – that expressed the ideal of action with no purpose but the achievement and display of excellence among one's equals.

This ideal of *purposelessness* was the perfection of the anti-banausic and anti-utilitarian; and it was the conscious expression of a leisured class whose hallmark was freedom from necessity and from dependence on labour for a livelihood. Consequently, the essential characteristic of the agonal spirit was 'a strong prejudice against everything banausic, everything that stood in the way of spiritual and gymnastic training, and completely against all work in paid dependence on others; and even farming done with one's own hands in time was hardly still regarded as respectable'.[40] The agonal ideal was the ideal of *kalokagathia*, gentlemanliness, 'the unity of nobility, wealth, and excellence'; while 'the banausic – i.e. farm-labour, handicrafts, retail trade, commerce, and the like – were despised. Noble work is only work with weapons, and for games and the state, not work for the necessities of life.'[41]

The essential difference between the fifth century and the preceding age for Burckhardt lay in 'the decline of the truly agonal'.[42] Instead of the 'noble victory without passion' which is the object of the agonal contest, 'the whole practice of the democracy in time became a false agon'. The spirit of the democratic age, as expressed in Pericles' Funeral Oration, was passion stimulated by endless restlessness and dissatisfaction, a wanton egoism that was reflected in cruel wars and the 'false agon' of show-trials, persecution, false witness and sycophancy, all of which was made inevitable by the democratization of civic life through public payment for service in war, juries and assemblies.

Finally, argues Burckhardt, the result of the moral corruption brought on by democracy and the decline of the truly agonal was that by the fourth century excellence was banished from the polis as the most talented citizens withdrew, at least in spirit, from the political realm and lost their attachment to the polis. This was an age of *political* decline, when wealth, though more dangerous to its possessors because of the persecution of the rich by the poor, was also increasingly valued for its own sake. What was most remarkable about the democracy, according to Burckhardt, was the 'enormous impudence' with which evil was openly done, a circumstance that has a parallel in the French revolutionary terror, though 'in Athens there must have been permanently more people who were evil in the highest degree and at the same time capable of acting than proportionately in any large city of the present day'.[43] 'Because of the democracy,' he writes, 'an enormous petulance developed, ... a true mob emerged, and people from this mob, which had grown very nervous, were able to compromise the entire state by actions of every kind. The chief evil remained that this so-called democracy, by depriving them of all security, drove the outstanding men to crime or apoliticism.'[44] In this respect, Burckhardt's judgment of Athenian democracy undoubtedly reflected his attitude toward the democratizing tendencies of his own day and the effect he felt they were having in driving men of culture like himself to the margins of public life.

Burckhardt sums up this account of Athenian history by again explaining the root cause of Athens's decline:

> The general phenomenon of Athenian life at this time is that people demanded rights instead of duties and pleasures instead of work, and here the fatal consequence of the anti-banausic attitude came to light. Since people did not perceive the blessings of truly strenuous work and wanted to live outside it, they had to seek other ways of achieving the good life and permitted themselves absolutely everything to get it.[45]

Burckhardt's apparently unequivocal attribution of Athens' 'decline' to the spread of an 'anti-banausic' attitude, however, is not without ambiguities. From the outset it is clear that the anti-banausic ideal is not, for him, evil in itself; indeed, it is the ideal he most admires, and the contempt for the 'banausic' which he castigates is a contempt he clearly shares. This attitude is disastrous only when it is adopted by the lower classes, instead of remaining the prerogative of the class to which it naturally and rightfully belongs: the aristocracy, whose disdain of labour is made possible and practical by command of the labour of others. The anti-banausic prejudice became the source of evil in Athens only when 'With the increasing establishment of democracy those strata upon which for the most part the Agon truly rested lost power and often their wealth as well.'[46]

The ambiguities do not end here. Burckhardt does not simply argue that Athens was corrupted by the spread of an anti-banausic prejudice to the lower classes. Side by side with this account of Athens's decline there runs an apparently contradictory view that the ultimate source of corruption was not the persistence and spread of the *anti*-banausic but rather the triumph of the banausic: 'If the banausics were powerful in the state already before and during the Peloponnesian War,' he writes, they became all-powerful after the restoration of the democracy;[47] and the final corruption of Athens which set in after the war was the result of this triumph and the transfer of power from aristocratic leaders of the banausic mob, like Pericles, to demagogues who were themselves banausic:

> Whatever writers may have thought about the lot of the banausic, it is certain that in Athens from the death of Pericles onwards tradesmen and craftsmen from the lower citizen classes pushed themselves forward and played a political role, despite the fact that they lacked a liberal education in music and gymnastics. They acted as spokesmen in the assembly now and held office, and since they did not want to be better than the great multitude, it was easier for them to manage the masses than it was for the aristocrats.[48]

Here again we encounter the juxtaposition of two apparently opposing views: that Athens was corrupted by the 'indolence' of its citizens, and the view that corruption was brought about by the extension of political power to those who were obliged to work for a living. Burckhardt, like his anti-democratic predecessors, seems unconscious of any contradiction between the myth of the idle mob and the conviction that the fatal flaw in Athenian democracy was that working people were citizens and that their 'banausic' spirit was allowed to put its stamp on Athenian political life. The resolution of this apparent contradiction is to be found, in Burckhardt as in Mitford, in the fact that 'indolence' and 'idleness' stand not for the freedom from labour – as in the case of the anti-banausic aristocracy which lived on the labour of others – but rather for the relative independence of the labouring poor who were not constantly preoccupied and disciplined by the compulsion to do 'work which the wealthy needed done' and who, in the case of Athens, were enabled by pay for public service to participate in politics.

Few historians today would accept Burckhardt's catastrophic vision of the evils perpetrated by the Athenian democracy, and few would be so sanguine about the virtues of the 'agonal' age or pass over so lightly the social conditions which made possible the leisure of the aristocracy, their dependence on the labour of others – for example, the widespread subjection of small farmers in the 'agonal' age which culminated in the reforms of Solon. But the view that a disdain for labour was a universal cultural ideal has been very persistent. That such an ideal existed among certain classes is undoubtedly true; it is certainly a prominent theme in the works of writers and thinkers like Plato, Aristotle, Xenophon or Aristophanes. In the case of a polis like Sparta, where citizens were excluded from 'menial' occupations and labour was reserved for subject populations, it might be possible to speak of a contempt for labour as a cultural ideal within the citizen body. It can even be argued (as we shall see in Chapter IV) that Burckhardt's tracing of this attitude to a source in the aristocratic culture of early Greece is convincing, and more plausible than the perhaps more conventional view that the anti-banausic prejudice has its source in the association of labour with slavery. His suggestion that the democracy was distinctive in that it blurred the line between rulers and producers also indicates a critically important fact about Athenian society, which we shall explore in later chapters. What is highly questionable is the assumption that the anti-democratic attitudes of a Plato or a Xenophon can be treated as universal cultural ideals in Athenian democracy, ascribed to the very 'banausics' whose daily activities are being condemned. Burckhardt's argument makes clear how such a generalization might become possible and precisely what it means. The proposition that a disdain for labour had spread to the lower classes depends, yet again, on the myth of the idle mob and the very specific conception of 'idleness' on which that myth rests. When historians argue, therefore, that a cultural devaluation of labour was one of the major ideological consequences of slavery, they are simply assuming what needs to be proved – that such an attitude existed as a general cultural norm; and it is not at all clear that such an assumption rests on any foundation more secure than the myth of the idle mob.

Fustel de Coulanges and the Thwarted Bourgeois–Liberal Republic of Athens

One final example may be instructive, because it has to do with a very distinguished and influential historian of the later nineteenth century whose political views were not as deeply conservative as Mitford's or Burckhardt's but who nevertheless echoes many of the same themes to be found in their work: Numa Denis Fustel de Coulanges, whose work is cited in Engels' *The Origin of the Family, Private Property and the State*, and who was a teacher of Emile Durkheim. Although Fustel wrote a ground-breaking work on the Roman colonate in which he expressed the view that slavery was a 'primordial fact' traceable to the very origins of society,[49] he does not explore that institution systematically in his famous work on ancient Greece and Rome, *The Ancient City*. He does, however, have something to say about the idle mob, the corruption of democracy by the multitude's freedom from labour, and the contempt for labour brought about by its association with slavery. What makes his work particularly interesting in the present context is that, while it is far less polemical than the other works we have discussed, and while it lays claim to an anthropological objectivity which insists on the *specificity* of ancient Greece and Rome, their incomparability to any nation in the modern world, Fustel's account of ancient institutions is still visibly marked by social attitudes of far more recent origin. This time, however, it is not the violent opposition to contemporary democratic trends of a Burckhardt but something more akin to the liberal faith in progress and bourgeois institutions.

Fustel looks at ancient civic institutions, and their fundamental differences from modern society, against the standard of the modern liberal state. The evolution of such a state is for him the measure of progress; and the development of human intelligence is in his view above all the evolution of liberal, perhaps utilitarian, ideas of society (with the help of Christianity). The history of Greece and Rome is always at least implicitly judged in terms of their contributions, or obstacles, to the evolution of bourgeois property and the liberal state. Indeed, despite the strong disclaimer at the very beginning of his book concerning the applicability of comparisons between the ancient Greek and Roman world and modern society, his analysis is often coloured by an anachronistic inclination to see in Greek and Roman society the rudiments – albeit aborted – of bourgeois principles, idealized bourgeois forms of property and state.

The message secreted in Fustel's insistence on the specificity of Greece and Rome, and on the danger of dreaming about reviving ancient institutions, is not only a scholarly one but also a political lesson for his own time. He seems to be warning his readers of the danger in impeding bourgeois progress or going beyond it to the disorders of mass democracy. People 'have deceived themselves about the liberty of the ancients, and on this very account liberty among the moderns has been put in peril', he writes. 'The last eighty years have clearly shown that one of the great difficulties which impede the march of modern society is the habit which it has of always keeping Greek and Roman antiquity before its eyes.'[50] Since *The Ancient City* was published in 1864, it is not too difficult to guess what historical events he has especially in mind. Again the French Revolution, with its invocations of classical antiquity, lurks menacingly in the background. This time, however, as we shall see, the principal lesson is that once set in train, revolutions have a way of not stopping at the salutary moment when they might establish a bourgeois republic, but tend inexorably to continue until they end in mob rule.

Fustel's perspective was not unique. Between 1750 and 1850 there had developed a tendency among French scholars to treat Athens as 'the model of the liberal and bourgeois society'.[51] Like the British, the French used ancient Greek history as a vehicle for contemporary political debates, adjusted to their own historical circumstances. Thus the example of Athens could be invoked for or against one or another aspect of modern French politics, the development of democracy, the phenomenon of revolution, and so on. (Athens as a commercial state, incidentally, makes a significant appearance here.) The striking thing about Fustel's argument is that, while he castigates his compatriots for 'always keeping Greek and Roman antiquity before [their] eyes', his own interpretation of ancient history is very much in the tradition of 'l'Athènes bourgeoise', as we shall see when we consider his account of the 'plebeian aristocracy'. The problem with all the exponents of this tradition is that when examining ancient history they seem always to keep modern France before their eyes.

Fustel's first premise is that progress in social institutions is a function of developments in human ideas and 'intelligence'. He particularly emphasizes the importance of religion in ancient Greece and Rome, but the evolution of ancient religious institutions is inseparable in his account from the evolution of property; and a central theme of his study is the 'progress' from a society in which 'the laws of property flow from religion' to one in which these laws 'flow from labour'. Precisely what he means by this will be seen in a moment. The religion of early Greece and Rome, writes Fustel, was at first a purely domestic religion of the hearth, based on the family as the primary social unit. As particularistic and antagonistic to *civic* life as this religion was, it had the essential and unique advantage of establishing and guaranteeing the right of property, 'this right from which all civilization springs'.[52] The Greeks and Romans, unlike other ancient peoples, 'from the earliest antiquity, always held to the idea of private property'; 'the idea of private property existed in the religion itself', based as that religion was on the individual hearth and family.[53] In its earliest form property was inalienable, because it was founded on religion rather than on labour and because it was based on the family, with its rights of succession and its inherent interest in the indivisible patrimony, making it a form of property particularly appropriate to a patrician class. Fustel therefore argues that the ancient religion was a patrician institution, and that the principle of aristocracy and the *civic* principle were mutually antagonistic. The liberation of property required the predominance of the *city* over the family, and civic law over paternal authority. Gradually, the city began to assume greater importance, having developed as a confederation of families and tribes; and a *civic* religion grew out of the domestic cult. The city, however, founded on religion as the family had been, still remained resistant to the development of property and the state in the forms that for Fustel are the most desirable.

Nevertheless, the ancient city – indeed the family itself – contained within it the seeds of its own destruction and progressive supersession. Fustel cites two major factors as the causes of this destruction: the relations of class and, of course, 'the natural development of the human mind'.[54] There ensued a series of revolutions beginning with the overthrow of monarchy and ending with the establishment of democracy. In the course of these revolutions, the cities of Greece and Rome seem to have laid foundations for the development of something like bourgeois property and the liberal state; but they were never able to overcome the particularism inherent in their civic religion, until the Roman Empire destroyed the municipal regime and Christianity finally established new social principles, particularly the separation of church and state, which would permit the development of new forms of property and state. Long before the end, however, Greece in particular had effectively destroyed whatever seeds of true progress it contained. The advent of democracy endangered the rights of property and nullified the advances of earlier revolutions which had almost established an aristocracy of wealth, a ruling class whose property was, as Fustel somewhat loosely puts it, acquired by labour (without specifying whose labour).

The first revolution (sounding suspiciously like the revolt of the nobles that set off the French Revolution)

which had overturned royalty had modified the exterior form of the government rather than changed the constitution of society. It had not been the work of the lower classes, who had an interest in destroying the old institutions, but of the aristocracy, who wished to maintain them. It had not been undertaken in order to overturn the ancient constitution of the family, but rather to preserve it.... The aristocracy had brought about a political revolution only to prevent a social one. They had taken the power in hand, less from the pleasure of ruling than to protect their old institutions, their ancient principles, their domestic worship, their paternal authority, the *regime* of the gens – in fine, the private law which the primitive religion had established.[55]

This political revolution, however, generated a social change. By contributing to the strength of the *city*, the aristocracy contributed to its own downfall, encouraging the dismemberment of the aristocratic gens, the breakdown of aristocratic unity aided by rivalry for political power, the disappearance of primogeniture, and, perhaps most important of all, the establishment of an arena for the development of class consciousness among the lower classes, who could meet in the city and share their 'desires and griefs'.[56] The consequence was the next major revolution, the disappearance of clientship and related developments, most dramatically exemplified in the case of Athens by the reforms of Solon. The essential meaning of this revolution for Fustel is that Solon 'had put aside the ancient religion of property', liberating property from its traditional bonds, and, above all, 'had wrested the earth from religion to give it to labor'.[57]

The lower orders, however, as yet had no real bond of unity; they had no leaders, no idea of authority not based on worship to oppose the traditional authority of the patricians. The emergence of such a leadership, a 'plebeian aristocracy', growing out of the new economic realities of the city, a class based on moneyed wealth derived from crafts, trade, and commerce, is for Fustel the single most important and progressive development to emerge from this series of revolutions:

> A sort of aristocracy was formed among the people. This was not an evil; the people ceased to be a confused mass, and began to resemble a well-constituted body. Having rank among themselves, they could select leaders without any longer having to take from the patricians the first ambitious man who wished to reign. This plebeian aristocracy soon had the qualities which ordinarily accompany wealth acquired by labor – that is to say, the feeling of personal worth, the love of tranquil liberty, and that spirit of wisdom which, though desiring improvements, fears risking too much.[58]

It is this third revolution, 'the entry of the plebs into the city', the overthrow of aristocratic rule and the privileges of birth, together with the 'end of the religious government of the city', achieved by the tyrants and finally by the reforms of Cleisthenes, that for Fustel held the greatest promise of progress – but *not* because it established democracy. On the contrary, he stresses that democracy was not the immediate consequence of this revolution. The only effective plebeian revolutions, he argues, were those in which a class immediately emerged to assume the authority of the aristocracy, a new class whose authority was based on wealth. Unfortunately, he continues, nowhere did the leadership of such a class last long. In Athens, the foundations for such a class were laid by Solon, who replaced rank based on birth with a system of political classes based purely on wealth. For a while this plebeian aristocracy was able to rule, and it brought to the city what Fustel calls the virtues of its class. While the traditional nobility 'had enabled human society to live, during several centuries with calmness and dignity', he writes,

> The aristocracy of wealth had another merit; it impressed upon society and the minds of men a new impulse. Having sprung from labor in all its forms, it honored and stimulated the laborer. This new government gave the most political importance to the most laborious, the most active, or the most skilful man; it was therefore favorable to industry and commerce. It was also favorable to intellectual progress; for the acquisition of this wealth, which was gained or lost, ordinarily, according to each one's merit, made instruction the first need, and intelligence the most powerful spring of human affairs. We are not, therefore, surprised that under this government Greece and Rome enlarged the limits of their intellectual culture, and advanced their civilization.[59]

This is a remarkable departure from the picture painted by Burckhardt. And yet we must be careful not to misunderstand Fustel when he sings the praises of the plebeian aristocracy for honouring and stimulating labour. In this new aristocracy, the modern bourgeois, or his own idealization of himself, is clearly recognizable. If this aristocracy was notable for its 'wealth acquired by labor', that labour can hardly have been its own, at least not entirely or even in large part. It was no more possible in Greece or Rome than it has been in any other society to amass substantial wealth without appropriating the labour of others. What Fustel seems to have in mind when he speaks of the special virtues attached to 'wealth acquired by labor' is a familiar defence of bourgeois property, property that is *productive*, in contrast to the passive, unproductive, and parasitical wealth of a rentier aristocracy. It has been very common in the modern age to treat labour, industry and productivity as the attributes not of labourers but of the capitalists who put them to work and who 'honour and stimulate' labour not by engaging in but by employing it. At any rate, as we shall see in a moment, Fustel's observations about the status of labour in Greece and Rome do not prevent him from concluding with a picture of Greek democracy in general which differs very little from the image of the idle mob, its contempt for labour, and the corruption of the state by the indolence of the multitude.

The values of the modern bourgeoisie are perhaps also visible in Fustel's account of political change in Greece and Rome after the triumph of the 'plebeian aristocracy'. The third revolution established a completely new principle of government, a new regulating principle which replaced religion as the basis of political authority and with it all claims to *absolute* political principles. The new principle of government was the 'public interest' – the Roman *res publica*, the Greek *koinon* – establishing that political constitutions 'should conform to the wants, the manners, and the interests of the men of each age', which could best be determined by consultation of the assembled citizens. The function of government also changed. It was 'no longer the regular performance of religious ceremonies. It was especially constituted to maintain order and peace within and dignity and power without.'[60] The *res publica* and *to koinon* as described by Fustel provided a suitable arena for the activities of the new aristocracy; and it sounds very much like the idealized liberal utilitarian state, a 'limited' constitutional state acting as a framework of security for the pursuit of private interests, with government as 'umpire' among conflicting interests.

Fustel's standpoint becomes even more clearly identifiable when he goes on to explain the reasons for the failure of this promising social experiment, particularly in Greece where degeneration was brought about by a fourth revolution, which established democracy. His comments on this development are again strikingly reminiscent of certain judgments on the French Revolution according to which a promising and progressive 'bourgeois revolution' degenerated into mob rule. Although on the whole he seems to believe that the decline was inevitable (in Greece as in France?), since 'the series of revolutions, once commenced, could not be arrested',[61] he does suggest one means by which the establishment of democracy might perhaps have been averted:

> The ruling class would perhaps have avoided the advent of democracy if they had been able to found what Thucydides calls [ολιγαρχια ισονομος], – that is to say, the government for a few, and liberty for all. But the Greeks had not a clear idea of liberty; individual liberty never had any guarantee among them.... The Greeks never knew how to reconcile civil with political equality. That the poor might be protected in their personal interests, it seemed necessary to them that they should have the right of suffrage, that they should be judges in the tribunal, and that they might be elected as magistrates.[62]

And here at last we come to the point where Fustel reverts to an all too familiar theme. Once democracy had been established, he argues, corruption was inevitable, because in Greek democracy there was no principle of order, no means of maintaining peace between classes, to replace autocratic political power:

> As there was no authority that was above rich and poor at the same time, and could constrain them to keep the peace, it could have been wished that economic principles and the conditions of labor had been such as to compel

the two classes to live on good terms. If, for example, the one had stood in need of the other, – if the wealthy could not have enriched themselves except by calling upon the poor for their labor, and the poor could have found the means of living by selling their labor to the rich, – then the inequality of fortunes would have stimulated the activity and the intelligence of man, and would not have begotten corruption and civil war.... The citizen found few employments, little to do; the want of occupation soon rendered him indolent. As he saw only slaves at work, he despised labour. Thus economic habits, moral dispositions, prejudices, all combined to prevent the poor man escaping from his misery and living honestly. Wealth and poverty were not constituted in a way to live together in peace.[63]

In other words, Greek democracy was torn by disorder and class conflict because it had neither the absolute political power of an earlier age to keep order among classes, nor the economic discipline of the modern age, in which political liberty is compatible with social order because the submission of the poor and their dependence on the wealthy are assured by the necessity of selling their labour-power. The chief defect of Greek democracy, it would seem, was that it was a democracy but not a modern bourgeois democracy in which political equality is relatively harmless, since the crucial issues between the classes are resolved in the 'economic' sphere.

The consequence was that the poor man, who had equality of political rights, began to see that he could use his political rights to gain equality of fortune, that as 'master of the votes, he might become master of the wealth of his city':[64]

He began by undertaking to live upon his right of voting. He asked to be paid for attending assembly, or for deciding causes in the courts. If the city was not rich enough to afford such an expense, the poor man had other resources. He sold his vote, and, as the occasions for voting were frequent, he could live.... These expedients did not suffice, and the poor man used more energetic means. He organized regular warfare against wealth.[65]

The result was civil war, the poor seeking to gain possession of wealth, the rich to retain or recover it. The democracy was dominated by material interests, and, above all, 'Men no longer saw the superior principle that consecrates the right of property. Each felt only his own wants, and measured his rights by them.'[66] All these evils could have been prevented if the upper classes had 'had intelligence or ability enough to direct the poor towards labor'.[67] As it was, 'no relation, no service, no labor united them'.

Thus, while Fustel remarks on the evils of poverty and social inequality which the democracy never succeeded in eradicating and which civic equality even rendered more obvious, he still sees advantages in class inequality, and he joins more conservative historians in apportioning blame and proposing solutions: again, the root of all evil was the indolence of the demos and its disdain of labour. Again, political institutions were used by the poor as a means of self-enrichment. Again, the solution would have been the tie which binds the poor to the rich by means of service, the dependence of labour.

There is one very curious thing about Fustel's account of Greek democracy. It turns out – though only in a footnote – that Athens was an exception to these rules about Greek democracy. Athens, he suggests, was spared the worst of the general disorder that plagued the democracies because the 'intelligent' and 'wise' people of Athens 'saw, from the time when this series of revolutions commenced, that they were moving towards a goal where labor alone could save society. They therefore encouraged it and rendered it honorable.'[68]

It seems odd that 'Greek democracy' should be characterized without reference to the most famous democracy, the only one about which there is anything like sufficient information to permit any judgment at all, while that one case, almost as an afterthought, is relegated to a footnote. At the same time, Fustel paints a picture of Athenian democracy in which ordinary citizens are so fully occupied in governing themselves that they have no time for their private affairs. He concludes from this that a man who had to labour for a livelihood could not be a citizen.[69] Perhaps Fustel was simply more concerned with the dangers of mass democracy in principle, as it might affect his own age, than he was in the details of Greek history. Or perhaps he did not after all mean to exclude Athens from the general condemnation of Greek democracy, since like other historians he was more concerned with the *independence* of the poor, their freedom from the necessity to sell their labour-power to the rich, than with their indolence – and this particular evil was at least as prevalent in Athens as in any other democracy. Whatever the reason, the weight of Fustel's account of Greek democracy is heavily on the side of the idle mob.

An Inversion of the Idle Mob: Marxism and the 'Slave Mode of Production'

Against this pervasive image, historical evidence to the contrary seems to have had little chance. All the evidence that the Athenian multitude, far from lacking employment and finding 'little to do', worked at productive and 'menial' occupations of all kinds, that much if not most production was in all likelihood carried on by citizens – peasants and craftsmen – rather than slaves (a point that will be discussed in detail in Chapter II), that public payments could do little more than repay a citizen for the occasional loss of a day's work in the performance of some public service – all this seems to pale by comparison. This eclipse of historical evidence by what can only be called ideology cannot simply be explained by the undeveloped state of historical scholarship or the unavailability of evidence, since, as we saw in the case of Boeckh, the myth and the historical evidence could exist side by side. But whatever the cause, the effects have been pervasive.

M.I. Finley has demonstrated that modern scholarship on ancient slavery has been dominated by moral and political considerations and that, since the publication of the *Communist Manifesto*, 'ancient slavery has been a battleground between Marxists and non-Marxists, a political issue rather than a historical phenomenon'.[70] The fierce debates surrounding the question of slavery which began in the 1960s and continue to this day have, he argues elsewhere, been marked by a 'polemical ferocity' that has as much to do with political antagonisms as with scholarly disagreements.[71] But if the slavery debate has become a political issue, it must be said that the political impetus predates the advent of Marxism and has its roots in earlier controversies generated by the growth of modern democracy, even if a systematic scholarship on slavery developed only later.

Finley's point, however, remains well taken, for there can be no question that the debate has long since been overtaken by disputes inspired by Marxism. Nevertheless, the old debate remains alive – indeed, it is precisely through the medium of Marxist theory that it has worked its most lasting effects. Paradoxically, though the myth of the idle mob originated in a conservative reaction to democracy, it has lived on in the Marxist conception of the 'slave mode of production', which has a very different political impulse. Now, when historians contend over whether slavery was 'basic' to Greek civilization, it is the Marxist meaning of that word that has pre-empted the debate;[72] and, although Marxist theory admits of interpretations rather different from the conventional view that the productive base of Athenian democracy was constituted by slavery, in the sense that slaves performed the bulk of material production in both agriculture and 'industry', that conventional view has until very recently dominated Marxist analysis and the controversies which it has provoked. This is true even in cases where the role of free labour has been acknowledged, at least to the extent that the 'slave mode of production' as a theoretical category has survived more or less intact throughout changes in the evidentiary base.

A brief look at Engels should suffice to demonstrate how the 'slave mode of production' is rooted in the myth of the idle mob. In

Anti-Dühring, Engels takes if for granted that not only industry but agriculture was mainly carried on by slaves in the 'heyday of Greece'[73], and maintains that

> Wherever *slavery* is the main form of production it turns labour into servile activity, consequently makes it dishonourable for freemen. Thus the way out of such a mode of production is barred, while on the other hand slavery is an impediment to more developed production, which urgently requires its removal. This contradiction spells the doom of all production based on slavery and of all communities based on it.... Greece too perished on account of slavery, Aristotle having already said that intercourse with slaves was demoralizing the citizens, not to mention the fact that slavery makes work impossible for the latter.[74]

Here we have what were to become the staples of later Marxist analyses, including the view (to which we shall return in Chapter IV) that it was slavery which impeded the development of technology in the ancient world. And in *The Origin of the Family, Private Property and the State*, assuming that there were eighteen slaves to every adult male citizen (a vastly exaggerated figure by today's scholarly standards), Engels elaborates on some of these themes:

> The class opposition on which the social and political institutions rested was no longer that of nobility and common people, but of slaves and free men, of protected persons and citizens.... The reason for the large number of slaves was that many of them worked together in manufactories in large rooms under overseers. But with the development of commerce and industry, wealth was accumulated and concentrated in a few hands, and the mass of free citizens were impoverished. Their only alternatives were to compete against slave labor with their own labor as handicraftsmen, which was considered base and vulgar and also offered very little prospect of success, or to become social scrap. Necessarily, in these circumstances, they did the latter, and as they formed the majority, they thereby brought about the downfall of the whole Athenian state. The downfall of Athens was not caused by democracy as the European lickspittle historians assert to flatter their princes, but by slavery, which banned the labor of free citizens.[75]

And later in the same work, echoing a judgment recorded many years before with Marx in the *German Ideology* that the ancient state was 'an association against a subjected producing class', Engels writes: 'The ancient state was, above all, the state of the slave owners for holding down the slaves'.[76]

So in the context of a view of democracy which distinguishes Engels fundamentally from the 'lickspittle historians', he nevertheless repeats their pronouncements about the idle mob and the contempt for labour associated with slavery. On these premises, he builds the characteristic Marxist argument about the class divisions between free men and slaves (overshadowing the divisions between appropriators and producers within the citizen body), and about the ancient state as an organization of citizen-appropriators against a producing class of slaves. Needless to say, Engels, who was not an ancient historian, relied on the secondary sources of his day, and was apparently very well read in them (in the *Origin*, for example, he cites both Grote and Fustel among others). There can be little doubt that his view of ancient Greece was deeply influenced by the purveyors of the 'idle mob', which dominated the field by default as defenders of democracy like Grote evaded the issue of slavery.

Much of this was to remain conventional in Marxist circles for a very long time, reinforced by the imposition of later Stalinist orthodoxies concerning the stages of historical development from primitive communism, through ancient slavery, to feudalism and capitalism. In a Left Book Club pamphlet published in 1938, Benjamin Farrington, no amateur polemicist but Professor of Classics at the University College of Swansea, could still write that

> With the peoples whom they called barbarians the Greeks certainly shared one ideal, which we see most successfully realised in Sparta, but which was also the basis of Athenian life – that all the hard work of field and factory should be shuffled off the shoulders of the citizen body and laid upon the backs of a depressed population of slaves.[77]

Farrington concludes by quoting Max Beer:

> The more I have studied the life of antiquity, ... the clearer it has become to me that the moral and political collapse of the old world was due chiefly to slavery – to unfree labour, to the despising of productive activity, and the resulting stagnation of the technology of labour.[78]

Things have begun to change. The most recent major Marxist work on the ancient Greek world, G.E.M. de Ste Croix's monumental *Class Struggle in the Ancient Greek World*, proceeds from the premise that small, free, independent producers were responsible for a 'substantial proportion' of total production and perhaps even 'the greater part of it' in 'most parts of the Greek (and Roman) world at most times'.[79] Although some of Ste Croix's arguments concerning Athenian slavery will be questioned in Chapter II, he has certainly shifted the Marxist analysis of ancient Greece on to a fruitful new course by taking seriously Marx's own suggestion that 'the really distinctive feature of each society is ... how the extraction of the surplus from the immediate producer is secured'.[80] For Ste Croix, then, ancient Athens would still be a 'slave society', not because slaves carried on the bulk of production but because, according to him, slavery was the principal form in which surplus was extracted by the dominant propertied classes and the condition for the leisured existence of these dominant classes. If, as we shall see, there are grounds for doubting his conclusion about surplus extraction in classical Athens, he has nonetheless asked the right question.

But if much has changed in Marxist analysis, there is still a good deal of theoretical life in the old 'slave mode of production' and in its associated axioms, for example concerning the degradation of labour and its stultifying effects on technological progress. The only other contemporary Marxist study of ancient Greece and Rome to match Ste Croix's in its scope and imaginative sweep, Perry Anderson's *Passages from Antiquity to Feudalism*, unequivocally embraces the 'slave mode of production' in a way that even Ste Croix hesitates to do (he prefers the notion of a 'slave economy' or 'slave society' in order to avoid any misconceptions about the predominance of slaves in production).[81] Though Anderson would not dissent from Ste Croix's qualifications concerning the role of slaves in production, he is more emphatic about the determinative effects of slavery on the whole of Athenian culture. In particular, he accepts the traditional Marxist view of its consequences for technological development and offers some sophisticated elaborations of the view that the degradation of labour associated with slavery impeded technological progress. Above all, he identifies as the hallmark of Athenian life a striking disparity between a stagnant technological base and a vigorous cultural superstructure, a contradiction he attributes to the 'slave mode of production'. All of these propositions will be questioned in what follows.

On the other side of the debate between Marxists and non-Marxists which has come to dominate the field, the residues of political preoccupations old and new remain. If their effects in the specialist literature are no longer as blatant as they once were, often appearing largely as sins of omission, elsewhere they can be very far-reaching indeed – as, for example, in the gross misapprehensions of a distinguished non-specialist like Hannah Arendt. She constructs a whole political philosophy, imbued with something like Burckhardt's agonal ideal, on the mistaken assumption that Aristotle's 'theory corresponds closely to reality' when he suggests that those who provide the material needs of the polis, including artisans and peasants, cannot be citizens.[82] Athenian citizens, she argues, to the extent that they were free from the necessity of labouring in order to live, were capable of a true political consciousness, in contrast to the masses in modern society, who since the French Revolution have intruded the 'social question' into the public space. The same principles and misconceptions inform her interpretation of the American Revolution (and of American history in general), which she regards as the one modern revolution impelled not by the 'social question' but by a more purely 'political' motive, the desire to found a new political order. The Founding Fathers – like Burckhardt's agonal heroes – were free from the imperatives of social need and therefore capable of understanding freedom. Unfortunately the promising beginnings were compromised very early in the history of the Republic, as it came increasingly under the influence of the European poor who washed up on its shores.[83] Leaving aside any weaknesses in Arendt's acquaintance with the facts of French or American history, it is tantalizing to speculate how different her historical judgments might have been had she been forced to attribute the glories of ancient Athens not to its agonal spirit but to the baleful influence of its 'banausic' citizens.

The myth of the idle mob has not yet died – or at least its legacy remains alive in a long line of progeny. There is much still to be done. It is not simply a matter of discovering what slaves in Athens did or did not do, though there remains a great deal to say about that. Finley has suggested that, if we are to redirect the investigation of slavery into more fruitful avenues, we should cease to ask whether slavery was *the* or even *a* 'basic' element in Greek civilization, 'or whether it caused this or that', and ask instead how it *functioned*.[84] He might have added that, if we are to ask how slavery 'functioned' in the democracy, we must also ask – as we shall in what follows – what was the function of democracy itself.

II

Slavery and the Peasant-Citizen

The Limits of Plausibility: Some Reflections on the Number and Location of Slaves in Athens

It is unlikely that the issue of slavery in classical Athens will ever be decisively resolved. With the exception of very general propositions about the 'importance' of slavery in Athenian society, nearly every major question remains in dispute: the number of slaves, the extent and distribution of slaveownership, the location of slaves in the economy. In other words, how important is important, and in what ways? While new and ingenious interpretations of the meagre evidence have never been wanting, there is little chance that enough new evidence will emerge to lay these fierce debates to rest. Still, the effort must be made. In particular, if we are to assess the role of slavery in maintaining the democracy, we must at least have some plausible idea of its role in sustaining life itself. In this still predominantly agrarian economy, the fundamental matter turns on the function of slavery in agricultural production, and it is to this question that the present chapter is primarily devoted. Some kind of resolution here is needed, too, in order to situate the labouring citizen, and especially the citizen-farmer, in the workings of the democracy.[1]

Let us look first at the parameters of plausibility by considering the numbers, what they suggest about the extent of slavery and about its principal locations. Instead of trying to resolve the perennial debate about the size of the slave population, we can arrive at some conclusions about the limits of possibility simply by exploring the implications of the *highest* current estimates. If we begin with the least restrictive assumptions about the number of slaves, we should be as well placed as possible to evaluate the likelihood that slaves carried the principal burden of basic – specifically agricultural – production in Athens.

Modern estimates of the number of slaves in classical Attica have varied widely, ranging, for example, from 20,000, as against a free population of 124,000, for the late fourth century BC to 106,000 for 323 BC, with a free population of 154,000. The latter figures appear in the article on 'Population (Greek)' in the *Oxford Classical Dictionary* (1970) over the names of A.W. Gomme and R.J. Hopper, and are based, with a few modifications, on Gomme's classic and often-cited *The Population of Athens.*[2] Let us take Gomme-Hopper as our point of departure because these figures represent among the highest estimates of slave-numbers still current in modern scholarship. These high figures, whether or not they are the most accurate, should provide the most generous basis for assessing the *prima facie* plausibility of widespread agricultural slavery in classical Athens.

Gomme and Hopper offer the following estimates for the years 431 and 323 BC, the peak periods:

	431 BC	*323 BC*
Total population of Attica	310,000	260,000
Citizens (with families)	172,000	112,000
Metics (with families)	28,500	42,000(?)
Slaves	110,000	106,000(?)

If we consider these figures in the light of certain other estimates concerning the geographical and occupational distribution of slaves, we obtain some astonishing results. Although little is known about occupational distributions, it is generally accepted that large numbers of slaves worked in the silver mines at Laureion. The major study on these mine slaves, S. Lauffer's *Die Bergwerkssklaven von Laureion*, estimates that as many as 30,000 slaves worked in the mines and processing mills at one time when they were in full operation, as in the late fourth century BC.[3] The mines were flourishing throughout much of the fifth century, before a decline toward the end of the Peloponnesian Wars and the revival in the second half of the fourth century.

Let us first, for the sake of argument, take Gomme–Hopper's maximum of 110,000 slaves for 431 and assume a figure somewhere between the extremes of modern estimates for mine slaves, leaning toward the conservative side – let us say 15–20,000. Where are the rest of the slaves, then? According to Gomme–Hopper, in 431, when about one-third of the citizen population lived in Athens, Piraeus, and environs, approximately two-thirds of the slaves lived within those boundaries. (In the course of the following century, the proportion of city-dwellers grew.) This would mean that about 73,000 slaves were located in the largely, though not entirely, urban area of Athens and its immediate surroundings, occupied as domestic servants, craftsmen and labourers in workshops, 'civil servants', policemen, entertainers, etc. After subtracting the mine slaves from the remaining 37,000, this would leave about 22–27,000 slaves for the areas in which the bulk of Attic agriculture was carried on. These would have to be distributed among the workshops of outlying towns and villages (remember that the area outside the urban centre of Athens was not all rural) and the households (often more than one) of the citizens living away from the city (two-thirds of the total citizen population, i.e. about 115,000, including families, according to Gomme–Hopper, of which perhaps 29,000 would be citizens), as well as country estates (often several) owned by citizens residing in the city. Then we must consider the fact that a reasonably wealthy household could easily employ several slaves just for domestic and personal services alone, without agricultural tasks – not only as personal attendants of various kinds, or for ordinary maintenance, cleaning, the preparation of food, or tending and teaching the children, but also in various household crafts such as weaving cloth and making clothes, making soap, etc. There is evidence which suggests that a household numbering fifteen slaves – apparently personal attendants for the various members of the household, rather than 'productive' labourers – was considered normal for a wealthy, and not necessarily the wealthiest, Greek. Such numbers appear, for example, in the last wills and testaments reported by Diogenes Laertius for the philosophers, Aristotle and Lykon.[4] While these reports may not be authentic, they do at least suggest what a Greek might regard as plausible. Plato, a moderately wealthy bachelor with what was probably a small household is reported to have freed one slave and left four others.[5] A small proportion of country households could thus easily exhaust the whole supply of rural slaves. It should be added that none of these calculations takes into account the fact that the total number of slaves would have included people of all ages and conditions, many of whom would not have been fit for heavy physical labour.

In 323, when according to Gomme–Hopper the metic population was substantially larger than in 431 while the citizen body was smaller and slaves somewhat less numerous, and when the proportion of city-dwellers had risen perhaps to three-quarters of the total population, the situation would hardly have been more favourable for agricultural slavery – especially if we take Lauffer's figure for mine slaves during the revival of the Laureion mines in the late fourth century. Needless to say, if Gomme–Hopper's large figures for the total slave population are rejected as too high – if, for example, we accept a 60–80,000 maximum in peak periods, [6] it becomes even more difficult to find enough slaves to produce a substantial agricultural labour-force.

Such literary evidence as there is pointing to the occupational distribution of slaves – and there is nothing even remotely conclusive – tends to confirm this picture, at least to the extent of suggesting a preponderance of slaves in domestic service and displaying little evidence of agricultural slavery. The best window on Athenian property relations is provided by the orators of the fourth century BC, in particular their legal speeches in the endless disputes about property which preoccupied the courts of the late democracy. Unfortunately, there is nothing comparable for the 'golden age' of the previous century; but since the proportion of slaves was if anything higher in the late fourth century than in the 'golden age', evidence drawn from the later period may at least tell us something about the outer limits of possibility.

The speeches of Demosthenes (including those designated as 'pseudo-Demosthenes'), the largest collection of its kind extant, will serve as the most comprehensive example. There is in his legal speeches a substantial number of references to slaves giving some indication of the work in which they were engaged (I have counted, conservatively, over fifty). Of these, at least two-thirds refer to domestic servants, often in the plural; and almost two-thirds of these are specifically designated as women – maidservants, perhaps sometimes concubines, nurses, etc. (though other references to servants may also include women). The next largest category – about one-third of the remainder – are engaged in what might be called 'white collar' services: as business agents, clerks or scribes, bank employees, a magistrate's assistant. (Some of these too may be domestic servants.) There are two or three references to servants, possibly domestics, assigned (temporarily?) to guard duty, in two cases protecting a mine; and one speech concerned specifically with mining refers to a number of mine slaves. Then there are two or three references to craftsmen, for example sackcloth weavers and colour grinders (both of these employed by the same man in houses owned by him, the first apparently in his own home – probably like other wealthy Athenians who made a business out of domestic crafts such as the production of clothing, a practice which Socrates recommends to his friend, Aristarchus, following the model of a certain Ceramon).[7] One passage seems to refer to ship slaves, another to prostitutes. Only four cases suggest labour on a farm, outside the house, and only one of these is unambiguous, referring to a group of slaves sometimes contracted out by their master for a wage as casual farm labourers. The others mention a shepherd, not necessarily, though probably, a slave; some servants who seem to be doing something away from the main house at the moment described in the speech; and a servant engaged at the relevant time in building a wall on a farm.[8]

None of this is conclusive and we cannot, of course, deduce the actual distribution of slaves in various occupations from the ratio of references in Demosthenes. That the picture is skewed by the nature of the legal cases in question is obvious. Certain categories of slaves may disappear altogether – for example, public slaves are unlikely to turn up in disputes having to do with private property. Most clearly under-represented are the mine slaves who are known to have constituted a substantial portion of the Athenian labour force, in numbers perhaps comparable to or surpassing domestic servants. The explanation for this disparity between their prominence in the economy and their insignificance in these legal speeches may simply be that, for all their importance in the Athenian economy, the silver mines comprised the wealth of a relatively small number of Athenian citizens, when compared with agricultural property;[9] and that these included, on the one hand, a number of very small leaseholders who could have worked the mines on their own, and on the other hand, a few of the richest men in Athens, who may alone have accounted for a very large number of slaves – such as the general Nicias, who was said to have leased out one thousand slaves for work in the mines. If nothing else, this would have reduced the statistical incidence of appearances in court by slaveowners involved in mining. We must, therefore, approach this literary evidence with caution. Nevertheless, the overwhelming preponderance of domestic slaves in the texts is at least suggestive, as is the striking elusiveness of slaves engaged in agricultural tasks (which cannot be explained away so easily, given the centrality of agricultural property). At any rate, this kind of evidence may gain some significance from its reinforcement of conclusions reached by other means.

Linguistic and Conceptual Ambiguities in the Evidence on Slavery

Scholarly opinion has generally tended toward the view that slavery was far less important in agriculture than in industry and trade, but new arguments have recently been offered in support of the contention that agricultural slavery in classical Attica was significant and widespread.[10] The terms of the debate have not been very clear. Everyone agrees that *some* slaves existed in the countryside and that *some* of them *sometimes* worked in the field; but it is difficult to determine at what point the incidence of slave labour in agriculture should be treated as significant or widespread. To some extent, the debate may just be about language and emphasis. In fact, it is not even clear what is meant by 'agricultural slavery'. On the assumption, however, that it means a permanent stock of slaves whose principal function is agricultural labour, and not simply domestic servants lending a hand in the fields now and then, and on the further assumption that 'significant' and 'widespread' mean that large landowners systematically and principally derived their wealth from slave labour and/or that slavery extended far down the social scale, used regularly and systematically on ordinary peasant holdings – on these two assumptions there is something to argue about.

Two works stand out as the most unequivocal recent statements in favour of the view that agricultural slavery was widespread in Athens: Michael Jameson's article 'Agriculture and Slavery in Classical Athens' and G.E.M. de Ste Croix's *The Class Struggle in the Ancient Greek World*. It will be argued in what follows that their case has not been made. Indeed, since these works represent the best that has so far been said in favour of such a view, the case can probably not be made at all, at least on the basis of available evidence.

The first and most striking point that confronts us is, as we have seen, that in the rather large body of surviving Greek literature – in sharp contrast to Roman sources – there is simply no direct evidence to indicate the importance of agricultural slavery. While the absence of evidence proves little and one should not make too much of arguments from silence (as Ste Croix so often points out), and while discussions of agriculture in general are surprisingly sparse in Greek literature, it does mean that the burden of proof lies more heavily on the advocates of Greek agricultural slavery than they have been willing to acknowledge.

The second point is that what textual evidence there is about agricultural labour in Athens is seldom unambiguous. The ambiguity begins at the most fundamental level, in the language itself. Ste Croix suggests that the Greeks and Romans were 'inhibited' from recognizing certain forms of unfree labour like serfdom and debt-bondage as distinct categories 'because they divided mankind into just two groups: free and slave'.[11] Yet he proceeds as if these conceptual difficulties affect only the 'intermediate' or 'mixed' categories between slavery and complete freedom, as if the conceptual apparatus of the Greeks and Romans should at least permit us unequivocally to identify *slaves* when they appear in the evidence. The Greek language in particular, however, does little to justify such confidence in the clarity with which Greek thought distinguished slaves from the rest of mankind. Indeed, nothing could be more effectively calculated to obscure the boundaries between slaves and other labourers than the language often used by classical Greek writers to describe how the work of society gets done.

In the case of early Greece, at least, even the dichotomy between servile and free is problematic. On the one hand, for example in Homeric language, both free labourer and slave can be referred to indiscriminately as *drēstēr*, 'one who works or serves'.[12] On the other hand, both master and servant might be contrasted with those defeated outsiders who are in but not of the community; and it has been suggested that the category *doulos* originally referred specifically to the 'not-belongingness' of these defeated ones rather than to their uniquely servile condition.[13] Indeed, from the 'heroic' and aristocratic vantage point of the Homeric epics, it would not be surprising to find *all* labourers regarded as servants, so that servile status would not be the distinctive characteristic of the slave.

What is more surprising is that the indeterminacy of Homer's vocabulary – and the ethical principles on which it was based – did not disappear from the language of classical literature as slavery grew in quantity and economic importance, even when the advent of democracy elevated the ordinary peasant and artisan to full citizenship and rendered the distinction between free man and slave more salient and decisive in practice. Ste Croix himself points out that the standard technical terms used by the Greeks to designate slaves – terms such as *doulos* and *andrapodon* – 'could be used loosely and even purely metaphorically'.[14] What he fails to tell us is how often the language of the most important texts leaves the labourer's juridical identity tantalizingly in doubt. Few languages can have had a greater variety of terms for those who work or *serve* than did classical Greek. It is striking how seldom their usage entails a clear distinction between free and unfree, and how often the usage adopted by the classical Athenian writers reflects the aristocratic ethic in which distinctions among the various kinds of servile and menial classes are of little moment.

The example of Xenophon is particularly instructive since his work, especially the *Oeconomicus*, has provided the richest source of evidence concerning the system of agricultural production in classical Athens.[15] In the *Oeconomicus*, which sets out the principles of estate management for precisely the kind of wealthy estate where we should most expect to find slaves working the land, the evidence turns out to be surprisingly elusive. Seldom, for example, are members of the work-force referred to as *douloi* – that is, more or less unambiguously as chattel slaves. In general, Xenophon uses a variety of other words which refer to servants or labourers without specifying their juridical status; and the context does not often permit us to identify a servant unequivocally as a slave. One relatively unambiguous passage refers to a bailiff as being 'bought' (XII 3), though the passage is less clear about whether Xenophon's model landlord, Ischomachus, himself normally buys his bailiffs.[16] Another (III 4) refers to servants (*oiketai*) in fetters (on *some* estates, though not specifically the one in question), which indicates slaves; as does another passage which speaks of the *oiketai* who are not allowed to breed without permission (IX 5). These texts refer more or less clearly to servants who are slaves, but they do not imply that all servants are slaves or give us any indication of how many are.

The word for servant most commonly used by Xenophon is *oiketēs*, which generally refers to household servants (though these could presumably work outside the house) but without distinction between free workers and slaves (e.g., in addition to the passages already mentioned, III 2, V 10, VII 35, VIII 22). Another term applied by Xenophon to servants, *diakonos*, 'one who serves or ministers' or an 'attendant', is often used in Greek to describe people who serve in a clearly non-servile status, such as officials in temples or religious guilds.[17] Xenophon uses it to describe both a household maid (VIII 10) and a steersman's mate (VIII 14). Ste Croix refers specifically to passages which purport to prove that bailiffs were typically slaves (about which more later), citing one in which Xenophon uses the word *therapōn* to refer (apparently) to a servant in charge of other servants, using *oiketēs* in the next sentence, apparently interchangeably with *therapōn* (XII 19). Especially in its earlier uses, *therapōn* could refer specifically to attendants who performed free services, in contrast to the *doulos* or slave, though it later came to mean simply 'servant' and could apply to slaves.[18] When Xenophon is referring specifically to people who labour in the fields, he most commonly employs derivatives of the verb *ergazesthai*, 'to work (or labour)', sometimes applied to manual labour in general, but more particularly to husbandry. All these words can refer to any kind of agricultural worker from the wage-labourer to the free husbandman himself, as well as to slaves. So, for example: 'even strong men cannot live without those who labour [cultivating the land]' (*ergazomenoi*: IV 15); or 'the earth yields food ... to *ergazomenoi*' (V 2); or 'what art repays the labourer (*ergazomenos*) more generously [than husbandry]?' (V 8).[19] Then there is the *ergastēr*, referring clearly to a labourer who works for a farmer (V 15), and the *ergatēs* again applied to a labourer working for a farmer. None of these words implies a particular juridical status. When immediately after the last passage, in V 16, Xenophon makes one of his rare unambiguous references to slaves, the passage can be read not as if he is equating *ergatai* with *douloi* but rather as if he is speaking of slaves (*douloi*) as a *sub*-category of *ergatai*. Having argued that a farmer (*geōrgos*) must encourage his labourers (*ergatai*) often, he goes on to suggest 'and slaves (*douloi*) need to be encouraged not less but even more than do free men (*eleutheroi*)', perhaps implying that the farmer's labourers may include both free men and slaves.

One unambiguous reference to agricultural labourers who are slaves (a passage in which he has Socrates repudiating the suggestion that the wealthy farmer should buy children to train them as *geōrgoi*, III 10) uses the term *geōrgoi*, the same word Xenophon uses most often to designate the farmer who *employs* labourers. In a famous text where he speaks of the debilitating effects of the banausic arts, he speaks of *ergatai* and *ergazomenoi* (here referring not to farm labourers but to artisans) in such a way that the terms may refer partly to slaves, but more explicitly to free craftsmen who make bad citizens because their practice of banausic arts weakens their minds and bodies and leaves them no leisure to attend to their friends or their city (IV 1–3). All this linguistic confusion does not prevent us from concluding that slaves were used on wealthy Greek estates, and especially in domestic service; but it significantly obscures our vision – much more than some historians admit – of the extent of agricultural slavery, its location (e.g., in the house or in the fields), and the ratio of slaves to free labourers.[20]

Although Plato and Aristotle are less useful as sources of concrete evidence about Greek economic practices, like Xenophon they do tell us something about the flexibility of the Greek language in referring to servants and labourers. For example in *Laws* (806E) Plato speaks of letting out land to *douloi*, thereby using this apparently unambiguous word for slave to describe a situation more suitable to serfs, *coloni*, or sharecroppers than to ordinary chattel slaves (which confirms Ste Croix's remark about the failure of the Greeks to recognize certain 'intermediate' forms of unfree labour). On the other hand, both Plato and Aristotle in varying degrees regard all manual labourers as properly servile, ideally to be excluded from the freedom of citizenship either as slaves, or perhaps as resident aliens (metics). This antidemocratic ethos and the blurring of distinctions to which it leads are exemplified by Plato in the *Statesman*. He first excludes all practitioners of 'contributory' or subsidiary arts – that is, all those engaged in productive activities and in supplying the community's basic needs – from a share in the art of politics (much as Aristotle does in his distinction between 'conditions' and 'parts').[21] He then goes on to consider the category of slaves and servants of all kinds (289C ff.). Here the term *hypēretēs* is used in both a literal and a broad or partly metaphorical sense to include everyone from the most menial, 'bought' personal servant or slave to the public servant or minister.[22]

What is especially significant about this passage is that Plato makes a clear distinction between people who are truly servile in the sense that they or their services are bought and sold, and others who serve in a less base and mercenary sense. In fact, the object of the argument is to disqualify the former from performing public services as statesmen. The effect of his analysis is that slaves – who are themselves acquired by purchase – are only one group within a larger servile category which includes those who place themselves voluntarily in a servile position by offering their services for hire to any employer. Such people are just as unambiguously unfit for politics as are slaves. Among them are not only wage-labourers but also merchants and traders, who act in effect as the hired hands of those engaged in productive arts whose products they distribute. Even if Plato's usage is partly metaphorical, it illustrates very well the aristocratic mentality which obscures the distinctions among people who work for their livelihood and perceives the differences among them as simply stages along a continuum of bondage and servility. The mentality of Plato, like that of Xenophon, is one in which all menial work ought ideally to be done by unfree labourers. The same point of view that affects the meaning of various words for 'servant' affects the meaning of 'freedom', since in aristocratic eyes juridical freedom alone does not entitle a man to be considered *eleutheros*. The conceptual and linguistic reflections of this mentality have produced not only metaphorical confusions but a flexibility of literal usage which considerably obscures our picture of Greek social life.

Historians are thus faced not only with a shortage of substantive evidence concerning slaves in Greek agriculture, but also with ambiguities in the relatively few references that do exist. The absence of positive references has been combined with other deductive and interpretative arguments – for example, about the size of holdings; the probable yield of agricultural land and the population it could sustain; the uneconomic character of agricultural slavery, especially on smallholdings, given the seasonal and irregular nature of agricultural work; and so on; and such arguments have been used to question the widespread employment of slaves and the importance of agricultural slavery in Greece.[23] It is conclusions of this sort that have recently been challenged, particularly by Jameson and Ste Croix.

Agricultural Slavery and the Peasant-Citizen

Michael Jameson's 'Agriculture and Slavery in Classical Athens' is the most important recent contribution to the argument that slavery was widespread and significant in Athenian production and, in particular, that this was so in agriculture. Although the standard of significance and the measure of 'widespread' remain unclear, it is Jameson's object to demonstrate that the utilization of slave labour in agricultural production went far down the social scale, in other words that the use of slave labour was the norm on ordinary peasant holdings: 'I would argue that at least in the conditions of the Classical period the addition of some slave help to the farmer's own capacity was essential for all but the richest and the poorest, that it extended the reach of the family's work force and that this permitted forms of intensification that enabled the farmer to be fully a citizen.'[24] (The 'richest' are excluded not, of course, because they owned no slaves, but because in such cases slaves did not serve simply as 'help to the farmer's own capacity'.) The extent and nature of slavery on properties owned by wealthy landowners do not come into question in Jameson's article, nor does he consider the situation of peasant farmers in relation to their wealthier compatriots, an oversight which, as we shall see, has serious implications for his analysis.

Jameson's argument is that population in Attica grew from the sixth through the late fifth century; that this demographic growth put pressure on existing resources and available land, as properties decreased in size; that this created a demand for intensified production, especially in the form of diversification of agriculture; and that slavery was the only available means to intensify production without incurring unacceptable social costs, that is, without compelling the Athenian farmer to sacrifice his civic and military roles: in other words, slavery was the condition for the unity of farmer and citizen.[25] There are some subsidiary arguments which are simply intended to demonstrate that the absence of references to agricultural slavery where one might expect to find them in epigraphic and literary sources tells us nothing 'one way or the other'.[26] Added to this are suggestions that slave labour in agriculture could have been rendered economical by regular year-round employment, if we assume a sufficient degree of diversification in response to a need for intensified production; but since much of this argument depends upon assuming precisely what needs to be proved – that there was a need for labour intensification of the kind and degree he describes – this argument tends to be circular. Fundamentally, the whole case turns on the proposition that 'slaveholding enabled the Athenian to be a participant in a democracy'.[27]

The attempt to relate the use of slavery to 'intensification' is questionable from the start.[28] Even if it could be shown conclusively that a clear increase in the demands made upon labour took place in the relevant period, what is there to show that this increase exceeded the capabilities of the peasant family itself, even when the head of the household performed civic duties? Suppose that before 'intensification' the family had too little to do. Do we know that the pre-intensification Attic peasant family was already taxed to the limits of its labouring capacities, that the growing pressures upon it exceeded both its ability to work longer hours and its capacity to increase output per hour of work, even granted the limited technical innovation so often attributed to Greek agriculture? 'Intensification' relative to what? And how much? This kind of argument simply will not work at such a level of abstraction.[29]

Jameson's propositions about demographic growth and intensification of production turn out to be rather vague and indeterminate. For example: 'As for the actual historic situation, perhaps we can begin with the proposition that from the VIth through the early Vth to the later Vth cent. the population of Attica grew, whatever the rate or the actual figures.'[30] Or: 'So far we have seen some hints of deviation from a hypothetical pattern of subsistence farming. Consideration of some calculations made for ancient agricultural conditions in general and comparison with modern data may help to show that a fair degree of intensification was practised by the IVth cent.'[31] This is followed by a short paragraph showing that, given normal grain yields, for a typical small Attic farm of 4–5 hectares '... to support a family with no other source of income, intensification, and with it very hard work, would be required'. Phrases like 'whatever the rate ...' or 'a fair degree' seem remarkably lame and nonchalant, especially since the 'rate' and the 'degree' are critical to his case.

Let us, however, make allowances for the fact that Jameson's argument is something of a 'thought experiment' and not an attempt to marshall the relevant evidence, and assume that he has made a case for substantial demographic growth in the relevant period and for a 'fair degree' of intensification. Let us focus on his central argument that the farmer's *citizenship* in a democracy, the demands it made upon him and his desire to preserve this status, compelled him to transfer agricultural labour to slaves.

It should be noted, first, that demographic pressures and insufficiences of peasant landholdings were not unique to classical Attica but have been recurring problems in agrarian societies dominated by peasant production. Nor have the 'intensification' of production, diversification and/or specialization been unusual in such societies.[32] Jameson's task therefore, is to identify what was peculiar to Athenian society which might account for the adoption of an unusual *solution* to these problems, the large-scale use of slave labour in agriculture. Jameson's answer is, of course, that the civic and military status of the Attic farmer is the *differentia specifica*. In fact, he is almost certainly right that this is what above all distinguishes the Attic peasant from peasants in other societies; but it is precisely this characteristic that makes the rest of Jameson's argument implausible. Far from explaining why the ordinary Attic farmer might have been compelled to transfer some of his 'intensified' labour to slaves, the citizenship of the Attic peasant actually *reduced* the need for labour intensification, in a sense offsetting demographic pressures, by limiting the need for surplus production in ways unknown in any other documented 'peasant' society.

Before this argument is elaborated, it would probably be wise to say a word about the description of Attic farmers as 'peasants', a designation which some may find contentious. Robin Osborne, for example, suggests that it is misleading to treat Attic smallholders as peasants 'in any strong sense of that word' for three principal reasons: that they lacked a 'distinct cultural tradition, that there was no clear division between town and country, and that there was no sharp dividing line between small and large landowners'.[33] Each of these points will be encountered in subsequent chapters. The town/country dichotomy is discussed at length in Chapter III, and the question of a 'peasant' culture is the subject of Chapter IV. In neither case is it a matter of disagreeing with Osborne about the distinctness of Athenian 'peasants'. On the contrary, it is precisely that distinctness which is the object of discussion. The separation between large and small landowners is more difficult, but it may be no less problematic in its application to other 'peasant' societies. As we shall see, there came a point in the evolution of relations between landlord and peasant when the power of rich landholders over poor began to resemble that of prosperous peasants over their poorer compatriots in mediaeval Europe, an economic power resting on superiority of landholdings rather than on 'extra-economic' powers of appropriation. While rich peasants may be in a position to exploit the poor by leasing out excesses of land, or hiring them as casual labour, there is in such cases no clear dividing line in the sense intended by Osborne – but then neither is there a clear separation between rich, exploiting peasants, on the one hand, and landlords whose exploitative power rests on superior property and not on a privileged juridical or political status.

Strictly speaking, then, we would have to reserve the word 'peasant' for those cases where such sharp juridical or political divisions exist. Purely 'economic' differences tend to exist on a continuum, in the absence of sharp divisions between absolute property and absolute propertylessness. At any rate, one of the critical issues in defining the character of Athenian farmers – and one of the main themes of this book – is how it came about that the division between landlords and peasants *lost* this dichotomous sharpness. To begin with a characterization of Attic smallholders as peasants is in a sense to formulate the principal historical questions that need to be answered about the development of the democracy, to establish what it is that needs to be explained, the processes of transformation which created the distinctness of the Attic smallholder. There is no intention here of claiming that Attic farmers in classical times were peasants in what

Osborne calls a 'strong sense of that word', if that means that they met every one of his strict criteria – which they clearly did not. But the significance of the *differences* between Athenian smallholders and others who may have a stronger claim to the word 'peasant' may be missed unless we begin with what they have in common.

Peasants have been defined – in contrast to 'primitive agriculturalists' – as cultivators who depend for their subsistence on certain rights in land and family labour, but who are involved in a 'wider economic system' which includes non-peasants. Essential to this definition is the fact that the peasant family operates as a productive unit (rather than as an 'entrepreneurial unit', as in the modern family farm).[34] In this sense, the small farmers of Attica can be called peasants. More specifically, peasants have been characterized as 'rural cultivators whose surpluses are transferred to a dominant group of rulers that uses the surpluses both to underwrite its own standard of living and to distribute the remainder to groups in society that do not farm but must be fed for their specific goods and services in turn'. The production of a 'fund of rent' – the payment in labour, produce, or money to someone who 'exercises an effective superior power, or *domain*, over a cultivator' – is, by this definition, regarded as the characteristic 'which critically distinguishes the peasant from the primitive cultivator',[35] whether that 'rent' takes the form of payments to private landlords or a tax or corvée labour for some state or religious authority. It has been a general characteristic of peasants that a large proportion of their surplus production has been accounted for by rent and/or taxes. What distinguishes the Attic peasant from others in this respect, as we shall see, is the limited degree to which he was subject to such obligations.

Clearly, the need to intensify production has varied in large part according to the extent of such obligations. Patterns of surplus *production*, therefore, have varied in response to the demands of surplus *appropriation*. These patterns have been determined not only by 'objective' factors of population, ecology and technology, cultural factors and the standard of expectations, but in particular by social and political relations and the balance of power between producing and appropriating classes. In fact, demographic pressures themselves cannot be considered in abstraction from these relations.[36] The level at which population growth begins to strain available resources and productive capacities varies *inter alia* according to how much production is syphoned off by leisured appropriators. This is especially true in non-capitalist societies where appropriating classes tend to extract surplus 'unproductively', increasing their surplus by coercively squeezing the direct producer rather than by enhancing the *productivity* of labour through technical improvements. The more surplus appropriated by non-producers, the lower the population 'ceiling', the level at which 'overpopulation' occurs, and the level at which population growth requires intensified production. That Jameson has failed to take account of such considerations is illustrated by the fact that his central concern is to identify the source of the poorer citizen's free time without asking about the source or degree of the rich citizen's wealth.

Athens can be contrasted in these respects with other ancient civilizations which were also subject to demographic pressures and technological limitations and where production was also sufficiently intensive to support elaborate material cultures as well as state-forms far more complex than the Athenian polis. In the ancient Near East, for example, wealthy ruling strata, monarchs, and religious institutions were supported not by chattel slavery but by the heavy dues and labour services of subject peasant populations. The difference does indeed seem to lie in Athenian *citizenship* and the social limitations that it placed upon surplus production. But the critical point here is that the demands of citizenship determined not only the form of surplus production but also its extent. The civic status of the small producer limited the pressures for intensified production by limiting the two principal forms of surplus-extraction, rent and tax. The wealth and power of landlords, and hence the demands they could make on the society's productive capacities, were restricted by the configuration of social and political power represented by the democracy, which limited opportunities for concentrating property and afforded legal protections to small producers against certain forms of dependence. As for the tax burden so often borne by peasants, not only was the Athenian state apparatus relatively simple, but exemption from regular taxation, as M.I. Finley has suggested, was a hallmark of 'that novel and rarely repeated phenomenon of classical antiquity, the incorporation of the peasant as a full member of the political community'. For the Greeks, '[a] tithe or other form of direct tax on the land ... was the mark of a tyranny'.[37] In this respect, classical Athens (and Rome before the growth of her empire) differed dramatically from other societies in which kingdoms and empires have rested on the backs of a tax-burdened peasantry.

The question then might be whether Athens could sustain the level of civic and military participation by ordinary producers required to preserve these restrictions on surplus extraction, without transferring labour from peasants to slaves. One could, however, just as well ask how peasants anywhere have been able to subsist on family labour while sustaining the level of surplus production required to maintain extremely wealthy landowners and a large and complex state apparatus. Rome, the one case in which slavery did develop on a large scale in the context of a peasant economy, was an exceptional case, characterized both by immense concentrations of wealth and by a growing imperial apparatus. The peasants' frequent and long absences on military campaigns during the period of imperial expansion (and their consequent unreliability as a labour supply) made them uniquely subject to dispossession and replacement by slaves.

It is instructive to compare classical Athens with Rome. Here is how Keith Hopkins describes Rome in the third century BC before her vast imperial expansion and before the massive influx of slaves into the Roman economy:

> ... the area governed directly by Rome in the early third century BC was not large and rich enough to support sizeable concentrations of wealth. The political system reflected the widespread obligation to bear arms and the widespread ownership of land; although far from democratic, it effectively limited the extent to which most citizens were exploited. The nobles collectively probably owned much of the best land, but typically had only modest estates. Few of the farms were large enough to require employment of non-family labour throughout the year. The bulk of agricultural land and of common land was exploited by small-holders or yeomen peasants, some of whom were partly dependent on the patronage of the prosperous.
>
> Most Romans were under-employed. Even independent yeomen living just above the level of minimum subsistence had plenty of time with nothing to do. An average peasant household producing its minimum subsistence on quite good arable land used up very much less than half of its own labour power. This chronic under-employment is still common in many peasant economies using dry farming. It was institutionalized in Rome in numerous public holidays and in popular participation in politics. Above all, under-employment allowed the state, when it could not extract a sufficient surplus of produce in the form of taxes, to tax labour instead.[38]

Since surplus labour was 'taxed' especially in the form of military service, argues Hopkins, the growth of the Empire and the concomitant increase of the military burden were particularly disruptive to the peasant economy and also compelled the rich to find an alternative labour supply:

> ... in the traditional agricultural system, the rich depended for the cultivation of their farms on the surplus labour of the free poor, employed as tenants, share-croppers or as occasional labourers. But the conquest of an empire increased the incidence of military service, and either took free labour away or increased its unreliability. Besides, as the estates of the rich increased in size, so did their need for labour.[39]

The dispossession of peasants absent for long periods on military duty, and with it the concentration of land in the hands of wealthy proprietors, form the background against which the growth of slavery took place. Thereafter, Rome was notable not only for her far-flung empire and the large state and military apparatus required to sustain it, but also for immense and almost unrestricted concentrations of property and huge disparities of wealth. 'What distinguished Rome was neither economic inequality nor exploitation,' P.A. Brunt has argued, 'but the enormity in the scale of both.'[40]

M.I. Finley appears, at first glance, to disagree with Hopkins' assessment of slavery in early Rome, suggesting that he gives too much weight to the effects of conquest and arguing that Rome was a 'slave society' before the period of imperial expansion.[41] On closer inspection, however, the differences between Finley and Hopkins seem not so very substantial. Finley's argument is simply that, while 'conquest' and imperial growth were critical factors in the *expansion* of the slave society, they do not account for its *emergence*. The growth of empire was important because it created 'the basis for large estates' and hence for new forms of slave utilization; and Finley agrees that an 'enormous leap' occurred after the Second Punic War.[42] Unless the disagreement concerns precisely how many slaves there were before and after the 'enormous leap' (which would be impossible to ascertain in any case, given the meagre evidence for the two centuries before 200 BC – as Finley points out), Finley's argument seems essentially similar to that of Hopkins. Both historians agree that there were slaves before the third century, but that an 'enormous leap' took place thereafter, in conjunction with the 'drastic reorganization of landholdings',[43] the concentration of property and the creation of large estates, associated with the process of imperial expansion. It is precisely this process of 'drastic' reorganization and concentration of property which seems never to have occurred in classical Athens.

Finley, it is true, stresses that Rome before the great 'leap' was already a 'slave society' and not simply a society with slaves; but we must remind ourselves of what that means: a slave society for Finley is one in which *large-scale* production in both the city and the countryside is dominated by slave labour – as in Greece and Rome where the permanent work force in 'establishments larger than the family unit … was composed of slaves'[44] – irrespective of the proportion of the society's production which is actually conducted in such large-scale establishments. Since Finley speaks of imperial conquest as the process which created the basis for large estates, it seems reasonable to assume that, in his view, Roman farms before that time were generally small and that agriculture was dominated by free men – even if such larger establishments as existed had a permanent work force of slaves.

At any rate, Finley's argument in no way affects the case against Jameson – except, perhaps, to confirm it. Jameson's suggestion that agricultural slaves were normally used by ordinary small farmers in classical Attica would seem to run counter to the conviction of both Hopkins and Finley that small-scale farming in both Greece and Rome was dominated by free men and permitted little scope for the use of slave-labour.

Athens during the classical period was closer to Hopkins' description of early Republican Rome than to the later Imperial model. With a relatively simple state apparatus; no systematic taxation (in fact, a system which obtained public revenues directly from the rich rather than by taxing the poor); without huge concentrations and disparities of wealth; with an 'empire' not unified or governed by a large administrative apparatus; and with a less onerous military burden – Athens had far less need, or ability, to tax the labouring capacities of her peasants than did Rome.

The contrast in military arrangements is especially striking. If the fate of the Roman peasant was largely determined by the military demands of imperial expansion, which made him vulnerable to dispossession and replacement by slave labour, the position of the Athenian peasant was almost exactly the reverse. Warfare in Athens was, if anything, tailored to the peasant farmer, with its character, methods, objectives, and timing circumscribed by the needs, capacities, and seasonal rhythms of the smallholder:

> The peasant basis of society determined the nature of warfare. Ancient Greek warfare was a notoriously odd business which depended upon heavily armed infantry (hoplites) who could operate efficiently only on level ground. But Greece is a country with a mountainous terrain which has few open plains. War was endemic in the Greek city; but it took place only over a very limited campaigning season. The peculiarities stem directly from the importance of the countryside. Heavily armed hoplite soldiers may be of no use off the more or less level plains, but when it is these plains which it is most important for the city to defend hoplites are the best instrument available. Long campaigns may be more cost-effective, but when the soldier is himself the farmer, keeping him from his fields is counter-productive. ... Most fighting in Archaic and Classical Greece was between neighbouring cities in disputes over border land. Much of this fighting was not so much warfare as piratical raiding not intended to threaten human life. ...
>
> These raids do not try to gain control of the disputed territory; they aim directly at the agricultural wealth of the region. The border dispute provides an excuse for a sheep-raid.
>
> Warfare like this, consisting of raids, was the perfect complement to farming. Gaining agricultural supplies by raiding was an alternative to

farming, a way of making up deficiencies in one's own supplies. ...

Hoplite warfare can easily be presented as an absurdity once the aims of fighting become the conquest of the town and the incorporation of its whole territory. The hoplite force cannot deal with an enemy which does not concern itself primarily with the plains. But as long as raids for agricultural booty lay but thinly concealed behind the military activities of Greek cities the plains were what was at issue. Hoplite warfare was perfectly adapted to the defence of the plains.[45]

These traditional patterns of warfare were gradually replaced by new techniques and strategies, accompanying new and more clearly political objectives; and it was Athens which often led the way, controlling the seas with an unequalled naval force and increasingly besieging towns. Such changes reduced the importance of the farmer-soldier, and one of the constant themes among critics of the fourth-century 'decline' is the increasing use of mercenary soldiers in place of the old peasant-citizen. But even these late developments never eradicated the citizen-soldier, 'and major wars continued to be decided most frequently by hoplite battles'.[46] The old pattern was finally broken only by the Macedonian conquest, which brought an end to the independent polis.

Athenian democracy in its formative and 'classical' periods, then, had at its core a citizen-soldier very different from the Roman legionary. It is not enough to say that the nature of warfare in Athens was determined by the importance of the countryside, or by the imperatives of the peasant-soldier. The Roman army too was a peasant army. But in Rome, the expansionary drive of the senatorial class took precedence over the smallholder's interests; and if keeping the farmer from his fields was 'counter-productive' for the peasant himself, it had no such deleterious effects on the landlord who amassed a fortune in the process or the latifundist who replaced the absent farmer with slave labour. Roman war, for all its peasant manpower, was not a peasant war, limited by the farmer's attachment to his land, the exigencies of a smallholder's livelihood, or the rhythms of the agricultural calendar, an 'alternative' or 'adjunct' to farming; it was indeed warfare for territory, aristocratic land-grabbing on a global scale. Nor does the formula 'citizen-soldier' adequately describe the Roman peasant, as it does, paradigmatically, the Athenian farmer; for as the military role of the Roman peasant grew to meet the needs of imperial expansion, his position as citizen declined. This is the context in which Roman slavery evolved.

The political differences between Athens and Rome, between Athenian democracy and the senatorial or imperial regimes of Rome, had other consequences, too, for their respective peasantries. If, as Keith Hopkins suggests, the political system of the early Roman

Republic restricted the extent to which citizens could be exploited, this was even more true of Athenian democracy. In fact, in a very important sense the essence of citizenship for the Athenian peasant was protection from certain kinds of surplus extraction, both in the form of taxation (as Finley pointed out in the passage quoted above), and in the form of dependence on the rich. In Rome, the transition from republic to empire at first permitted the rich to avoid the burden of state revenue without transferring the full fiscal weight of empire to the peasants, by exploiting the provinces; but eventually, in contrast to Athens, the tax burden was increasingly shifted to the poor, while the public financial burden of the rich diminished even further.[47] In Athens, no such decline of the peasant as citizen took place while she remained an independent polis.

It is true that the relative unavailability of Athenian free producers for exploitation was itself a critical factor leading to the growth of slavery. In a sense, the free time of the poor was won at the expense of slave labour for the rich. This, however, tells us little about the use of slaves by the small proprietors themselves, which is Jameson's principal concern. Furthermore, while the relative freedom of the Athenian small producer encouraged slave utilization by the rich, that freedom itself placed *limits* on what the rich could do even with slaves. The relations between appropriating classes and free producers restricted not only the total amount of surplus production in general but also the extent and form of slave-exploitation itself. In particular, the configuration of class power between producing and appropriating citizens in Athens obstructed the concentration of property which could have made possible more intensive forms of slave production like the latifundial slavery of Rome.

The Roman case, then, was quite exceptional in its demands on the peasantry and its need for an alternative labour force. At the very least, it is no more difficult to believe that the Athenian peasant-citizen could both subsist on family labour and sustain an unusual degree of civic participation than it is to believe that peasants elsewhere (apart from Rome during *part* of her history and in *parts* of the Empire) have been able to live on family labour while still sustaining a complex state apparatus and great concentrations of wealth (e.g. in the ancient kingdoms of the Near East and Asia, early modern 'absolutist' France, etc.).

In all such cases, a significant factor in explaining these possibilities may be what has often been called, somewhat misleadingly, the 'chronic underemployment' of peasant economies, to which Keith Hopkins refers. It is a commonplace that peasant economies have been generally characterized by 'underproduction' (at least according to the standards of productivity demanded by modern capitalism) and by uneven rhythms of work, often with long 'unproductive' periods. These rhythms are, of course, determined in part by environmental and ecological factors, the weather, seasonal cycles, and so on. Production is also restricted by the size and quality of peasant holdings, which are often insufficient to support the family and may require the farmer to undertake labour for others as a casual labourer, sharecropper, or tenant in order to make ends meet. Analysts have also identified essential characteristics of the domestic unit as a unit of production which work against – or limit its demand for – production beyond the needs of family subsistence, and tend toward an under-utilization even of existing resources and technologies, in the absence of external compulsion.[48] The 'inefficiency' of peasant production, the tendency to absorb surplus work-hours by increasing labour input and effectively reducing labour-productivity, has also been noted. The implication is that, according to circumstances, peasants with smallholdings generally must either seek work outside their households on someone else's land, as tenants or casual hired labourers, or keep their essentially 'underemployed' families busy at home by maintaining a more labour-intensive (and cheaper) system of production and suppressing technical improvements in labour productivity.[49]

The very idea of 'underemployment' or 'hidden unemployment' as applied to peasant economies has been criticized by scholars sensitive to anachronisms and the inapplicability of values and categories derived from the capitalist economy with its unprecedented need and capacity for maximum productivity, or from the rhythms of industrial production and the factory which knows no seasons. These criticisms, however, merely reinforce the argument being made here. Without denying the characteristics of peasant production described by others in the language of 'underemployment', critics reject this designation precisely on the grounds that it assumes, among other things, that the model peasant is a full-time agriculturalist. This assumption 'represents a gross distortion of the varied and complex tasks which peasants may undertake during the course of a single day'.[50] So the concept of underemployment treats time not devoted to farming as 'rest' or 'idleness', when in fact the *typical* peasant is one who devotes only part of his time to agricultural production and much of it to other activities: crafts; trading; communal work, including the performance of various functions for cult and village; and a variety of tasks which in more 'developed' economies would be performed by full-time specialists.

So whether we accept the formulation that small peasants are typically 'underemployed', or reject the concept of 'underemployment' and recognize not only non-agricultural and even non-productive and 'extra-economic' activities as essential to the social function of the peasant, it remains true that *all* peasants to a greater or lesser extent must divide their time between productive and unproductive activities, as well as between household and communal functions. We must add to these considerations the fact that time devoted to productive activities is itself normally divided between production for the peasant's own family (as well as, quite commonly, assistance to his peasant neighbours) and surplus labour for landlord, state, or religious establishment.

With all this in mind, it becomes far less difficult to imagine an Attic peasant family, relatively free of the need to create massive wealth for rich compatriots or to support an immense political superstructure, sustaining itself without alien labour, while the head of the household remains able to perform his civic and military functions; though we should not exaggerate the amount of time spent by ordinary peasants attending assemblies and juries, the democratic ideal notwithstanding.[51] At the same time, the political importance of the *village* as the bedrock of the democratic state (more on this in the next chapter) discouraged changes in residence patterns, keeping people attached to their village communities, and reinforcing adherence to subsistence strategies in agriculture.[52] Some ordinary peasants may have had a slave, male or female, who lived as part of the family and shared in all its activities; but we should not underestimate how difficult it would have been for a peasant family, living always close to the margin – and this would include not just the poorest but the many who had holdings of a few acres – and typically 'underemployed', to solve its problems of subsistence by adding to the household yet more permanent and alien mouths to feed.

Jameson's contention that slave labour was the norm on the ordinary peasant holding is, therefore, hardly convincing. As for slavery on large estates, he presumably regards the question as settled and unproblematic. It is true, of course, that the case being made here *against* the widespread use of slaves by peasants is based in large part on the fact that small farmers were relatively free from the necessity to produce a surplus for larger landholders and that this freedom was paid for to some extent by the labour of slaves on wealthier farms. We should not, however, go to the other extreme and underestimate the degree to which Athenian citizen-farmers were themselves exploited, producing wealth for their rich compatriots as tenants, sharecroppers, or casual hired labourers. The question of slave-utilization by wealthy proprietors cannot be separated from this issue; and it cannot be taken for granted that, if the use of slaves by peasants is problematic, at least we can be sure of the degree to which wealthy Athenians relied on slaves to produce their wealth.

Ste Croix and the Debate on Agricultural Slavery

These issues are highlighted in the work of G.E.M. de Ste Croix. Since Ste Croix regards Jameson's article as the *only* recent study to assign slavery its proper role and to present the evidence accurately, he presumably accepts its reasoning about slavery on peasant holdings.[53] His own arguments, however, seem at least implicitly to have more to do with larger landowners, though we are never told how far down the social scale we should take examples drawn from literary accounts of wealthy Athenians. At any rate, Ste Croix's discussion, more than Jameson's, allows us to assess the state of the evidence concerning agricultural slavery on the larger properties where we should most expect to find it.

Ste Croix quite justly points out that the absence of evidence is no proof of non-existence but goes on, rather less judiciously, to maintain emphatically that 'a great deal of slave labour' was employed on the land, 'contrary to what is sometimes said.'[54] He does not himself support this assertion by direct evidence (of which there is little) or even by calculation and deduction based on what is known about crop yields, the size of landholdings, etc., but relies on an interpretation of literary texts. Above all, however, he depends on the abstract and speculative assumption that unfree labour, in the absence of hired labour, is the most profitable method of surplus extraction. In the end, much of his argument, as we shall see, turns on this assumption: the best case in favour of widespread agricultural slavery, he maintains, is to be found not in any available positive evidence but in the *a priori* preferability of unfree labour and wage-labour as modes of exploitation. Since, he argues, wage-labour was rare in Athens, there must have been a great deal of slavery.

Something needs to be said about this first premise before we turn to Ste Croix's use of the literary evidence. Ste Croix argues that slavery was the best means of extracting 'the largest possible surplus from the primary producers' under the prevailing conditions.[55] This proposition is based on a more general rule that unfree labour and hired labour are the only ways of consistently achieving a large surplus – in contrast to the appropriation of rents from free producers, or other forms of appropriation, such as taxation or compulsory services, made possible by control of the state machine: 'to ensure a really large surplus for a long period, the bulk of the primary producers must either be made to give unfree labour, under the constraint of slavery or serfdom or debt bondage, or they must be driven to sell their labour power for a wage'.[56] Under the conditions prevailing in ancient Greece and Rome, slavery was the best available means of extraction,

... having regard to the low level of productivity, and also to the fact that *free hired* labour was scarce, largely confined to unskilled or seasonal work, and not at all mobile, whereas slaves were available in large numbers and at prices the lowness of which is astonishing, in comparison with what is known of slave prices in other societies.[57]

This argument leaves the critical questions unanswered, and unasked. Ste Croix, to begin with, generally underplays the disadvantages of slavery which might put in question his primary assumption about its inherent superiority over other modes of exploitation – such as the difficulties and costs of supervision (which in Athens would have been aggravated by the fact that wealthy landowners often held their property in scattered parcels rather than large estates) or the problems arising out of the fact that the master's investment is embodied not simply in means of production or labour-time but in the very person of the slave.[58] More importantly, the argument is surprisingly ahistorical. The suggestion that unfree labour and hired labour are two intrinsically preferable forms and that in Athens slavery was the chief alternative in the absence of hired labour does not advance the issue very far. Hired labour has, after all, never been the predominant form of surplus appropriation until the very recent and localized predominance of capitalist appropriation. Where wage-labour has existed in pre-capitalist or non-capitalist economies, it has generally been an adjunct to other forms of labour and surplus appropriation, often as a means of supplementing the incomes of smallholders whose land – whether owned or held conditionally – has been insufficient for subsistence. In such cases, wage-labour has tended to be casual or seasonal, employed particularly at the harvest. Wage-labour as a predominant form presupposes a labour-force composed of people who are juridically free but devoid of land or any other property essential to production – whether held in ownership or some kind of conditional possession such as tenancy – and therefore dependent for their livelihood upon the sale of their labour-power for a wage on a regular, continuous basis. The predominance of such a labour-force has been unique to the capitalist economy which emerged in early modern Europe. In non-capitalist economies, where peasants have tended to dominate production, propertied classes have derived their wealth primarily from rents, labour services, dues, fines, taxes, tithes, or tributes, imposed upon producers who have been in various ways dependent upon them, either in legal bondage, e.g. as serfs or debt-bondsmen, or in otherwise subordinate positions, as sharecroppers or tenants.

Various modes of appropriating surplus from peasant producers who owe part of their labour or produce – in kind or in money – to landlords have existed throughout recorded history and throughout the world. At the same time, large-scale chattel slavery has been rare.[59] Wage-labour cannot, therefore, in any historically meaningful sense be regarded as the chief alternative whose non-availability proves the importance of slavery.

It is worth adding that Ste Croix seems to assume that the necessity of accumulation characteristic of capitalism is a universal law of nature, and that every system needs a maximum surplus in the way that capitalism does. Equally unhelpful is his habit of lumping chattel slavery together with all other forms of unfree labour such as serfdom and debt-bondage. Why slavery and not other forms of unfree labour, and why in Greece and not elsewhere in the ancient world (or virtually anywhere else at any time), even under similar conditions of low productivity and a similar 'unavailability' of wage-labour? How do we account for the large surpluses produced and appropriated in other ancient civilizations in the Near East and Asia where, although neither chattel slavery nor wage-labour played a major role, there existed elaborate material cultures and state apparatuses and luxuriously leisured ruling classes? And if we grant that forms of *unfree* labour other than slavery were unavailable in Athens (notably because of the political status of peasants and artisans), Ste Croix gives no adequate reason – as we shall see – for assuming that slavery remained the only eligible option. If we consider the importance of tenancy and sharecropping of various kinds throughout history, it is difficult to take seriously his easy dismissal of rent-extraction from free producers as a major source of wealth, on the a priori ground that unfree labour is in principle more profitable than free.

In fact, the very idea of an a priori superiority inherent in a mode of exploitation is ill-conceived. There can be no doubt that for the Greek and Roman propertied classes slavery was a lucrative means of surplus extraction and that the degree of control they derived from the outright ownership of labourers as chattel property afforded them great advantages. 'Yet,' writes M.I. Finley,

> for all the advantages (or apparent advantages), slavery was a late and relatively infrequent form of involuntary labour, in world history generally and in ancient history in particular. Advantages and disadvantages are not essences but historical attributes that come and go under changing social and economic conditions.[60]

Ste Croix's attempt to construct an argument in the absence of positive evidence therefore rests on a very weak foundation. Now let us see how he deals with such positive evidence as there is.

In Appendix II of his book, he sums up what he regards as the most important textual evidence. It must be said that, if there are convincing arguments available to make his case, Ste Croix fails to produce them. Indeed, his evidence here is alarmingly thin, and he uses it much less carefully than his painstaking scholarship elsewhere leads one to expect. The evidence is hardly conclusive and does little more than prove at best that agricultural slaves existed, especially on large estates (which no one denies). Ste Croix fails to acknowledge the difficulties posed by the imprecision and ambiguity of the language in the texts he cites, though many of his examples are precisely the problematic ones mentioned in our own discussion of Xenophon. More significant, however, is his rather liberal interpretation of the evidence.

Apart from references to various passages in Xenophon, Aristophanes and Demosthenes which Ste Croix cites largely without quotation or discussion, his case in favour of agricultural slavery consists of two principal elements: a discussion of the famous passage in Thucydides about the escape of more than 20,000 slaves during the occupation of Decelea; and the 'negative' argument that in the absence of hired labour, slavery was the best available means by which Athenian landowners could have made 'appreciable incomes' – an argument that relies on evidence concerning hired labour rather than slavery.[61]

Let us look first at the discussion of the passage from Thucydides, to which Ste Croix here devotes nearly half of his argument. Thucydides (VII 27.5) refers to more than 20,000 slaves who escaped from Attica during the Spartan occupation of Decelea.[62] This is a passage which commentators often cite in their estimates of the slave population. Ste Croix makes a great deal of the phrase '*more than*' 20,000, suggesting that many historians have misquoted this phrase as if it said a *total* of 20,000. From this Ste Croix concludes that Thucydides must have had in mind a maximum of hardly less than 30,000. Having established to his own satisfaction that the number of escaped slaves was as high as 30,000, Ste Croix goes on to the next phrase which suggests that a great part – or, as Ste Croix prefers to interpret it, the greater part – of these slaves were *cheirotechnai*. This word, which normally refers to craftsmen or artisans, he translates more generally as skilled men or experts; and because they were skilled, it seems to him unlikely that they were largely mine-slaves, as many scholars have supposed.

It could be argued, first of all, that the debate about numbers is futile, since Thucydides himself could hardly have known the figures with any degree of precision or certainty. Nevertheless, even if the figures must remain speculative, we can at least accept that there were large numbers of skilled workmen among the slaves. Ste Croix, however, is on weaker ground if he assumes that these *cheirotechnai* are unlikely to have been miners simply on the grounds that workers in the mines would not have been regarded as 'skilled'. In fact, the evidence suggests that a miner could be thought of as a craftsman – *cheirotechnēs, technitēs,* or *dēmiourgos*; and such men, like other craftsmen, left visible testimony to the pride they took in their *technē*.[63]

It may be fair to say that not all or perhaps even most of the *cheirotechnai* are likely to have been mine slaves or even workers in the various processing operations connected with the silver mines. There may have been other kinds of craftsmen from the villages and towns in the *chōra*. But having asserted that the deserters were mainly skilled workers, Ste Croix makes a leap in his argument which is truly breathtaking in its inconsequence. He simply adds: '... no doubt including agricultural specialists such as vine-dressers, who would have better opportunities for running away than e.g. mine-slaves'.[64] That breezy phrase is the sum of the evidence which Ste Croix extracts from Thucydides to prove that agricultural slavery was prevalent in classical Athens.

Jameson, incidentally, uses this passage in Thucydides to support his own case on agricultural slavery in a way that directly contradicts Ste Croix. He denies that *cheirotechnai* were 'the majority', 'the greater part', rather than simply 'a large part'; and, more particularly, he questions the assumption that these skilled workers included significant numbers of agricultural experts, supposing instead that they 'came largely from the *ergasteria* in the mining district and elsewhere'.[65] He believes nonetheless that the passage as a whole implies 'significant losses in farm labour'. His reason for this conclusion seems to be simply that the passage speaks of the Attic *chōra* and its losses, which (if I understand him correctly) presumably means that the slaves who escaped were largely from the countryside. Even if this is so, however, it tells us little about how many lost slaves were farm labourers. Thucydides refers not simply to the loss of slaves but to the general disruption of agriculture caused by the enemy's domination of the countryside. In any case, the slave-population of the *chōra* would certainly have included mineworkers and domestic servants, as well as the skilled craftsmen who laboured in the villages and small townships scattered throughout Attica. (It is, after all, important to remember that 'urban' craftsmen cannot have been confined to the city of Athens.) Indeed, taken together, these types of slaves could, as we have seen, conceivably account for most of the 'more than 20,000', leaving little room for real agricultural slaves. At any rate, however this passage is interpreted, the very least that can be said is that it leaves us none the wiser about the proportion of Attic slaves who functioned as agricultural labourers.

Another striking example of Ste Croix's mode of interpretation occurs in his citation of a passage from Xenophon's *Memorabilia* to prove that 'Even the overseer or manager ... of an estate in Attica (or elsewhere) would normally be a slave or a freedman.'[66] It may be so, but the text in question tells us nothing of the kind. In this passage (*Mem.* II 8, esp. 3–4), Eutherus, apparently once a man of property, tells Socrates that since his return from the war he has been forced to work for a living with his hands (literally, his body). He and Socrates then go on to discuss what Eutherus might do when he becomes too old for physical labour, and Socrates suggests that he might hire himself out as an overseer to manage a wealthier man's estate. Eutherus replies that it would be hard for him to submit to servitude (*douleia*).

Now why this passage should be cited as evidence that bailiffs or overseers were normally slaves is far from clear. On the contrary, it could be taken to mean that the notion of a free hired bailiff was quite normal. What the text does suggest is that Athenians, and more particularly men accustomed to the independent life of the propertied class, were reluctant to accept salaried employment, which was generally regarded as a dependent condition. From this point of view, such employment would constitute *douleia*. Ste Croix cites the exchange between Socrates and Eutherus much earlier in the book to illustrate the attitude of Athenians toward hired labour.[67] But while Xenophon's words can legitimately be used to illustrate a particular attitude toward hired labour or salaried employment they cannot be used – as Ste Croix uses them in the earlier reference – to support the contention that hired labour was rare in Athens. However widespread the disdain for such dependence might be, it tells us nothing about the number of people who may have had no choice but to accept it – as Xenophon's Eutherus may have been forced to do, like other citizens with insufficient property, let alone the many who were classed as *thētes* and who were therefore officially propertyless or at least in possession of minimal property.[68] In this connection it is worth noting another passage, from Xenophon's *Ways and Means*, which seems to suggest that many Athenians who lacked the strength to work with their hands might be happy to earn a living as managers (IV 22). However widely accepted the upper-class norm of true *eleutheria* may have been among Athenians, it is clear that a great many citizens could not actually live in accordance with it. Reasoning as Ste Croix does here, one might equally conclude, given the strictures against the banausic life so often repeated by aristocratic writers, that few Athenians engaged in manual labour at all.[69] At any rate, the important point now is that the passage in question tells us nothing at all about the prevalence of slave-bailiffs or even about their very existence.

Ste Croix does not rest his case on positive evidence alone. On the contrary, he suggests that perhaps the most telling argument for the importance of slaves in Athenian agriculture is the negative one:

> that hired labour, the only alternative way in which Athenian land-owners could have made appreciable incomes out of their property (as we know they did), or indeed any profit at all (apart from leasing), was evidently rare and confined mainly to the season of harvest, vintage and olive-picking.[70]

This argument immediately raises a host of problems. The first is that in order to support his contention that wage-labour was rare, Ste Croix appears to rely on a methodological principle he has himself emphatically rejected: treating the infrequency of references as testimony to the rarity of the institution.[71] The rejection of this principle is the basis of his argument in favour of agricultural slavery. As positive evidence, he cites three passages from Xenophon's *Memorabilia* to prove the comparative insignificance of hired labour.[72] One is the story of Eutherus already mentioned, which proves nothing one way or the other except that some formerly wealthy Athenians were reluctant to accept salaried employment. Another is a well-known exchange (II 7.2–6) in which Aristarchus complains that since the revolution (the coup of the Thirty Tyrants) he has had a household full of relatives, largely women, to support. He has no income from his landed property, which has been seized by enemies, nor from his house property, since there are so few people left in the city to rent it. Socrates cites the example of Ceramon (and others) who, with many mouths to feed, manages to support his family and still save enough to be rich. Aristarchus points out that Ceramon's dependants are largely slaves, while his own are free persons. The implication is that such free persons cannot be expected to do manual work – a notion which Socrates in this instance rejects, suggesting that Aristarchus put his womenfolk to work to produce marketable goods.

Now whatever this passage may do to suggest that upper-class Athenians despised manual labour (and that Socrates, who often accepts the anti-democratic views of his wealthy companions and patrons, at least on this occasion takes a different view – though, significantly, only in the case of women), it is really stretching the point to argue that the text tells us anything much about hired labour. It is not even clear that Ste Croix is right to interpret this exchange between Socrates and Aristarchus as indicating that 'in Xenophon's opinion the average upper-class Athenian of his day automatically assumed that a really profitable manufacturing business would be slave-worked';[73] but even if this is so, we are hardly entitled to draw the general and unequivocal conclusion that 'the labour exploited by the propertied class is that of slaves'. The passage refers to very specific cases in which wealthy men use the domestic skills of their household members – slave or free – to make saleable domestic items like bread or clothing. We are even less entitled to draw any conclusions about slaves in agriculture, and still less about the use of hired labour in the Athenian economy in general. In fact, the argument is rather circular: if the rarity of wage-labour is supposed to prove the prevalence of slavery, we cannot use the same text to prove both the importance of slavery *and* the rarity of wage-labour – quite apart from the fact that there is here no reference to *agricultural* labour at all.

The other passage cited by Ste Croix in his discussion of hired labour (*Memorabilia* III 11, esp. 4) seems to suggest that there are three obvious ways of acquiring wealth in Athens: to have a farm, a house to let, or craftsmen. This may very well be true; but again, it is far from clear what it proves about hired labour – or indeed about slavery. Xenophon tells us nothing here about how or by whom the farm in question would be worked. Nor, for that matter, is Ste Croix necessarily entitled to turn the craftsmen (*cheirotechnai*) into *slave*-craftsmen. Xenophon may have slaves in mind, but we can hardly assume this if we are to use the text as proof that slaves were used to the exclusion of hired labour. We are even less entitled to assume that the *farm* is worked by slaves – which is the crucial point for Ste Croix in his argument that the rarity of wage-labour is the most telling case for the prevalence of slavery in agriculture.

It is, of course, more than probable that hired labour, at least regular hired work as distinct from casual or seasonal wage-labour among free men, was relatively rare in Athens. Nevertheless, the very evidence Ste Croix produces indicates that it was not as unimportant to the Attic economy as he suggests. Ste Croix cites all the texts – and they are indeed infrequent – which he has been able to discover referring to hired labour in Athenian agriculture.[74] What is significant about these references is not just their infrequency, but the fact that they include passages which make it clear that the use of wage-labour in harvesting was typical – so much so that the word 'harvester' was virtually synonymous with 'hired man'. So, for example, in *Hiero* (VI 10), Xenophon writes that tyrants hire guards just like harvesters. Similarly, Demosthenes (XVIII 51) denounces Aeschines as not a friend but a hireling of Philip and Alexander, 'unless a harvester or other hired man is to be called the friend and guest-friend of the man who pays his wages'. The implication seems to be that harvesting was typically done by hired labourers (at least on larger farms). Given the importance of harvesting in a primarily agrarian economy, this is no small matter.

Even to say, as Ste Croix does, that wage-labour was 'confined mainly to the seasons of harvest, vintage and olive-picking' is already to say a great deal.[75] It hardly supports his own conclusion that hired labour was unimportant if it was the typical form of harvest labour, and if the harvest accounted for a very substantial part of agricultural labour, as it has commonly done in agrarian economies.[76] It is possible that some of the hired labourers were slaves let out by contractors; but this needs at least to be argued, not assumed. In any case, the strong possibility that an essential part of agricultural labour was typically performed by hired labour raises serious questions about Ste Croix's 'negative' argument for the prevalence of agricultural slavery.

A further question is raised by the negative argument. Here again Ste Croix's case is built upon the assumption that slavery and hired labour were the only alternative ways 'in which Athenian landowners could have made appreciable incomes out of their property ... or indeed any profit at all'.[77] Significantly, he adds parenthetically the phrase '(apart from leasing)'. The rest of the argument proceeds as if the parenthetical possibility did not exist. Indeed the 'negative' argument in favour of agricultural slavery depends upon the assumption that no reasonable alternative other than wage-labour was available. Ste Croix fails, however, to explain why we should so readily dismiss the option of leasing, except to reiterate the assertion that '... leasing cannot be expected to yield nearly as much profit as working land directly with slave labour...'.[78] Since various forms of tenancy and sharecropping have been among the most common modes of surplus extraction throughout history, this cavalier dismissal is especially puzzling. Here again Ste Croix falls back on his unproved assumption about the inherently superior profitability of slavery, which, of course, in abstraction proves nothing at all. Quite apart from whether the 'social costs' involved were quantifiable, even Ste Croix himself acknowledges that the circumstances surrounding slave-exploitation may be such as to offset its inherent profitability. Indeed, he even suggests that these circumstances may render leasing preferable. For example, discussing the rise of the colonate in Rome, he writes of

> the additional time and effort which a landowner working his estate directly with slave-labour would have to expend in order to get the best results, compared with the landlord who leased out his land, and the impetus this would give to leasing. ... Over all, farms which were leased would normally have required less attention from their owners, and this would have partly discounted the higher profits to be expected from land worked directly with slaves.[79]

The need for direct supervision is a limitation on the advantages of slavery that might be said to inhere in the nature of slavery itself. This is quite apart from the many other conditions and qualifications that need to be taken into account in accordance with the principle that the desirability of any form of exploitation is not a universal 'essence' but a 'historical attribute'. Ste Croix generally neglects this principle in his assessment of leasing as an alternative to slavery; and to the extent that he takes it into account, the presumption is almost always a priori in favour of slavery. For instance, in his argument for the prevalence of slavery he cites Columella (I 7.4-7) to illustrate that leasing was considered undesirable by Roman writers, except under certain limited circumstances, notably when the landowner could not regularly supervise the work himself.[80] The passage could, however, as easily be read as an argument in favour of tenancy. Columella here outlines the many dangers attendant upon slave estates not personally supervised by the landlord and recommends leasing in such cases. The possibility of regular personal supervision could certainly not be taken for granted in Rome for a variety of reasons, not least the tendency for the holdings of large proprietors to be widely dispersed, and the political pre-occupations which kept many landowners in the city of Rome and away from their farms (I 1.19).

The dispersion of landholdings was typical in Attica as well, and constant supervision of slaves would also interfere with social and political activities (a point that Jameson, incidentally, overlooks).[81] We might conclude, then, that Columella's principle was operative there too. At any rate, if we are entitled to speculate in the absence of positive evidence and draw conclusions about the frequency of certain labour-forms from their advantages, a case could be made for the view that tenancy or sharecropping must have been fairly common because they had certain significant advantages over other forms, given the general drawbacks of slavery and its need for supervision and given the historical circumstances of class relations and political conditions.

It might be somewhat imprudent to draw this conclusion in the absence of positive evidence, and the fact is that the evidence for tenancy in classical Athens is relatively sparse (as indeed is the evidence for other specific forms of labour). One notable exception is Lysias VII 4-11, which, surveying the history of one particular plot, catalogues a series of lettings as if this were the most natural disposition of land.[82] Still, we should perhaps not expect, in the surviving literature, to find references allowing us to distinguish among peasants and the various ways in which they may have held their land. The smallholders who made up the bulk of Athenian proprietors are of little concern to someone like Xenophon, writing in the *Oeconomicus* about large estates. Where they are mentioned, we are unlikely to be informed about the status of their land, any more than we might be in English literary references to 'husbandmen' or 'farmers', which would not normally permit us to distinguish among the forms of tenure such people enjoyed.

Consider, for example, a passage from one of the older Robin Hood ballads, the *Gest of Robyne Hode* (stanzas 13–14), where Robin states his principles to Little John:

> But loke ye do no husbonde harme
> That tilleth with his ploughe
> No more ye shall no gode yeman
> That walketh by grene-wode shawe;
> Ne no knyght ne no squyer
> That wol be gode felawe.

The 'husbonde' here is evidently a cultivator with a landholding of some kind who probably possesses a plough-team; but we have no way of knowing in what form or on what conditions he holds the land, just as we can rarely be sure about the status of the Greek *georgos* or *ergazomenos*. In fact, as R.H. Hilton points out in a discussion of rural society in late mediaeval England, in the many literary works depicting country life we cannot normally distinguish among peasants of various kinds, their forms of tenure or even their degrees of freedom, at a time when the distinction between free and villein was still important in manorial documentation. 'A normal contrast in literature is between "lords and common people"...', he writes. 'Country people are referred to as "tillers" or husbandmen, normally without distinction of status.'[83] Thus, words like 'tiller', or 'husbandman', or 'ploughman' can cover a wide range of peasant tenures, from free tenures to tenancies in villeinage.

Similar ambiguities have attached historically to other words in English having to do with the status of people who cultivate the land. The word 'farmer' itself is a case in point (see *OED*). Originally the farmer or 'fermor' (like the French *fermier*) was specifically a tenant and sometimes a bailiff or steward – someone to whom land was 'farmed' out by a wealthier landlord to be managed or worked (like Xenophon's manager?); but for a time this meaning coexisted with the more general meaning of 'farmer' as applied to anyone who cultivates the land. Among other things, this conflation of meaning may suggest the frequency with which farm labour was done by tenants. The 'yeoman', generally regarded as the model prosperous peasant, was originally by definition a nobleman's servant or attendant (see *OED*); and in the heyday of the English yeomanry, Sir Thomas Smith, writing in the 1560s, could speak of yeomen as both *freemen* or 40-shilling freeholders (i.e., part of the Parliamentary electorate) and '(for the most part) fermors to gentlemen', that is, tenants working the land of lords, knights, and gentlemen.[84] In fact, the seemingly clear-cut concept of 'freehold' included certain kinds of tenancy.

The often ambiguous shadings of meaning in the spectrum between dependent labourer, tenant, and freeholder reflects the complicated spectrum of conditions and tenures typical of smallholders in many parts of the world. This is especially true where there is no concept of 'absolute' private property but rather various shades of conditional property; where there is no clear dividing line between outright ownership and mere possession or occupancy; and where there is no rigid dichotomy between property and propertylessness of the kind that exists in modern capitalist society. The indeterminacy of peasant conditions and tenures would have been especially characteristic of classical Greece, which, before the development of Roman property law, had no clear legal conception of *ownership* at all.[85]

In the light of these considerations, it is at least worth suggesting that historians have not made as much as they could of the available literary evidence. One especially tantalizing example will illustrate the possibilities – and the difficulties – secreted in the texts.

At the beginning of the *Oeconomicus* Xenophon raises the possibility that a man can be put in charge of another's estate and practise the art of estate management without himself owning land (I 3–4). The passage clearly refers not to a slave-bailiff but to a free manager. Ste Croix takes this to be one of the rare Greek references to hired labour, and in any case quickly dismisses it as a 'hypothetical point' in a text which otherwise assumes that overseers are slaves. He argues that Xenophon is simply trying to illustrate hypothetically 'the fact that what you do for yourself you can also do for others', and that elsewhere in the book (XII–XV) Xenophon always taks for granted that the overseer will be a slave.[86] The text could, however, be read in quite a different sense. First, it may demonstrate that the notion of free managers was quite normal in Athens. Thus, everything that follows on the art of estate management applies to owner-manager and non-owning manager alike. It is important to note that, even if the later passages cited by Ste Croix refer to slave-bailiffs, they do not necessarily in any way affect Xenophon's original suggestion about the free manager. Although Xenophon speaks here of turning over or entrusting (*epitrepein*) an estate to such a manager, he does not actually refer to the manager himself as *epitropos* or *epistatēs*, the terms he later uses to describe the bailiff or steward. The free manager in the opening passage is, like the landlord, spoken of as someone who fulfils the role of *oikonomos* (I 2) or *oikonomikos* (I 3). So Xenophon may be thinking here of a different person from the bailiff discussed in detail later on (XI 25–XV 10). What the free manager does is not simply to act as bailiff in the sense intended by the later passages but rather, like the landowner and in his stead, to practise the art of estate management (*oikonomia*), an art which includes the procuring, training, and general supervision of good bailiffs and labourers. In other words, the free man referred to at the outset apparently stands in lieu of the landlord, not of the bailiff.[87]

The bailiff discussed in XI 25–XV 10 probably is a slave, literally 'bought'; but even here there are some ambiguities. It is clear, for example, that the bailiff is permitted to profit from his activities and, indeed, that a certain degree of passion for material gain may actually be a desirable quality in a manager (XII 15–16). He may even be enabled to grow rich; and his master may treat him like a free man (*eleutheros*) and even a gentleman (*kalos kagathos*). At the very least, this reflects the profound complexity of the slave condition, illustrating that the juridical category of slavery might incorporate conditions shading into other less dependent forms of labour.

It is even possible that Xenophon is indifferent to the juridical status of bailiffs, who could be either slaves or free. The suggestion that they may be 'treated like' *eleutheroi* is not by itself an indication that they are slaves, since even a free hired manager or tenant might not be regarded as *eleutheros*. 'The free man', as Finley points out, 'was one who neither lived under the constraint of, nor was employed for the benefit of, another; who lived preferably on his ancestral plot of land, with its shrines and ancestral tombs.'[88] At any rate, if the bailiff is a slave, we should be careful about how we generalize from this example. The advice about the bailiff is given by Xenophon's model landlord, Ischomachus, an exceptionally rich man.[89] His extreme wealth (by Athenian standards) makes his example in general a difficult one for others to follow; and his daily activities (XI 14–18) are certainly those of a very rich man with considerable leisure. Since those activities include regular visits to the farm in question, we may presume that this farm meets the condition for a slave-run estate, regular supervision by the landlord, which was surely not possible on all estates.[90]

Let us return, then, to the free manager of I 3–4, who apparently plays the part of an *oikonomos*, not simply that of a bailiff. The most important point is that Xenophon may not be speaking here of a hired manager at all, in the sense of a salaried employee, but rather of some kind of tenant. The critical passage reads as follows: Having been asked by Socrates whether a man who understands the art of estate management can earn money managing another's estate even if he owns no property himself, Critobulus replies, 'Of course; and he could bring in good rewards if, having taken over an estate, he pays what is due and produces a surplus to increase the estate' (I 4).[91] What is striking about this passage is that it conjures up a manager who is responsible for certain outgoings or dues, especially payments to the landlord, and whose earnings are determined by the amount of surplus he produces over the outgoings. This is certainly not the position of a hired man or salaried employee in any strict sense, implying the receipt of a fixed wage or salary. Such a man would not be responsible for outgoings, nor would his earnings be directly determined by the surplus over outgoings. The conditions described here are much more like those of a tenant who takes over a piece of land, assuming responsibility for all its burdens and costs, paying a portion of his earnings to the landlord, and keeping for himself whatever he produces over and above his rents and expenses.

It is true that the word used to describe this 'manager's' earnings is *misthos*, the word most commonly used to refer to a wage. *Misthos* can, however, mean 'reward' or 'recompense' in a more general sense; and, for example, the verb *misthophorein* can mean either 'to work for hire' *or* 'to bring in rent or profit'. Furthermore, there are etymological and historical reasons for supposing that a close connection existed between the 'hired' manager and the tenant or sharecropper. There is a close etymological relationship between *misthos* and *misthōsis*, 'wage' and 'rent'. The *misthōtos* is a hired man; the *misthōtēs* can be a rent-payer or tenant.[92] The linguistic fluidity between the words for *paying* rent and *receiving* a wage probably suggests a real structural and historical connection between them which is not conveyed by the clear and even antithetical difference between rent and wage in the modern sense. In his study of Athenian law, Douglas M. MacDowell makes the following suggestion about the possible historical transmutation of *misthos* into *misthōsis*:

> By lease it was possible to obtain use of property without acquiring ownership of it. The word for lease or rent is *misthosis*, and the connection of that word with *misthos* ('fee', 'wages') suggests the following course of development. A landowner might employ a man to work a piece of his land, giving him a fixed amount of the produce each year (*misthos*) and keeping the rest himself. Then, to encourage the labourer to work hard, the landowner might agree to take only a fixed amount of the produce each year, allowing the labourer to keep the rest; in practical effect, this would mean that the labourer had a lease of the piece of land and paid a fixed rent for it.[93]

In other words, the fixed rent as outgoing is not here diametrically opposed to the fixed 'wage' as income (the term 'wage' in this context is in any case misleading); both characterize a relationship between landlord and tenant, in which one man is paid for working or managing another's land, and payment is made by means of dividing the tenant's product between himself and the landlord. In both cases, the earnings derived from working for someone else might be a *misthos*.

The critical point here is that, whether the tenant receives a fixed wage or pays a fixed rent, he is regarded as someone employed to work or manage another's land. The form in which he receives his share does not alter his position in this respect, even if it may affect his earnings or his attitude toward productivity. That the ancients included certain kinds of tenancy among the several ways in which a landlord might employ a farm manager to work his land – in other words, that they may have regarded tenancy as a kind of 'hired' labour – is suggested at least by Roman sources.[94] Cato, for example, seems to have in mind a gradual continuum from letting out a whole piece of land to a sharecropping tenant, to letting out a piece of it for a specific purpose (e.g., tending a vineyard), to letting or contracting out a specific task (e.g., gathering olives) to be performed by hired labourers (*De Re Rustica* 136–7, 144). In each case, people are paid to perform agricultural labour, though depending on the comprehensiveness and the duration of the task – which may range from taking charge of a whole estate all year round, to performing a specific and narrowly defined seasonal task such as harvesting a particular crop – payment can range from a share of the farm's entire yield (either as a fixed share of the crop or the share that is left after rent) to a wage.

A mixture of various rent-forms, fixed or variable, ranged along a continuous scale, extracted in various ways by landlords from tenants and sharecroppers with varying degrees of security of tenure according to prevailing needs and possibilities, has been typical of many agrarian economies. At the very least, we must entertain the possibility that such forms of tenancy, leasing, or 'management' – and not just slavery or wage-labour – were available as significant options to Athenian landowners looking for ways to exploit labour 'profitably'. Indeed, since wealthy Athenians so often owned several smaller properties rather than large concentrations of land, 'farming' out these smallholdings in one form or another may have been the easiest way.

What, then, might the Attic countryside in classical times have looked like? Most properties would be worked by peasants and their families. Often these smallholders would, as in other peasant communities, assist their neighbours, especially at harvest time.[95] Some smallholders would be able to afford a slave or two, whose principal functions would probably be in the house, but who might lend a hand in the fields. Land owned by wealthy citizens would, in the typical case of small scattered properties, be let out to tenants or sharecroppers, who would work the land in much the same way as any other peasant, using principally family labour. Larger estates – of which there were relatively few – could be supervised directly by the landowner or by bailiffs. In such cases, the basic permanent stock of farm labourers would consist of slaves, but this stock would not be very large. It is possible, too, that the size of a farm would not be the sole consideration, since even a small home-farm, owned by a wealthy leisured proprietor as one of several fragmented holdings, might be worked by slaves, even if his other properties were farmed by peasant labour. Casual labour would probably be available for hire at all times in the form of propertyless citizens and the many small farmers whose properties (whether owned or leased) were insufficient to support their families. These labourers would be especially busy at the harvest, but would be available for various kinds of work throughout the year. It would be to the advantage of the landowner to employ them whenever possible – buying their labour-power at very low wages and only when needed – instead of investing in slaves and incurring the risks and responsibilities of owning their *persons*, keeping them alive and (relatively) well through both productive and unproductive periods. As long as the concentration of property remained limited and peasant tenures reasonably secure, and while even large landowners often held their properties in separate scattered parcels, the scope for labour on the land beyond that of the peasant family unit would continue to be restricted.[96] This picture cannot, of course, be confirmed by positive proof, but it is historically plausible and fits the available evidence. Unless and until new evidence emerges different from what now exists, 'widespread' agricultural slavery must seem very much more fanciful.

The bulk of Athenian slaves, then, would be found in domestic service and in the silver mines, the two areas of labour which they more or less monopolized. The rest – relatively few, if we assume something less than the maximum estimates of slave numbers – would be scattered throughout the division of labour: apart from small numbers in agriculture, they would work in public service (what Finley has called the lower civil service), including the Scythian archers who represented the nearest thing to an Athenian police force – functions in which slaves predominated over citizens; various crafts, entertainment, and so on. The large numbers in the mines and in domestic service were certainly 'essential' to the Athenian economy, and their absence, if such a thing can be imagined, would have transformed Athenian society. Silver was vital to the Athenian economy; and an Athens without domestic servants – that is, an Athens without wealthy households, or one in which poor citizens served in the households of their wealthy compatriots – would have been something very different from the Athenian democracy. And the productive functions of the household crafts which supplied many of the citizens' daily needs, in the absence of large-scale production for the market, should not be underestimated. But if slaves undoubtedly belonged to the essence of Athenian life, it was in a very different sense from that suggested by the 'slave mode of production' which displaces the labouring citizen from the heart of the productive 'base'.

The Polis and the Peasant-Citizen

The Liberation of Labour: From 'Redistributive' Kingdom to Tribute-Free Polis

There is a sense in which Burckhardt and the others were right when they singled out as an essential characteristic of Athenian democracy the fact that the poor were free, or relatively so, from the compulsion to 'do work which the rich needed done'. This claim, as we saw, must be distinguished from the simple myth of the idle mob, according to which the poor were excessively free from work as such, leaving slaves to carry on the labour of day-to-day life while citizens disported themselves in the assembly, the theatre, and especially in the courts, where the poor were constantly occupied in persecuting and expropriating the rich. If the idle mob bears little resemblance to historical reality, there is an important grain of truth in the more subtle proposition with which the myth is often associated, namely that, while the multitude did work for a livelihood, the bonds between rich and poor in Athens were weak to the extent that the two classes were not firmly bound to one another by the ties of dependence that link master and servant.

The independence of the labouring poor, which for Mitford and Burckhardt was the major source of Athens's ills, may indeed supply the key to Athenian democracy. To put it this way is already to recognize that, even if an intimate connection undoubtedly existed between the freedom of the citizen and the bondage of the slave, that connection did not take the simple form suggested by the myth of the idle mob or by its Marxist inversion, the slave mode of production. The connection between democracy and slavery is not simply that the labour of slaves made possible the leisure which citizens could devote to political activity. The connection is to be found in the *independence* of the citizens, not in their leisure nor in the relegation of productive labour to slaves.

To put it another way – and this may be taken as the central thesis of the present study – the distinctive characteristic of Athenian democracy was not the degree to which it was based on dependent labour, the labour of slaves, but on the contrary, the extent to which it *excluded* dependence from the sphere of production, that is, the extent to which production rested on free, independent labour to the exclusion of labour in varying forms and degrees of juridical dependence or political subjection. Athenian slavery, then, must be explained in relation to other forms of labour which were *ruled out* by the democracy. It should be treated not as the productive base of the democracy but rather as a form of dependence permitted and encouraged by a system of production dominated by free and independent producers and growing, as it were, in the interstices of that system. The central question about Athenian slavery would then be what social needs remained to be filled by some kind of dependent labour which the dominant forms of free labour were unable to accommodate.

There are two common ways of formulating the historical connection between the rise of democracy and the growth of slavery. The first suggests that an increase in the supply of slaves, by whatever means, made the democracy possible by liberating the citizen body for civic participation. This 'explanation' begs every important question and is, in any case, chronologically flawed. Nowhere in Greece does slavery seem to have been economically important until the sixth century BC, and in Athens it reached its peak rather later than in other prosperous cities.[1] Even if we hesitate to accept the convention which identifies the Solonian reforms (594/3 BC?) as the founding moment of Athenian democracy, they certainly represent a critical turning-point in the liberation of the peasantry; and in that sense, it can be said with reasonable confidence that Athenian democracy had implanted its roots before slavery became a significant factor in the Attic economy. The alternative explanation of the connection between democracy and slavery is that the growth of the democracy and the status it accorded to the poorer citizens of Athens, peasants and artisans, made them unavailable as dependent labour, thereby creating an incentive for their wealthier compatriots to seek alternative modes of exploitation. M.I. Finley, for example has argued that 'The peasantry had won their personal freedom and their tenure on the land through struggle, in which they also won citizenship, membership in the community, the polis. This in itself was something radically new in the world, and it led in turn to the second remarkable innovation, a slave society'.[2]

This seems the most fruitful line to follow, though it requires considerable elaboration and specification. We need to know, first, precisely what social functions the peasant-citizen was no longer available to perform and what limits his existence placed on the possible forms in which labour could be organized in the polis. If it was not labour as such which was precluded by the status of citizenship, and certainly not the agricultural labour that constituted the material base of this agrarian society, then what possibilities *did* citizenship foreclose, and where were the spaces which slavery could grow to fill? It must also be said, however, that slaves did not simply step directly into places left vacant by peasant-citizens. The very existence of that unique social formation, the distinctive relations between landlords and peasants embodied in the polis, and the democracy in particular, not only created new economic opportunities but also restricted the possibilities of production and appropriation – for example, by limiting the concentration of property and thereby, as we have seen, limiting the scope of slave-utilization itself. So we need to know a great deal more about the needs, possibilities, and limits created by this 'radically new' phenomenon, the peasant-citizen, if we are to understand the functions of both democracy and slavery.

One way of defining the significance of the peasant-citizen (and increasingly also the artisan-citizen) might be to consider this phenomenon against the background of other peasant societies, beginning with the communities of early Greece before the advent of the polis, and those Greek states which never saw the full development of either the peasant-citizen or large-scale chattel slavery, notably Sparta, Thessaly, and the city-states of Crete. In all these cases, agriculture and production in general were dominated by people who were politically subject to or juridically dependent upon privileged classes or a central authority to whom they were obliged to render tribute and/or labour services in one form or another. In fact, this is a characteristic which these states had in common with most known advanced civilizations of the ancient world. The generality of such social arrangements is what makes it useful to characterize the contrasting situation of Athenian democracy in terms of its exclusion of dependence from the sphere of production, instead of emphasizing, as is more commonly done, the predominance of dependent labour in the form of chattel slavery. In comparison to the conditions of other advanced civilizations of the ancient world – and indeed many later societies – the absence of a dependent peasantry and the establishment of a regime of free smallholders stands out in sharp relief.[3]

The following description of the 'redistributive' kingdoms of the ancient world can serve as a point of departure:

All large-scale economies in kind were run with the help of the principle of redistribution. The kingdom of Hammurabi in Babylonia and, in particular, the New Kingdom of Egypt were centralized despotisms of a bureaucratic type founded on such an economy. The household of the patriarchal family was reproduced here on an enormously enlarged scale, while its 'communistic' distribution was graded, involving sharply differentiated rations. A vast number of storehouses was ready to receive the produce of the peasant's activity, whether he was cattle breeder, hunter, baker, brewer, potter, weaver, or whatever else. The produce was minutely registered and, in so far as it was not consumed locally, transferred from smaller to larger storehouses until it reached the central administration situated at the court of the Pharaoh. There were separate treasure houses for cloth, works of art, ornamental objects, cosmetics, silverware, the royal wardrobe; there were huge grain stores, arsenals, and wine cellars.

But redistribution on the scale practiced by the pyramid builders was not restricted to economies which knew not money. Indeed, all archaic kingdoms made use of metal currencies for the payment of taxes and salaries, but relied for the rest on payments in kind from granaries and warehouses of every description, from which they distributed the most varied goods for use and consumption mainly to the nonproducing part of the population, that is, to the officials, the military, and the leisure class. This was the system practiced in ancient China, in the empire of the Incas, in the kingdoms of India, and also in Babylonia. In these, and many other civilizations of vast economic achievement, an elaborate division of labor was worked by the mechanism of redistribution.[4]

Such 'redistributive' systems could be associated with various forms of land tenure, though possession would typically entail certain obligations to the central authority to which all the land would often belong at least in principle. In the case of the wealthy and privileged classes, the right to land was likely to be associated with some official function or public office. For the peasant, the possession of land, in whatever form, would mean obligation to an overlord, in the form of tax, tribute, or labour services, rendered directly to a local landlord or to the central authority. The chain of redistribution, of appropriation, transfer, and storage, began here, with the labour of the peasants whose produce fed landlords, officials and kings, and whose corvée labour built palaces and pyramids. The peasant's condition was by definition one of juridical dependence or political subjection.

It is now generally agreed that some such redistributive system prevailed in Bronze Age Greece, at least in the later Minoan and Mycenaean kingdoms, albeit on a generally smaller scale than the other major kingdoms and empires of the ancient world. The mythical labyrinth of King Minos, for example, is recognizable in the ruins of the palace at Knossos as the remnants of the myriad storage chambers so expressive of the redistributive mechanism; and the decipherment of Linear B, whatever controversies it may still occasion, testifies without much ambiguity to a vast system of record-keeping, the inventories and obligations of a redistributive economy. Although little is known about the peasants of Bronze Age Greece, archaeologists and historians have reconstructed a picture of these ancient kingdoms in which the palace at the centre is the terminus for a chain of appropriation beginning in the surrounding villages with the labour of peasants, bound to local landlords, officials, and the central authority through a system of tribute and probably corvée labour. This bureacratic network of obligation seems to have been organized through a system of land tenure in which

> much (and perhaps all) land was held with an office, status, or occupation, and ... obligations to and from the centre were calculated and met by allocations and quotas of land and products (agricultural, industrial, and intellectual). We must imagine a situation in which officials, soldiers, craftsmen, herders, and farmers all held land (or worked on the land) on condition that they rendered either appropriate services or quotas of products, industrial or agricultural as the case may be.[5]

This picture is confirmed, as Finley remarks, by 'the absence of any indication of rent (in "money" or kind)'. Although Finley fails to pursue the implications of this observation, the absence of rent suggests that, while property was held by *individuals* and there existed a right of individual appropriation, it would be misleading to think in terms of *private* property, which obscures the *public* or *political* character of appropriation and property rights. This distinction between *individual* appropriation and *private property* (a distinction Finley does *not* make) should be kept in mind in what follows.

The disappearance of this state-form remains one of the most tantalizing mysteries of ancient history. Few historical transformations have been more dramatic than the inexplicable change that occurred from the redistributive kingdoms of Bronze Age Greece to the polis-form, the small independent 'city-state', with its roots in the so-called Dark Age after the mysterious cataclysm. The palace-civilization, its administrative apparatus and its system of appropriation, storage and redistribution, simply vanished. Perhaps the most telling and conspicuous token of this transformation is the apparent disappearance of writing in Greece for several centuries. Once the need for compulsive record-keeping so characteristic of the palace-economy had evaporated, it was to be a long time before new social needs and possibilities created new literary and intellectual forms, together with a new and more versatile system of writing, the Greek alphabet.

Too little is known about the period intervening between the ancient kingdoms and the polis to allow any confident hypotheses about the historical processes leading from one to the other. By the time the evidence again becomes sufficient to construct a coherent picture of Greek society in the so-called Archaic Age, forms of social and political organization radically different from those of the Mycenaean states have already emerged, bearing little resemblance to the highly stratified, 'bureaucratic' kingdoms, with their systems of property and distribution. It is surely right, as Anthony Snodgrass has urged, to treat the Archaic Age as a period of major importance, instead of simply as a prelude to the greatness of classical Greece; and he is surely right to insist on the 'structural revolution' which set in train the developments that constituted the uniqueness of Greek social, political, and cultural forms. This is the period which, as Snodgrass points out, saw the emergence of the small independent state, the autonomous polis consisting of a town and surrounding territory, with its principle of *citizenship*, the community of free citizens and the concomitant ideas of individuality and freedom which uniquely pervaded Greek culture and account for much that is specific to Greek art, philosophy and literature. But we still have little basis for speculating about how these revolutionary developments emerged out of the ruins of the very different social formations which predominated in Greece in the preceding centuries.

It may be possible, however, to guess at certain continuities between the ancient kingdoms and the later polis by looking at what we might call – with great caution – some cases of arrested development in Greece. Without necessarily discovering causes or even suggesting an unbroken process of evolution, we may at least find social and political forms that in principle bridge the gap between the redistributive kingdom and the regime of the peasant-citizen. In particular, we may find in the *penestai*, helots or serfs of Thessaly, Sparta and Crete various forms of tributary relationship which represent points along a continuum between the palace-centred tributary system and the citizen-community of independent peasants whose citizenship is betokened by their freedom from tribute. The disappearance of tributary relationships, ranging from the political serfdom of the redistributive kingdom through the communal yet individualized bondage of the helots to the looser and highly personal ties of clientship, was accompanied by the massive growth of chattel slavery in those parts of Greece where the liberation of the peasant was most complete.

Thessaly, Sparta and Crete, despite the substantial differences among them, had certain major similarities that may, as Snodgrass has argued, entitle us to group them together as a distinct category 'offering a model of conservative political development' against which the achievements of a democratic polis like Athens can be measured.[6] In all these cases, the peasantry was in various states of juridical dependence or political subjection, and the lands of the citizen community were worked by serfs of one kind or another. In Thessaly, the *penestai* ('labourers' or 'poor men') were probably dependent peasants who were obliged to render part of their produce to their overlords in exchange for certain rights. The helots of Sparta, about whom much more is known, were a dependent population subject collectively to the Spartan state but individually allotted to individual members of the Spartiate community. They worked the land, again in exchange for certain rights, turning over part of their produce to their overlords. In the cities of Crete, there existed two categories of serf, private and public. In all these cases there also existed another category somewhere between the dependent serfs and their masters: the *perioikoi*, peasants living in the surrounding countryside who, although juridically free, were without rights of citizenship and politically subject to the state. These states, together with some others such as Argos and Lokris, about which less is known but which seem to have had various categories of dependent or underprivileged populations, also tended to be aristocratic and militaristic, and some form of monarchy may have survived longer here than in other Greek states. These also appear to have been 'conquest-states' in which the subject groups were indigenous populations ruled by alien occupiers. This 'conservative' model, argues Snodgrass, may show

> what might have been the general result, had the more radical developments in other Archaic states never happened. There might have been considerable political and military achievements, on this hypothesis, but not many cultural ones; ... The total achievement might have compared with that of the Etruscan or Phoenician cities.[7]

There were other cases, such as Boeotia – where apparently high census qualifications for active citizenship produced a kind of 'periokic' group – or Corinth, which began with a highly exclusive aristocracy ruling over a population whose lands it had occupied but ended with a more extended citizen body instead of the serfdoms of Sparta or Crete. The most dramatic contrast, of course, is provided by Athens, where the reforms of Solon, consolidated and extended by the evolution of democracy, put an end to all serf-like conditions and tributary relations at a moment when Athens seemed to be 'regressing into the pattern of the serf-based states'.[8]

The special conditions of the 'conquest-states' may make it

dangerous to generalize from their circumstances to a universal model of juridical and political dependence midway between the redistributive states of Bronze Age Greece and the polis of the peasant-citizen. We cannot just infer a simple process of evolution from the Mycenaean kingdoms to less centralized, more fragmented forms of tributary relationship, especially given the scale of destruction and depopulation which intervened – although the case of Crete, as we shall see in a moment, is suggestive. But some continuities are not precluded, and it is difficult to imagine that the Mycenaean legacy had no bearing on what came after. At the very least, we may permit ourselves to construct a kind of analytic continuum which may help to illuminate the distinctiveness of the democratic polis – or even the polis in general, whose distinctive characteristics were most fully developed in the democracy.

R.F. Willetts has summed up the transformation of the Cretan economy after the fall of the Mycenaean kingdoms in a way that may shed light on the larger question of the polis not only as a unique political formation but also as a distinctive form of property relations and the organization of labour:

> The political form of the new economy was the city-state. By the development of the city-state in its classical form, the old village commune, with its traditions of common ownership, was to be changed into a community of peasant proprietors, engaged in independent production for the market. However, this process was far from uniform. The peasant proprietors of Athens achieved their status after protracted class struggles culminating in a democratic revolution. The peasants of historical Crete never achieved their independence. In Crete, the traditions of common ownership based on the village commune were joined to a system of tributary exaction which the Dorian aristocracies durably consolidated.
> ... A form of land tenure thus developed which was based on the inherited Minoan–Mycenaean, as modified by Doric, tribalism. ... The cultivators became vassals, serfs. Dorian supremacy was achieved through the exactions of a tributary system imposed upon surviving forms of the primitive village commune.[9]

Without getting involved in the vexed question of the 'Dorian invasions' (or, for that matter, in other historical controversies not immediately relevant to the present question, such as debates concerning the nature and extent of Greek production for the market), we can perhaps extract from Willetts's summary an account of the relation between the redistributive economy of Bronze Age Crete and the later system of serfdom. The suggestion here is that, irrespective of the special conditions of conquest, there was a continuity between the state-appropriation of the Bronze Age kingdoms and the tributary relations of Cretan serfdom. The common thread joining the two is the subject village commune, the community of peasants, collectively bound to a ruling 'caste' whose political dominance also entails the right to exact tribute. In the earlier forms, that tribute might be regarded as akin to a *tax* in kind, the tribute owed to a centralized state. In the later case, tribute has, as it were, become more individualized, a kind of *rent*. The replacement of the redistributive kingdom by the municipal form of the polis in this case means that the instrument of appropriation is no longer a 'bureaucratic' state but a community of citizens, a community of proprietors with individual rights of appropriation, though these rights are still determined by membership in the state. For the dependent peasant, the decentralization of the polity and the growing individuation of property also means an individuation of dependence: the collectively subject peasant village gives way increasingly to the individual relationship between serf and master, and probably also increasing bondage to the soil, as the peasant becomes attached to the overlord's *household*, instead of to the extended patriarchal 'household' of the redistributive kingdom.

Kings and Landlords, Subjects and Citizens: From the Fall of the Mycenaean Kingdoms to the Reforms of Solon

This structural connection (if that is not putting it too strongly) between the different forms of peasant dependence and tribute need not, of course, imply that a widespread historical process of transition from one to the other took place throughout Greece. Nevertheless, it is worth considering the possibility that some kind of continuity existed between the Mycenaean kingdoms and later systems of labour and land tenure even in those poleis which were to issue in very different social arrangements. The most important case, and indeed one of the very few cases about which enough is known to justify speculation, is Athens, among the handful of sites for which there is evidence of continuous occupation throughout the dark age. Always keeping in mind the uncertainties of the archaeological record, which is particularly unhelpful on precisely such questions about social relations, we may nevertheless be entitled to suppose that Mycenaean institutions left their mark, not only on that part of Attica inhabited without interruption but also on those depopulated parts of the countryside which may have been gradually resettled in a process of 'internal colonization' by aristocrats and their followers moving out from an occupied centre.

To speak of continuities is not to deny the tremendous differences between the early kingdoms and the states which emerged from their ruins. But it is possible to become so preoccupied with *difference* that historical processes disappear altogether. It seems implausible in the extreme that a new social order emerged in Greece which owed nothing to its predecessors and which followed a course of development no different from what might have occurred had the powerful Mycenaean kingdoms never existed, and had the Greek polis evolved out of a pristine 'tribal' community.

On one point in particular this picture is unsatisfactory. When Greek society re-emerges from the obscurity of the dark age, one feature is especially striking: the presence of a clearly defined ruling class, a privileged nobility based on individual property. 'In the Homeric poems,' writes Finley, 'the property regime, in particular, was already fully stabilised. How the original divisions and settlements were made is scarcely visible, for that had all taken place in the past and belongs to the prehistory of the society. The regime that we see in the poems was, above all, one of private ownership.'[10]

No available anthropological evidence from other societies has provided analogous cases which might help to account for such a development out of a pristine 'primitive' social order. Anthropology offers no comparable examples of a 'fully stabilized' regime of property, with this degree of individuation, in combination with a political organization so rudimentary as to invite comparison with tribal chieftainship. In fact, early anthropological speculations about the origins of private property in general tended to be deeply coloured by the (false) example of Greece, *before* archaeological discoveries revolutionized perceptions of early Greek civilization. The image of a tribal order which, through a process of internal differentiation, produces class divisions and private property has always been bedevilled by this misleading example, originally constructed in complete, and unavoidable, ignorance of its 'prehistory'.

But Homeric society did, after all, have a long and complex 'prehistory', and that included the Mycenaean kingdoms, with their elaborate state apparatus and their systems of bureaucratic land tenure. There is, then, no need to imagine the anomaly of a 'stable property regime' evolving in the context of a virtually stateless society. Here, however, it may be necessary to introduce a qualification into Finley's characterization of the Homeric property regime. He acknowledges the difficulties associated with the concept of 'private property':

> I do not propose to enter into the largely sterile controversies over the applicability of words like 'private' and 'ownership' to primitive and archaic

holdings. It is enough to indicate that there was free, untrammelled right to dispose of all movable wealth – a right vested in a *filius familias* as well as in a *pater familias*; that the continuous circulation of wealth, chiefly by gift, was one of the major topics of the society; and that the transmission of a man's estate by inheritance, the movables and immovables together, was taken for granted as the normal procedure upon his death.[11]

There is, however, one important qualification which Finley does not take into account, and that is the extent to which rights of appropriation may still have rested on 'extra-economic' powers, juridical, political and military, that is, the extent to which property in 'Homeric' society still retained the character of political, albeit individual, appropriation, despite the disappearance of the state apparatus. Again, we may need to apply the distinction between *private* and *individual* property, in order to acknowledge the specificity of what has been called 'political' appropriation. Conditional tenures of the type associated with the Mycenaean state no longer existed, of course; and it is probably true, as Finley argues, that nothing like feudal relations occurred in 'Homeric' society. But there can be little doubt that the lords of the epics represent a dominant class whose powers of appropriation rested not simply on superior property but on exclusive extra-economic powers, juridical, military, and political. There may have been little left of what might be called a state apparatus at all, but what there was remained embodied in this hereditary nobility. It might be less misleading, then, at least to reserve judgment on the degree of *privacy* in Homeric private property, and to speak instead of a stable regime of individual appropriation.

It might be possible to make sense out of Homeric 'private property' if we assume that the administrative distribution of property originally linked with 'office, status, or occupation' in the bureaucratic-redistributive state became clearly individual property as the administrative apparatus disappeared. Perhaps what we see in the Homeric property regime are the decapitated remnants of that bureaucratic system. At least, we should not allow ourselves to be misled by the apparently antithetical differences between the two systems of property – the one collective and public (in principle) in the sense that it derived conditionally from the state, the other individual (if not, perhaps, completely 'private'). However much we may have come to think of *state* and *individual* as antithetical principles, we cannot overlook the possibility that the emergence of a stable property regime in Greece *presupposed* an earlier system of 'bureaucratic' property and could not have existed without it.

The specificity of Greek development – and perhaps of Western private property in general – may be traceable to the special and mysterious circumstances which as it were liberated individual appropriation by depriving the bureaucratic–redistributive system of the state which stood at its head. A profound transformation certainly, but a historical continuity nonetheless. It may, indeed, be easier to accept this kind of continuity than to imagine the establishment of a stable property regime in the virtual absence of a state, as a complete break between the Mycenaean and 'Homeric' orders would require us to do. More generally, a process of this kind might help to account for the distinctive evolution of private property in the West, in which the critical turning-point may have been precisely the unique *individuation* of political appropriation that ensued from the destruction of the Mycenaean state apparatus.

At any rate, there has been some speculation that the 'Homeric' lords may be the descendants of a kind of provincial nobility, local officials with property rights who served as administrative conduits for the central authority of the Mycenaean states. This view gains some support from the curious fact that the 'kings' of the epics are normally called not *wanax*, as are the true kings recorded in Linear B inscriptions, but rather *basileis*, the title of a lower rank local official.[12] Such etymological speculations may be dangerous, especially given the extent of the destruction suffered by the Mycenaean social order and its palace economy; but this notion has certain attractions as a means of accounting for at least some notable features of 'Homeric' society and its class of hero-nobles, not only their very existence as a propertied class but perhaps also their *apartness* from the community of peasant householders which barely appears in the epics, as if it belonged to another world.[13]

The lords of the epics are often described as something akin to tribal chieftains, albeit well on their way to the privileged status of a propertied aristocracy; but this analogy fails not only to account for the existence of the property regime but to capture the *separateness* of this dominant group. They do not altogether give the impression of a hierarchy growing organically out of a single community; instead, they bear the marks of 'apartheid' which divided ruling and subject communities in Mycenaean times. The social gulf between these two communities – possibly at one time including residential separation – seems greater than any differences of wealth that could have been sustained by the materially impoverished society which succeeded the downfall of the prosperous Mycenaean states; but if this is so, it may simply confirm that the economic privilege of this aristocracy originated in the 'extra-economic' powers of the bureaucratic–redistributive state.

It is, of course, possible that the division between lords and common people represents not a direct continuity from the days of the palace economy, of appropriating states and subject peasant villages, but a new internal polarization, in which a growing opposition between aristocrats and commoners begins to resemble the division between ruling and subject communities, like the two societies of Bronze Age Greece. Very likely the truth lies somewhere in between these two possibilities. The new aristocracy may have owed its origins to the bureaucratic regime of the ancient kingdoms; but with its wealth and power considerably depleted by the cataclysm and without the support of the state from which it sprang, aristocrats relied on their remaining advantages of superior property and a monopoly of jurisdiction to rebuild their strength and widen the gulf between ruling and ruled. Whatever the explanation, what we see as Greece emerges from the dark age is still – or again – a dichotomous relationship between two societies 'separated by that social gulf created and maintained by the lack of laws, customs, and a way of life in common'.[14] And though Homer only tells the story of the ruling society, we can see, too, a dominant community with a monopoly of juridical, political, military and religious powers which, though feeble and precarious in comparison to the centralized force of the bureaucratic state, can still function as a means of extracting surplus from subordinate peasant communities, in the manner of Hesiod's 'gift-eating basileis' who use their judicial powers as a means of appropriation.

Throughout this discussion speculation is, of course, the operative word, for the evidence concerning the social arrangements of archaic Greece is weakest on precisely those points which are most important to our question. When the silence of the dark age is broken by the Homeric epics, we learn virtually nothing about the lives and conditions of the less exalted classes outside the immediate households of the hero-nobles. Hesiod tells us something about the more prosperous peasant at least in Boeotia, but even here there is hardly enough to advance our speculations very far. Until the reforms of Solon we remain largely in the dark about the forms of land and labour which produce the wealth of the rich. Although we know something about Solon and even more about the subsequent effects of his reforms, we cannot be sure of their significance because we know so little about the prior conditions to which those reforms were meant to respond. Still, there is at least enough to permit some educated speculation.

A great deal turns on the meaning of Solon's *seisachtheia*, the famous 'shaking off of burdens'. It is known that Solon abolished debt-bondage, forbidding loans on the security of the person which could issue in enslavement in case of default. The *seisachtheia* itself, however, is more problematic and remains in dispute among historians. It is commonly understood that this reform refers above all to the *hektemoroi*, those who were obliged to pay a specified portion of their produce to someone else; but the status of these *hektemoroi* is a matter of controversy. In the past, it was generally assumed that this condition was the result of defaulting on a mortgage or loan, the consequence of which was to place the land of the debtor in bondage and some portion of his labour with it. There is, however, no mention of debt in Solon's own account of the reforms concerning this 'enslaved' land. It may also be significant that in Solon's day Athens could hardly be considered a money economy, and that coinage was a later invention than was traditionally assumed. This is important to the extent that it casts doubt on the range of possibilities for incurring debts of the kind and magnitude suggested by the status of hektemorage.[15] In general, it is difficult to imagine how debt in the sense that it is commonly understood could have accounted for the vast numbers of people who were apparently involved, even if Aristotle is exaggerating when he suggests that all the poor in Athens on the eve of Solon's reforms were serfs (*pelatai* and *hektemoroi*) to the wealthy few (*Ath. Pol.* 2 and 5). Furthermore, as Antony Andrewes points out, the word translated as 'debt' is χρέος (as in Aristotle, *Ath. Pol.* 6), a term 'which embraces other kinds of obligation than those that arise from borrowing; it would include rent or taxes or other kinds of dues'.[16]

With all these considerations in mind, it has become increasingly common to regard hektemorage as something other than a condition into which some free peasants had lapsed by defaulting on debts. It seems likely that, as Andrewes suggests, hektemorage represents 'an old-established system for tilling what might be called the lands of the rich', whether in the form of 'a feudal state of hereditary serfdom', as Rhodes proposes, or a relation of clientship between peasants and aristocrats, as Murray argues following Fustel de Coulanges.[17] In other words, the 'debts' which Solon cancelled were the obligations of rent or tribute owed by a dependent peasant to a lord. The practice of enslavement for debt, which certainly did exist, must itself be reinterpreted as part of a more general system of dependence. As Oswyn Murray writes,

> It is characteristic of such forms of servitude that they are not primarily responses to economic pressures, but are rather an extension of the social system in general, and more particularly the system of land tenure; that is, such slaves are not usually created by a form of 'bankruptcy', but rather they exist in a stratified society in which inferiors may be liable to perform services for their superiors, and where 'debt-slavery' is the lowest level to which a man may be born or sink for a variety of reasons often non-economic: 'men

are not much accustomed in any society to lend to the poor'. The law is in the hands of the rich, and therefore enforces obligations by depriving the poor of existing rights; the poor may want protection (or have it forced on them); the rich are more concerned with manpower for military or civil purposes than with loan capital or interest, for labour is more valuable than surplus goods in a pre-monetary economy; and debt-slavery is often closely connected with forms of land tenure, because its prime function is usually to provide agricultural labour.[18]

These interpretations would certainly be more consistent with Aristotle's account of the widespread division of Attica into wealthy landlords and their poor serfs. If this is so, Solon's *seisachtheia* constitutes a more substantial structural change than the cancellation of debt in the narrow sense would suggest, abolishing the last remaining forms of dependence and tribute to which Athenian peasants were subject. In fact, even a narrower construction of the cancelled 'debts' would permit us to interpret Solon's reforms as putting an end once and for all to peasant dependence in Attica. In any case, the status of *hektemoroi* and *pelatai*, together with land designated as *epimortos* (subject to a share, a *morté*) henceforth had no place in Athenian social arrangements.

The ascription to Solon of a more revolutionary reform than simply the cancellation of debts need not contradict his own claim to have resisted the demand for redistribution, as long as we remember that the concept of *ownership* was far more indeterminate and fluid in ancient Greece than in modern times or even in ancient Rome. In the absence of clearly defined legal concepts of property, and with the continuum of conditional property which, as we have seen, is typical of pre-capitalist economies, it is possible, indeed likely, that even dependent peasants like the *hektemoroi* enjoyed certain rights of possession which remained in principle secure as long as they continued to pay their dues.[19] Thus Solon would have done something less than redistribute land by transferring property formerly owned by large landowners to new owners among the poor peasants. At the same time, if the cancellation of debt, even in the broader sense, may have been less than the poor would have wished, its significance should not be underestimated.

Oswyn Murray, who regards the 'shaking off of burdens' as 'primarily a social revolution, the abolition of the relation of clientship between peasants and aristocrats', offers some tantalizing suggestions as to the origins of this system of clientship (a system which, on closer inspection, seems not very different from Rhodes' 'feudal' relations):

it might perhaps be a remnant of the old Mycenean land tenure system, where the peasantry was subordinate to the local *basileis* and ultimately to the royal palace, which was essentially an office of administration and a storehouse for contributions in kind; or the origin of the system might be later, in a voluntary 'feudal' contract of mutual help entered into during the unsettled migration period; or it may reflect the conditions under which Attica was repopulated in the mid eighth century. The essential character of the developed system is that it is one of 'conditional tenure' in which the peasant owns the land, subject to a traditional payment in service or kind: such a system, even after its abolition, could well explain the fierce local loyalties and private fiefs of the Athenian aristocracy that persisted during the next few generations.[20]

The suggestion that the relations of clientship or 'feudal' obligation have their roots in the Mycenaean land tenure system is attractive because of the structural affinities between the various forms of peasant tribute; and if we accept this suggestion, it is even easier to postulate an evolutionary process from one to the other in Athens than in the case of the 'conquest-states' where extraneous factors intervene. But even if we assume a later development of these relations of dependence in Attica, more or less unrelated to the earlier systems of centralized tribute, we can at least apply our analytic continuum to illuminate the distinctiveness of the tribute-free peasantry which dominated the agrarian scene after the Solonian reforms.

It should be said, however, that if 'debt' in the conventional sense seems an unlikely explanation of hektemorage, and if the very notion of debt in ancient Attica must be reconsidered in the light of its weak or non-existent cash economy, there may be other senses of 'borrowing' and 'lending' which do make sense in the context of a non-monetary society and which may indicate the kinds of relations that existed between landlords and peasants after the Solonian reforms. Osborne, for example, emphasizes the continuing importance of borrowing and lending even in the absence of a developed cash economy:

> ... concentration on the way in which Solon made it illegal for one Athenian to enslave another has obscured the fact that the nature of the agrarian society made it inevitable that less formal structures of dependence continued to exist. Throughout Classical antiquity, lending and borrowing were important ways in which local communities acquired a clear, if flexible, structure of groups of distinct status. It is arguable that few Greek cities, perhaps none at all, became sufficiently converted to a cash-based economy to replace these ties with the more extensive ties of dependence which money loans make possible. While money loans did become a very important means by which the rich could meet financial obligations without selling off real property, they seem to have played no significant part in the peasant's fight for survival.[21]

As long as we understand borrowing and lending in terms not implying money transactions, it is possible to imagine a variety of arrangements by which the poor might have gained access – at a price, if not in money then in service or kind – to the wealth of the rich, including (and perhaps especially) their land in the form of tenancies. The relations thus established between landlord and tenant would not be the secondary result of some penalty for default on a mortgage or loan but would be the immediate object of the transaction between them, a non-monetary exchange of labour for access to property. The relationship would not be juridical or political, in the sense that it would not be based on the 'lender's' privileged juridical status or political superiority, nor on the 'borrower's' juridical dependence or political subjection. It would be an 'economic' relationship, based on the lender's superior property, but still deriving its specific character from the absence of a 'cash nexus'. It is even possible that such arrangements already existed in pre-Solonian times alongside more traditional forms of dependence in which peasants were subject to a dominant class with claims on their labour resting on a monopoly of public power. Such an account of 'borrowing' would be entirely consistent with, for example, Antony Andrewes's explanation of pre-Solonian 'debt', since obligations of 'rent' would themselves 'arise from borrowing'. In the post-Solonian era, the more 'informal' economic arrangements would have entirely replaced the traditional forms of juridical dependence.

That the Greeks thought of such tenancy arrangements as comparable to loans is suggested by the tendency to talk about rent-producing properties in the same terms as interest-bearing loans, as sources of revenue or ways of making property productive of a return (for example, in Dem. XXIX 60, where a word generally applied to interest, *tokos* – a metaphorical extension of the word for childbirth, parturition, or offspring – is applied to the rent from a property). A particularly suggestive passage occurs in Isocrates's *Areopagiticus* (especially 31–6), which describes an alleged golden age when relations between rich and poor were harmonious because the rich 'shared' their wealth with the poor. In contrast to his own unhappy time, when the rich allegedly live in fear of confiscatory claims upon their wealth, in the good old days 'the result of their dealing honourably with each other was that the ownership of property was secured to those to whom it rightfully belonged, while the enjoyment of property was shared by all the citizens who needed it' (Loeb Library translation). One of the principal methods of 'sharing' or 'lending' was 'handing over lands [to the poor] at moderate rentals', which we need not understand as entailing money rents. This passage is generally dismissed as a pretty conceit, fabricated by Isocrates as a means of denouncing what he regards as the corruptions of the 'radical' democracy, when the rich hesitate to 'lend' to the poor and try to conceal their wealth for fear of the multitude's unbridled greed and the tendency of the courts to show excessive solicitude for the poor, instead of adhering strictly to the law. But perhaps Isocrates, for all the limitations of his account as a historical record, may be telling us something important which sheds light both on the vexed question of 'debt' in early Greece and on the ways in which Athenian landlords may have appropriated wealth after the Solonian reforms.

At any rate, Athenian agriculture – and hence the material base of Athenian society – after Solon was dominated by independent smallholders. It is likely that many of them were subject to various kinds of rent, or perhaps the kind of obligation incurred by 'sharing' in the wealth of the rich; but relations of juridical dependence were banished for the duration of Athens's existence as an independent polis. The growth of democratic institutions removed the last vestiges of political subjection which might have served as a means for privileged classes to extract tribute from the peasantry. The status of taxation in Athens which we have already noted – the view that direct taxation is tyrannical, and the remarkable absence of taxation as an object of grievance among the poor, in contrast to other societies in which peasants have carried the burden of a tax-hungry state – testifies to the firm implantation of this smallholder's regime.

Landlords and Peasants from Solon to Cleisthenes

Let us then try to reconstruct the development of social relations in the Attic countryside. When the ruling society of Bronze Age Greece was shattered – by whatever mysterious means – it left behind the subject peasant communities on which it had been superimposed. Perhaps, too, there remained fragments of its ruling apparatus in the shape of local aristocracies. But if the epics still bear the traces of this traditional division between ruling and subject communities, there is, of course, a critical difference. The Homeric lords are not securely bound together by a strongly centralized state. Indeed, one can hardly speak here of a state at all. It was not only the palace economy that disappeared with the Mycenaean state, but the institutional bonds of unity within the ruling society, as well as the strong coercive force which ensured the subjection of subordinate communities.

Lords and peasants thus increasingly confronted one another not as two opposed communities, but as *individuals* and as *classes*. The resulting balance of forces was inevitably unstable: on the one hand, a propertied class with economic and juridical superiority sufficient to squeeze the peasantry but lacking the unifying force, the check on intra-class competition and conflict, and the coercive support provided by a strongly centralized state; on the other hand, an increasingly restive peasantry chafing at the bonds of personal dependence, the economic vulnerability of the smallholder aggravated by juridical restrictions. It need hardly be added that the growing dependence of the dominant class on the military assistance of its subordinates, the hoplite infantry of the more prosperous peasantry, can only have added to the instability of this regime and the pressure to alter the balance of rural class power.

This, then, was the situation confronted by Solon, who set out to deal with both aristocratic factionalism and peasant discontent.[22] To some extent, his reforms simply acknowledged what had already taken place. The aristocracy, now on its own without the bureaucratic state and with no secure political substitute, could no longer rely on its monopoly of extra-economic power. Its appropriative capacities increasingly depended on the 'economic' advantage of wealthy land-ownership. Even without juridical relations of dependence, however, superior property might permit landlords to profit from the vulner-ability of the smallholder, as marginal peasant proprietors were compelled by economic necessity to rely on their wealthier compatriots to supplement their precarious livelihoods, as tenants, sharecroppers or casual labourers.[23] At the same time, the benefits of superior property were enhanced as general prosperity grew and new opportunities arose for the fruitful use of wealth in trade and a growing urban economy.

But in order to stabilize the situation and protect the economic advantages of the landlords, some political reorganization was required, some juridical and political apparatus to sustain and reproduce the new relations on the land. Solon refused to redistribute land, and left the economic vulnerability of the peasants untouched; but he removed the extra-economic encumbrances that burdened peasant land, and thereby gave juridical recognition to the changing relations between landlord and peasant. Popular grievances were also met by eroding other lordly extra-economic powers through political reforms enhancing the citizenship rights of the demos, and especially reform of the courts. These reforms made inroads into the monopoly of jurisdiction by 'gift-eating' lords, in particular by instituting procedures permitting any citizen to initiate a prosecution on behalf of any other injured party, and by providing for appeals to popular law courts.

Solon's famous classification of the Athenian citizen-body into *economic* categories, based on land-yields instead of on distinctions of birth, can be interpreted in this light. Although the new economic criterion certainly had the effect of admitting into the highest class, and hence to certain exclusive offices, prosperous men without the distinction of noble birth, Solon's system should be construed as acknowledging not the growth of a trade-based 'bourgeoisie' (such as still appears in some historical accounts) but a change in the nature of landlordly power, from an increasingly unreliable extra-economic superiority to the economic dominance of landed wealth.

Solon's solution to the inherent instability of this class-divided but virtually acephalous social order – a solution whose logic would be pursued by subsequent Athenian reformers – was in effect to strengthen the civic community, the community of citizens, as against other traditional principles of social organization. Probably no other solution was possible. Certainly the kind of dispensation which many centuries later was to bring an end to the instabilities of European feudalism – the process of 'feudal centralization' that created the early modern monarchies – was in this case unavailable, if only because the balance of power between landlords and peasants was not as unequal in Greece and because the aristocracy was simply not strong enough both to sustain a monarchical power and at the same time to protect its own power in the face of a centralized monarchy. The Greek solution had the advantage of submitting the aristocracy to the jurisdiction of the civic community and disposing of a significant element in peasant grievances. However, it also created its own logic of process and its own instabilities – no longer the age-old opposition between ruling and subject communities but a new dynamic of inter- and intra-class conflict. In the polis, as a self-governing community of citizens in which landlords and peasants met as individuals and classes in a single community rather than as two opposed societies, it might be difficult to halt the sharing-out of extra-economic powers once begun. The new political powers embodied in the polis themselves became a bone of contention both among members of the dominant class, and between them and subordinate classes.

The phenomenon of *tyranny* can be explained in the light of these new relations.[24] It marks a turning-point in the evolution of the aristocracy as no longer a separate society but the dominant class of a civic community, part of a citizen body and subject to its jurisdiction. In that sense, tyranny expressed both the strength and the weakness of the aristocracy. On the one hand, the tyrannies can be seen as aristocratic efforts to harness the new political order to their own advantage – and to some extent they succeeded; on the other hand, tyranny also expressed the need of aristocrats for support from the demos and their inclination to intra-class competition, as one or another aristocratic family sought predominance over the rest. Their method of consolidating personal power was to reinforce the polis community far more substantially than had the Solonian reforms, with measures to unify the state, create some form of public finance, establish state cults and public ceremonies, continue Solon's reform of the courts in the direction of a public system of justice, and so on. Whatever the intentions and successes of individual aristocratic dynasties, the incorporation of the aristocracy into the civic community also had the effect of diluting aristocratic power. There is no need to attribute democratic motives to the tyrants who introduced measures designed to help small farmers – such as the state loans of the Pisistratid tyranny[25] – in order to acknowledge that one consequence of strengthening the polis community was to invite or consolidate challenges to exclusive aristocratic power from less privileged members of the civic community.

The paradoxical logic of this process is summed up in the reforms of Cleisthenes, whose motives may have been no different from those of any other aspirant to tyrannical power on behalf of his own aristocratic dynasty, but who constructed his base of support in a way that was bound to weaken his class. Following a new path opened up by the polis itself – or perhaps taking to its logical conclusion the method of the tyrants – he enlisted the support not of other members of his class, in the traditional aristocratic way, but of the demos which constituted the bulk of the polis community. He thus became – inadvertently? – the architect of the democratic constitution and for many the democracy's true founder. It is significant that the principal means by which he transformed the constitution of the polis was, as we shall see in the following section, to establish the *village*, the age-old arena of peasant activity, as the basic constituent unit of the state and the locus of civic identity. The personal dramas of the succession from Solon to the tyrants to Cleisthenes should not disguise the fact that even if Cleisthenes was pursuing personal or dynastic ambitions when he 'politicised the Attic country-side'[26] (and we can never be sure what his motives were), he was doing so (successfully) in a way which conformed to the new realities of class relations on the land.

Village and State in Democratic Athens

One especially important expression of the unique political status enjoyed by the Athenian peasantry is the political role of the village. In this respect, Athens seems to have been unique even among Greek democracies,[27] and much else that is distinctive about the Athenian polis and its culture is arguably traceable to this, perhaps the most literally democratic, feature of the democracy. Throughout history, the peasant has typically been also the 'villager', not only a village-dweller but one for whom the village constitutes the primary community beyond the household. It is the primary political unit through which he is administered and often taxed, but also often the only one in which he exercises any degree of self-government, and the principal instrument of self-defence against the depredations of landlord and state. The 'nucleated' settlement, a cluster of dwellings surrounded by agricultural land worked by the villagers, has probably always been more common in peasant societies than the isolated farmsteads scattered throughout the countryside so typical of commercial farming in the modern age. It is a pattern which still persists, for example, in the Mediterranean today, and has existed in all parts of the world extending as far back in time as archaeological records allow us to go. As Robin Osborne has convincingly argued in his account of settlement patterns in ancient Attica (an argument that, incidentally, could only have been strengthened by an acknowledgment that such patterns have probably been more a rule than an exception throughout history), this was also the dominant pattern here, where the evidence overwhelmingly testifies to the rarity of isolated farmsteads worked by farmers residing on their land away from a nucleated settlement.[28] The ubiquity of this settlement pattern serves to confirm Osborne's view that it has not been enforced by geography but 'must have been a product of human choice', a choice that has had as much to do with social and political needs as with 'economic rationality'.[29]

Some particularly informative examples of such village settlements and their 'extra-economic' functions are provided by mediaeval Europe. Here is how one prominent historian has characterized the mediaeval West:

> One fact is outstanding: in the civilization of the ninth and tenth centuries the rural way of life was universal. ...
>
> Another thing is also certain. It was a countryside created by man around a few fixed points of settlement ... They [the peasants] give the impression of belonging to villages.
>
> Indeed the countryman's life was very rarely conducted in solitude. Dwelling houses appear to have been close together and very seldom isolated. ... [I]n the present state of researches it merely appears that the village, whatever its size or shape, provided the normal background of human existence. In Saxon England, for example, the village served as the basis for the levying and collection of taxes. Around these fixed points was laid out the pattern of the cultivated land, and particularly the network of trackways and paths, which appear in the landscape of today as the most tenacious relic of our ancient heritage, the reality which provides the starting point for archeological study of the village territory.[30]

Another similar account of mediaeval country life, specifically in England, illustrates the social and administrative functions the village might perform:

> The manorial estate was not the only institution to organize and to regulate the agricultural activities and lives of medieval country-folk. The village and the community of men inhabiting it provided a collateral or an alternative system of ties, rights and obligations. The village, like the manor, was ubiquitous, since the overwhelming majority of medieval country-folk lived in group settlements of one kind or another. ... The most obvious characteristic of the village was its topography. It was a collective, i.e. grouped, settlement; and the form of grouping most characteristic of the medieval countryside was that of a 'nucleated' village consisting of a cluster of households round a natural centre, topographical or economic – a well, a pond, a village green – which would also include or be contiguous with the site of the village church. Its other characteristic was, so to speak, constitutional or tenurial. A typical village was bound to a manor with an exclusive link, which can best be expressed by the formula of 'one manor, one vill'. The third feature was social and administrative. The inhabitants of a typical village formed a village community collectively administered and possessing formal and informal bodies, courts, assemblies, 'chests' and gilds, which issued and administered the rules of husbandry, watched over local customs of tenure and inheritance, and enforced local peace and order. As many of these functions also belonged to the lord and his manor, they were frequently exercised by the village courts functioning also as organs of manorial administration and in fact presided over by manorial officials.[31]

The mediaeval village, then, was a place of residence, a community of peasants, the arena in which they collectively regulated much of their daily life and productive activity, but also a unit through which their overlords dominated them and extracted their surplus. In these respects, the mediaeval village shares many characteristics with other peasant communities throughout the world at various times throughout history. Although its peculiar relation to the manor is, of course, a distinctive feature of Western feudalism, there is nothing unusual about the dependence of the village upon, and its subordination to, a superior administrative power, or its function as a medium of surplus extraction. The role of the village as a basis for the levying and collection of taxes or tributes, for example, is a recurrent theme in the history of peasant societies. Indeed, the domination and exploitation of the village by 'alien political hierarchies' is often treated as a defining characteristic of peasant society, a corollary of that definition, which we encountered in a previous chapter, according to which the peasant is a rural cultivator distinguished by the 'production of a fund of rent' or the transfer of his surplus to a dominant group of rulers.[32]

The dual character of the peasant village as a self-contained and to some extent self-regulating community, and at the same time a medium of domination and exploitation – as well as the universality of this social form – is succinctly conveyed by Teodor Shanin in his general account of the peasantry as 'a political factor':

> In the setting of the village community or peasant commune, the peasant reaches a level of nearly total social self-sufficiency. The appropriation and division of land, marriage, social and religious needs are generally taken care of at the village level. A common interest in commune rights as well as in providing for productive activity requiring the participation of more than one family generates co-operation, generally coupled with some type of grass-roots democracy. The characteristics of the peasant village – its members being born into a single community, undergoing similar life-experiences and necessarily involved in close, personal interaction – with a consequent absence of anonymity – make for the highly traditional and conformist culture peculiar to a rural community. All this makes the word *mir* (meaning 'the world' or 'peace') used by the Russian peasants to refer to their village commune, a significant description of its function. The village is the peasant's world. A society of small producers consists of innumerable village segments generally, dominated and exploited by alien, political hierarchies.[33]

Osborne's persuasive picture of Attic country life suggests that the village there may have performed many of the same social functions as peasant communities have done elsewhere. Certainly there is considerable evidence of the importance in Attica of local ties and the function of the village community in determining patterns of landholding and organizing the social life of Athenian farmers.[34] The critical difference between the Attic village and the 'typical' peasant community lies in the relation between the village and the larger political organization in which it was embedded. Shanin describes the peasant commune as both socially self-sufficient and politically dependent; it is self-contained both in the sense that it constitutes virtually the whole of the peasant's world and in the sense that the world of its rulers is *alien*. In other words, the peasant commune is by definition dominated and exploited by 'alien, political hierarchies', political entities to which the peasant in no way belongs except as *subject*. The relation between state and village is the dichotomous relation between ruler and subject, as well as between producer and appropriator, whether in the nexus of feudal lord and serf, manor and village, or redistributive state and tribute-paying peasantry. This dichotomous relationship was to a certain extent compromised throughout the Graeco–Roman world wherever the peasant was granted the status of citizenship, even when, as in Rome, the peasant's civic status was limited. But nowhere has the typical pattern been broken as completely as it was in the democratic polis in Athens. The breakdown of the opposition between village and state was the very foundation of Athenian democracy, as the village community became the basic constituent unit of the polis.

The reforms of Cleisthenes are commonly regarded as having established the organizational basis of Athenian democracy. Although the intention and significance of his reforms remain in dispute, there can be little doubt that his system of *demes* – the smallest constituent units of the new political order – had the effect of reposing political power in the ordinary people of Athens, the demos, to a degree unprecedented in the known ancient world. These demes, which seem to have varied greatly in size, from hamlets to the equivalent of mediaeval English market towns, were largely based on existing villages (*demoi*), most corresponding to single villages, though new and artificial units may have been created in some cases.[35] By this means, Cleisthenes, in Osborne's words, 'politicised the Attic countryside and rooted political identity there'.[36]

It was through his deme that a man became a citizen, retaining his deme-identity – the mark of his citizenship – throughout changes of residence. The association of citizenship with the local identity of the deme among other things freed the right of citizenship from aristocratic control. It was also in the local democracy of the deme that peasants probably played their most active political role. If it remained true that the central assembly in Athens was generally dominated by wealthier citizens, especially those who maintained a residence in the city as well as owning properties in the countryside and especially in the demes where they were inscribed as citizens, there was no discontinuity between the polis and the deme.[37] The deme was the basic constituent unit of the polis and not simply its subject. All demesmen had the same civic rights and were entitled to attend the central assembly and serve on the juries through which so much of what we would consider *political* business was done; there was no distinction between villager and townsman in this respect, or between peasant and landlord. Every citizen could become *demarch*, the chief official of the deme through whom the local administration of the polis was mediated – and, in fact, the evidence is that demarchs were generally men of moderate means and relatively humble status.[38] Every citizen could also serve on the *boulē*, the council which set the central assembly's agenda – in fact, it is likely that most citizens must have sat on the *boulē* at least once.[39]

If the exigencies of labour, distance from Athens, and certain exclusive offices continued to give the advantage to wealthier citizens in the assembly at Athens, and if the most active politicians at the centre always tended to come from prosperous families, the fact remains that the democracy was unique in both principle and practice. In principle, it granted full civic status to ordinary peasants and artisans, and in practice such people actually did participate not only in local self-government through the deme assemblies, but also – if not as regularly as their wealthier compatriots – in the administration of the polis as a whole. The democracy no doubt worked imperfectly; but by giving (in Osborne's words[40]) political status to the villages, breaking down the discontinuity between village and state, between the peasant community and the political order, it radically transformed the character of both.

There is a sense in which even non-democratic city-states in the Graeco–Roman world granted a distinctive political status to the countryside. As M.I. Finley has pointed out, 'Ancient cities in the great majority counted farmers, whether working or gentlemen farmers, men whose economic interest lay chiefly and often exclusively in the land, as the core of their citizenry.'[41] This accounts to a great extent for the particular relationship between town and country which many commentators, with the model of the mediaeval town in mind, have singled out as a distinctive feature of classical antiquity. It may at first seem remarkable that such a highly urbanized civilization, where so many people lived in cities and where a highly developed urban culture was able to flourish, could coexist with a relatively undeveloped urban economy. For the Greeks and Romans, it was agriculture and not trade or manufacture that constituted the basis of civilized life, that is, a life with *cities*.[42] The association of urbanism with agriculture, which from the perspective of mediaeval Europe on the one hand and industrial capitalism on the other looks like a contradiction in terms, made perfect sense to the ancients whose vibrant urban culture was supported by predominantly agrarian economies; and it made sense precisely because the role of the city was in the first instance *political* as much as, or even more than, economic – though this distinction can be misleading in the case of pre-capitalist societies where the 'economic' power of appropriation depends so directly upon juridical status and political power.

In contrast to other advanced civilizations where political power found its point of concentration in royal palaces or theocratic temples, the seats of kings and priests, state power in the polis was as it were diffused throughout the city, the arena of activity for a community of citizens. It is perhaps in this sense more than in any other that the problematic notion of the 'city-state' conveys a useful meaning. The *city* was also the *state* both in the sense that it developed as a site of political activity (even more than it did, for example, as a marketplace), and in the sense that the territory which it governed was united with it in a single whole without rigid boundaries between town and country, between ruling, appropriating state and subject, producing villages.

If all this was true to a greater or lesser extent of the ancient 'city-state' in general, it was, of course, especially true of the democratic polis. If the 'core' of the citizenry in other city-states consisted in great part of farmers, it was only in the democracy that 'working farmers' and not simply 'gentlemen farmers' were counted among citizens with full civic status. It was here that the typical opposition between appropriators at the political centre and peasants in a subject hinterland had been most effectively annihilated; and it was here that the boundary between village and state was most completely broken down.

Town and Country in Attica

Athens was among the most urbanized of ancient cities, 'the most populous city of the Graeco–Roman world in its day'.[43] The polis most often cited as the counter-model to Athens, Sparta with its subject peasant population, hardly developed a city or an urban culture at all. It is certainly a striking fact that, while the polis with the greatest *political* division between the ruling centre and the subject periphery had the least significant physical division between town and country, the most advanced urban culture of the Graeco-Roman world was also the one in which the institutional boundary between town and country was at its weakest. This paradox serves to emphasize the political function of the city.

The conceptual distinction between town and country in Athens was correspondingly weak. As many commentators have pointed out, just as 'there was no sharp dividing line between city and countryside (*chōra*) either in political status or religion',[44] the conceptual distinction between town and country, or town-dwellers and countrymen, remained ill-defined and ambiguous. Even the tendency to contrast the urbane and sophisticated townsman with the rough and boorish countryman, which appears especially in Attic comedy, was not without ambiguities. 'The Athenians,' argues Humphreys, 'distinguished the city type, the *asteios* – sophisticated, witty, cunning – from the rustic, *agroikos* ...; but there is little sign of a grouping of interests, of a conscious solidarity, corresponding to the division of economic activity and manners.'[45] In fact, the distinction may have been even less clearly defined than Humphreys suggests, and more deeply coloured by the political unity that joined city and countryside. Osborne, for example, interprets the distinction between the *asteios* and the *agroikos* in a particularly suggestive way:

This is not a distinction between the man who lives inside the walls of the city and the man who lives outside, it is a distinction based on behaviour, and in particular on political behaviour. ... Living in the country certainly may make it more difficult to be urbane ... but it does not produce the boor.[46]

The difference between these types, then, lies above all in the extent to which they exercise their right to participate in politics at the centre of the polis, a right that is at least in principle open to countryman and town-dweller alike. The idea of *Athens*, the city, in contrast to the *chōra* of Attica is itself a *political* concept rather than a geographical notation: for example, while countrymen are *Athenaioi*, women, wherever they reside, because they lack political rights and 'hence have no special connection with the city and indeed ... are excluded from just those areas which distinguish city life', are never *Athenaiai* but *Attikai gynaikes*, not Athenians but Attic women.[47] Much the same can be said, as Osborne suggests, about the deme-identity. Whereas a male villager, as a citizen, would be identified by his *demotikon*, his deme name, the countrywoman might be identified by her husband's or her father's deme, but in her own right was simply someone who lived in a particular village.

Humphreys has suggested that the critical factor in determining the difference between the urban–rural continuum which characterized ancient Athens, and the urban–rural dichotomy of, for example, Hellenistic Alexandria or the cities of mediaeval Europe, is not the level of economic specialization nor the size and density of the urban population, but rather the presence or absence of 'middlemen' – feudal lords, patrons or economic entrepreneurs – whose position in some way depends on maintaining such a dichotomy. In Athens, she argues, the countryman's relation with the city and its institutions was direct, not mediated through middlemen: 'The Athenian countryman had a close and direct relationship with the city; he voted in its assembly, bought and sold in its markets, took part in its religious festivals, sued in its courts, had the same political rights and obligations – including that of military service – as the urban population.'[48] This is, perhaps, just another way of saying that the unity of town and country, which reached its peak in Athenian democracy, as well as the 'disproportion' between the degree of urbanization and the size of the urban economy, can be attributed in large part to the political status of the peasantry.

In fact, the political importance of the village seems to have reinforced the attachment to subsistence strategies in agriculture; and there is a striking absence of evidence for local markets in Attica, in sharp contrast to their prevalence in Rome.[49] The paradox is thus complete: the political elevation of the village, signalling the breakdown of the age-old division between ruling centre and subject countryside, encouraged the growth of the city, while at the same time and by the same means it placed limits on the development of the urban economy.

If the political function of the city helps to account for a level of urbanization not commensurate with the development of the urban economy, it still remains to ask how it was possible to sustain this political function and this degree of urbanization upon a material base that was more rural than urban. More particularly, how was it possible for people whose livelihood and wealth were so overwhelmingly derived from the land to be so active in the city, especially in the case of the most active citizens whose prominent role in the political life at the centre was facilitated by more or less permanent residence in the city? There is a temptation here to revert to the traditional view that the life of citizenship was dependent upon slavery, in the straightforward sense that the leisure of one was dependent upon the labour of the other. The flaws in this equation have already been examined in our discussion of slavery in Athenian agriculture.

In the case of the working farmer, the peasant – keeping in mind that in practice he tended to be more active in the local politics of his deme than in the city centre, that agricultural labour was marked by sharp seasonal fluctuations which left the farmer 'underemployed' at various times in the year, and that some peasants lived in or near the city while farming lands in its immediate surroundings – we need to remember the ways in which the democracy limited the demands on surplus production, whether by peasants or even by slaves. In a sense, even to ask the question about the city's material base in the way we have done is to make unwarranted assumptions about the level of surplus production required to sustain the democracy. If the political role of the peasant made unique demands on his time, we must also remember the demands that were *not* made on his labour. There was no large state apparatus to sustain, no royal bureaucracy, no massive and wealthy ecclesiastical establishment, no huge disparities of wealth marked by conspicuous luxury, aristocratic magnificence and a flourishing market for manufactured luxury goods;[50] and military obligations were circumscribed by the capacities, objectives and rhythms of the smallholder. In short, the social, political and economic demands upon the tax and rent fund – in the form of rents, fees, dues, tithes, tributes, taxes and labour services – typically produced by peasants elsewhere were relatively limited. Even if, as seems likely, Athenian peasants produced more of their richer compatriots' wealth, through rents of one kind or another, than is supposed by those who insist on the importance of slavery in agriculture, the demands on peasant-produced surplus – and indeed, on surplus production in general – were restricted in

Athens. This would, of course, have been especially true during the period in the fifth century BC (about which more later in this chapter) when so much of Athens's income was derived from imperial revenues.

As for the wealthiest landowners who may have resided in the city at a distance from their scattered rural properties, there is no doubt that they relied at least in part on slave-labour; but the fact of their residence in the city while their wealth was principally derived from the countryside by itself tells us nothing about the importance of agricultural slavery. History provides ample evidence of absentee landlordism without chattel slavery. In fact, especially given the typically fragmented landholdings in Athens, the long-term absence of the landlord might itself have argued against the consignment of farming to slaves.

The Nexus of Freedom and Slavery in Democratic Athens

And yet, after all this is said it must still be acknowledged that Athenian democracy was inextricably bound up with slavery on a scale unprecedented in the ancient world. The very least that can be said is that the freedom of the peasantry in various ways encouraged the growth of an alternative form of dependent labour, chattel slavery, and that in one way or another the freedom of the citizen and the degradation of the slave were but two sides of the same coin. It may, then, seem immaterial whether we regard slavery as cause or effect, whether we treat slavery as the condition which made possible the freedom of the peasant or whether, on the contrary, we look upon the freedom of the peasant as the condition for the growth of slavery. And it may seem especially perverse to argue that in the first instance the essential feature of the democracy is the degree to which dependence was excluded from the sphere of production.

Nevertheless, it remains the basic premise of this study that only by viewing the democracy from this perspective can that unique political formation and the role of slavery within it be understood. At this angle of vision it becomes possible to appreciate the significance not only of certain political institutions but also, as we shall see in the next chapter, certain cultural forms and attitudes that are specific to the democracy. And we can also begin to answer the question raised at the outset of this chapter: if the consolidation of a free peasantry left or created certain social needs which were met by the growth of slavery, what were those needs and how did slavery fill them? This formulation of the question may also provide us with a check against which to judge the inadequate positive evidence concerning the location of slaves in the

Athenian economy by giving us some indication of where we might expect to find them, provided, of course, that we do not allow our expectations to become self-fulfilling prophecies.

The first point that needs to be stressed is that, if the democracy and the status of the free producing classes within it encouraged the growth of slavery, they also shaped and limited the ways in which slave-labour could be utilized. Slavery no less than any other Athenian institution existed within the context of social and political relations which restricted the scope of appropriation and the concentration of property. The domination of agricultural production by free smallholders meant that the possibilities of slave-utilization were limited in some areas and encouraged in others.[51]

On the one hand, as we have seen, the exploitation of slaves in agricultural production was restricted by the regime of smallholders and by the fragmentation of property that went with it. Other kinds of production, insofar as they fell outside the traditional domain of the peasant, in principle allowed more room for slavery, and any growth in the urban economy created new space for slave production. No doubt the democracy encouraged the development of the urban economy in various ways – for example, by making the city such an important centre of social activity, by increasing the importance of foreign trade, and perhaps even by compelling the rich to seek alternative sources of wealth to the extent that secure peasant tenures and the independence of the smallholder limited appropriation on the land. But while growth in the non-agricultural sector certainly expanded the possibilities of slave-exploitation, the silver mines are the only unambiguous case of substantial growth, producing Athens's most important export, in great part by means of slave-labour. The importance of trade and commerce in general, or the scope for large-scale manufacture, should not be exaggerated; and it must be kept in mind that any encouragement the democracy might have given to growth in the urban economy would have been at least partially offset by the limitations imposed by democracy on the expansion of a market, insofar as the democratic polis represented a consolidation of the smallholders' regime. The reinforcement of subsistence strategies by the political importance of the village has already been noted. In any case, smallholders themselves constitute a notoriously 'inelastic' market; and the restrictions on the concentration of wealth would have curtailed the consumption of manufactured goods by wealthier landowners, who in other times and places – particularly mediaeval Europe – have constituted the major market for the luxury goods typically producd by craftsmen in pre-capitalist societies.[52]

On the other hand, the independence of the peasantry meant that certain kinds of labour services, apart from agricultural production, which in other peasant societies have been drawn from the peasant family – notably various kinds of domestic service for the rich, as well as corvée labour both public and private – insofar as they continued to exist at all had to be performed by some other kind of dependent labour force not associated with the peasant family. As a general rule, it might be expected that slavery would grow most dramatically in those areas left vacant by the transformation of the peasant's relation to landlord and state: the detachment of his household from dependence on that of the lord, and his conversion from subject to citizen. The one limited the forms in which the peasant could be made to work for the lord, excluding those that entail personal bondage to landlord or land; the other limited the forms in which he could be made to work for the state, curtailing the scope of taxation and corvée labour.

What these limitations might mean can be illustrated by contrasting this case to others in which such restrictions did not apply. We have already noted the differences between the Athenian peasantry and others throughout history with respect to taxation and corvée labour. Let us consider more closely the position of the peasant in relation to an individual overlord. Ancient Crete and Sparta may again serve as counter-examples.

The laws of Gortyn bear witness to a form of serfdom in Crete clearly distinguishable from chattel slavery, though the latter also existed on a limited scale. Serfs had a legal and social status which allowed them the tenure of houses and movable property, including livestock, as well as the rights of marriage and divorce.[53] In short, the serf, like any other peasant, was entitled to family and household, and the peasant family was undoubtedly the basic unit of production here as elsewhere in peasant societies, probably working land which the family itself occupied. At the same time, the household, the house and the land they occupied and worked, were part of the ancestral estate allotted to one of the Cretan rulers. As the Cretan word *woikeus* suggests, the serf was attached to the household of a lord, and it was by virtue of this attachment to the overlord's estate that the serf was obliged to pay tribute. It is reasonable to suppose that here, as in other cases where peasant families have been juridically tied to the household of an overlord, such attachment entailed services above and beyond agricultural labour, especially domestic service of various kinds carried out by members of the peasant family. There also existed categories of debt-bondage in which a formerly free person might be reduced to a condition comparable to that of serfs.

Roughly similar conditions existed in Sparta, where the helots possessed certain rights, maintaining their own families and occupying land, while remaining bound to their Spartan overlords to whom they owed tribute and very likely a variety of labour services. In both cases, the right of the masters to exact tribute or labour services was mediated by the state and their membership in it as a citizen community ruling over a subject population. In this sense, the surplus labour appropriated by the Cretan or Spartan overlord was, again, perhaps a direct descendant of the tribute exacted by the redistributive state; and this inextricable unity of economic and political power, in which the right of private appropriation rested upon possession of the state, had as its corollary a relatively undeveloped privatization of property.

The implications of attachment to an overlord's estate are much clearer, of course, in the far better documented case of mediaeval Europe. A particularly useful illustration is the *familia* of the eleventh and twelfth centuries:

The numbers of landlords were great and they belonged to all ranks of society. Twelfth-century documents record peasants who owned more land than they could cultivate themselves, who leased out plots to other villagers less well provided for, and who acquired in this way economic power over their tenants. It is true that to have power over men as well as land was a less common privilege, but we may assume that every noble family, monastery or chapter controlling and exploiting a *familia*, a group of dependent peasants, in its vicinity formed the centre of a domestic lordship. The importance of this kind of economic domination was indisputable, since it was certainly most highly valued by twelfth-century lords. ... The most highly prized of a lord's possessions were neither his fields nor the amount of gold and jewellery locked away in his inner chamber, nor were these objects of envy to others. The real wealth of that period was to be found only in the 'family'.

The complex social group known as the 'family' included first of all the domestics. It contained also peasants set up in their own homes; some, but not all, of the lord's tenants; freeholders who had become clients; and occasionally tenants of other lords. ... What then did he [the lord] expect from them?

Above all he expected them to work. The eleventh- and twelfth-century 'family' constituted before all else a reservoir of manpower into which the master could dip freely for help in the cultivation of his demesne. The first duty of a dependant consisted in 'service', by which was meant that he was bound to fulfil all his lord's orders. ... A diploma given in 1035 by the king of Germany, Conrad II, laid down the powers of the abbot of Limbourg over 'the unmarried sons (of men of his *familia*); he may place whoever he wishes in the kitchen, whoever he wishes in the bakery, whoever he wishes to do the laundry, whoever he wishes to look after the stable, and he may assign whoever he wishes to do each task. As for those who are married, the abbot may appoint them at will to be cellarers, seedsmen, collectors of tolls, or foresters. ...'

We may well think that in the eleventh century the essential economic value of the *familia* centred on this group of domestic servants. The men whom the master had housed in their own cabins (*cases*), were still obliged, it is true, to perform personal service, as distinct from the charges and labour services incumbent on their tenancy. They came to work in the household on certain days; their wives wove the lord's flax and wool at home or in the workshops of the 'hall', they fashioned at home various wooden objects for use on the demesne. But this labour supply remained insufficient. Their master mainly expected from them what was later called in Germany *Gesindedienst*: he wanted them to rear children and put them at his disposal when they were old enough to serve. Like the servile *manses* of Carolingian times, the cabins inhabited by the men of the *familia* were nurseries of young domestic workers.[54]

It can be stated as a general rule that 'power over men' in the sense here intended – that is, the power to command the service of dependent labourers who are obliged to serve by virtue of their juridical or political status – is typically the most highly prized possession of the propertied classes in pre-capitalist societies. And although in such societies, and especially when the money economy is undeveloped, the attachment of non-kin to the household by various juridical means has been a common method of procuring regular personal service beyond the work of the family or the obligations of kinship, chattel slavery has not been the predominant or even the preferred form in which such power has been exercised. Indeed, one of the disadvantages of chattel slavery may be that the slave, unlike the dependent peasant, is less likely to be accompanied by a subject *household*, available as a source of labour and a 'nursery' of workers. A broad spectrum of peasant dependence, ranging from serfdom to clientship, has been a far more widespread way of commanding a variety of labour services.

It is this spectrum of dependence that was precluded by the democracy in Athens; and it can be argued that the kind of economic power still exerted by Athenian landlords over their poorer compatriots did not extend much beyond the forms described by Duby as belonging to those prosperous peasants in the twelfth century 'who owned more land than they could cultivate themselves' and leased out the excess to tenants. This kind of economic power, or that of the landlord over the casual wage-labourers who supplemented his work force in times of special need, was certainly not inconsiderable or unprofitable; but it was more limited in its scope than various forms of peasant dependence, and it left open whole areas of personal service which dependent peasants, serfs, and clients have performed throughout history.

To be a citizen, to belong to the polis, was precisely not to belong to an *oikos* other than one's own. We should not be surprised to find these empty spaces filled by the one remaining form of attachment to the master's household – chattel slavery. In his relations with free peasants, the dominance of the Athenian landlord over his fellow citizens rested not on exclusive possession of the state and its tributary system, nor on a privileged juridical status, but on possession of more and better property. And the juridical status of the slave was itself determined by the replacement of traditional tributary relations with the relations of private property, as personal servitude became synonymous with the reduction of human beings to chattel property.

In a society where agricultural production was dominated by smallholders whose availability for personal service to the rich and public service to the state, except as citizens and soldiers, was limited; where a degree of freedom from personal dependence unequalled in any other advanced civilization of the time had produced a culture in which independence and self-sufficiency were among the most prized and deep-seated values, where might one except to find room for the labour of slaves? Is it too much to say that we might expect to find the largest space for slavery precisely where the evidence suggests it was: in domestic service; in long-term employment, public and private, whether in the most degraded and servile occupations such as mining, or in managerial positions; and in those areas of production outside the traditional domain of the peasant citizen; in other words, in the interstices of the peasant regime, and not in the society's agrarian material base?

The Smallholders' Regime and the Subordination of Women

The other major form of dependence in the democracy, the sub-ordination of women, can perhaps also be illuminated by considering it in the context of the peasant regime. There is, of course, nothing unique in the democracy's exclusion of women from the political sphere, nor did the subordination of women originate with the democracy. Nevertheless, it remains a remarkable feature of Greek history that the position of women seems to have declined as the democracy evolved, and that in non-democratic states – notably Sparta and possibly the Cretan cities (if the laws of Gortyn are any indication of a more general disposition in Crete) – they enjoyed a more privileged status, especially in their rights of property. For example, while Athenian heiresses (*epikleroi*) were obliged to marry the next-of-kin in order to preserve the family property, Spartan women could inherit in their own right. And while aristocratic women in Athens were increasingly confined to their quarters in the home as the aristocratic household economy gave way to the 'city-state' and indeed to a decline in the unchallenged superiority of the aristocracy in general, their Spartan counterparts experienced a degree of freedom which deeply offended non-Spartan Greeks.

Here some cautions must be introduced. The privileged position of Spartan women, for example, is unlikely to tell us much about their helot subordinates; conversely, the limited freedom and mobility of aristocratic women in Athens were not matched by comparable restrictions on poor women, who in practice had considerable freedom of movement, to go about their necessary business, perhaps sometimes to labour as artisans and shopkeepers. In other words, class distinctions must be made. And care must be taken not to misconstrue the meaning of female privilege in a case like Sparta, where the unusual freedom of women was the obverse of a uniquely dominant male ethos, the product of the proverbial Spartan militarization of all social life in what amounted to a permanent military occupation by the Spartiate community of an exploited subject people, the helots, and to a lesser degree the *perioikoi.* The result of this garrison state was to subordinate family life to the male community of the mess, the bonding of age-groups and the soldier's solidarity. If Spartiate women were unusually free, it was as a mirror image of the dominant male community, imitative of and always subordinate to it – even if the military preoccupations of the men had the effect of devolving upon women a unique degree of participation in the control of landed property.[55]

It may be necessary to qualify the proposition that the status of women in general declined with the advent of democracy, especially since we know so little about the condition of women of subordinate classes in earlier times, and not a great deal about them even in the democratic age. We may accept that the deterioration in the status of aristocratic women had ideological consequences in the cultural derogation of women in general.[56] But we can make no safe assumptions about the peasant household, or about the effects of the democracy on its patriarchal structure.

Such qualifications notwithstanding, there remains something to be explained, even if we confine ourselves to the one well-documented fact which is most commonly accepted as testimony to a decline in the status of women in general, that is, their effective deprivation of property rights. It is far beyond the scope of this study to speculate about the origins of women's subordination or sexual divisions of labour; but taking as a point of departure a society in which male dominance, the patriarchal family, patrilineal descent and patrilocal marriage were already well established, as they were in most parts of

Greece, there may still be something to add to the already substantial literature on the status of women in ancient Greece concerning the tendency of the democracy to reinforce and aggravate some of these patterns. In particular, it is worth considering how the liberation of the peasantry and the emergence of the peasant-citizen may have contributed to the restriction of women's property rights.

One general point needs to be stressed at the outset. In pre-capitalist societies where powers of appropriation are typically grounded in juridical privilege and political authority – the 'power over men' which commands the services of labourers in various conditions of juridical dependence or political subjection – there is a premium on political rights without parallel in capitalist societies. In capitalism, claims on the labour of others rest on the property of the capitalist and the propertylessness of the labourer and can coexist with formal juridical/political freedom and equality – even to the extent of universal suffrage. In pre-capitalist societies political rights are, as it were, a scarce resource, and there is an absolute limit on their distribution, a very restrictive limit beyond which the extension of citizenship endangers the very foundations of the social order and its system of appropriation. Political rights in class-divided pre-capitalist societies are by definition exclusive. The exclusion of pre-capitalist peasant-producers from full political rights, if not as universal and complete as the exclusion of women, certainly counts as a general rule – a rule spectacularly breached by Athenian democracy.

But if the exclusion of women from politics belongs to this general picture of political exclusiveness, it remains to be said that political rights have throughout most of human history tended to be male prerogatives – for whatever reason. The prestige attached to that political role has in turn reinforced the dominance of the male in the household, even one whose own political rights have been severely restricted or confined to his village community. In the peasant family, the political elevation of the male has intersected with other factors disposing the household to a strongly hierarchical and perhaps coercive structure, not the least of which is the household's dual function as a 'home' and the principal unit of production at the same time – more particularly the productive unit which must answer to the exploitative demands of landlords and states.[57] The organizational requirements of exploitative production, which tend toward a coercive hierarchy, may help to explain the especially pronounced patriarchal structure so often observed in peasant households.

In democratic Athens, then, it is possible that two countervailing pressures were at work in determining the condition of women. On the one hand, to the extent that the burden of exploitation was lightened by the political status of the working farmer in the democracy, some of the pressures for a hierarchical and coercive household regime may have been alleviated. On the other hand, the privileged political status of the male widened the gap between men and women, and perhaps pressures for the cultural devaluation of women were reinforced as the extension of citizenship carried with it a concomitant ideological impulse to harden the remaining principles of exclusion. Unfortunately, we cannot know which of these forces prevailed in the day-to-day life of the peasant family, but we can perhaps reformulate the question to ask how the transformation in the function of the peasant household – the change in its economic role as peasants were liberated from traditional tributary relations – affected the property rights of women in general.

Let us begin with the peasant household as the principal unit of production, drawing on the labour not only of the household head but of his family. It stands to reason that the condition of the household and the roles of its various members will vary according to the demands placed upon its labouring capacities. The dependent peasant household which must produce not only for its own consumption but to create the wealth of landlords and states will face more onerous demands on the labouring capacities of all its members than will the free peasant household subject to limited claims on its labour by landlords and states – or at least this is so unless and until the free farmer is subjected to a new kind of demand, the competitive pressures of a capitalist market. The Attic peasant household was subject to limited external demands, with restricted claims on its labour from landlords and states and with no competitive market. It is possible that in this respect it has had no exact historical parallel.

However, if the external demands on the productive capacities of the peasant household were limited in Athens, the peasant family faced another stringent pressure: the need to protect the family property. The smallholder's stance toward his property must always be primarily protective – literally conservative, neither liberal (in 'conspicuous consumption') nor acquisitive as the larger landholder can afford to be. In a sense, the burden of conservation lies even more heavily on the free smallholder than on the dependent peasant who derives a certain security of possession from the fact that his landholding is the condition of his labour for the overlord. It is precisely in this sense that 'power over men' was the most highly prized possession of the pre-capitalist lord. Land without dependent labourers attached to it was of little value to him. Peasants with free claims to land presented a different problem for the landlord, one resolution of which was the exploitation of their relative weakness and economic vulnerability to the point of dispossession, whether through debt, foreclosure, purchase or outright expropriation. The free peasant must then conserve his property against the threat of dispossession, and also against excessive morcellization – or at least he must strike some kind of balance between the need to provide for his children (a constraint which, though it applies to wealthy landlords too, operates differently for the smallholder with no reserves to ensure the livelihoods of disinherited offspring) and the need to keep the property sufficiently intact to preserve its viability, a particularly stringent constraint where holdings are already close to the margins of survival.

Here may be part of the answer to our question concerning property rights in the democracy. It may not be possible to determine the historical reasons for the particularly restrictive disposition of female property rights, but their *consequences* are at least suggestive. The restrictions on women's property rights appear to have had 'one good result':

> If property is fairly widely distributed in the first place, and if (as in all or nearly all Greek states) marriage is patrilocal, so that the girl leaves her father's clan and, taking with her whatever she possesses either as dowry or in her own right, goes to join her husband's family, then to keep women propertyless may well help to prevent property from accumulating rapidly in the hands of the richer families. ... At Sparta, the fact that daughters could inherit in their own right and that the *patrouchos* (the Spartan equivalent of the Athenian *epikleros*) did not have to marry the next-of-kin must have played a major part in bringing about the concentration of property in a few hands which reduced the number of adult male Spartan citizens (the *homoioi*) from eight or nine thousand to hardly more than a thousand by the date of the battle of Leuctra in 371 BC. ... In Athens ... there could be no such thing as a daughter inheriting in her own right, and the *epikleros* had to marry the next-of-kin and thus keep the property in the family. This would help to preserve family property, and would work against automatic accumulation by the already rich through the processes of marriage and inheritance; and the resulting greater equality of property among citizen families is likely to have been one of the factors making for the exceptional strength and stability of the Athenian democracy.[58]

In other words, yet again, Athenian democracy, in its disposition of property rights as in its political institutions or its military arrangements, was uniquely determined by the logic of the smallholders' regime. The particular ways in which it was so determined must, however, be further specified, for it is difficult to think of any other historical example of just this kind of regime, with just this balance of contradictory forces at work. On the one hand, like other peasants, the Athenian smallholder was subject to the pressures of poverty and marginal property; he was not the undisputed master of the Attic countryside but, like other peasants before and after him, coexisted with landlords and the threats their superior wealth represented. On the other hand, he was uniquely well situated to impose his logic of self-preservation on the whole community; he had the strength, as it were, to turn his weakness into law. On the one hand, he was uniquely free of juridical disabilities or political subjection, in contrast to his counterparts elsewhere. On the other hand, unlike the juridically free and propertyless producer in a capitalist order, he continued to live in a society where appropriation, and the relations between appropriators and producers, were inextricably linked to political rights and juridical privilege and not yet determined by purely 'economic' power and the laws of the market. In this context, the possession of citizenship had a particular salience and exclusiveness.

This is the context in which the status of the Attic woman must be situated. Women have always served a multiple function in the peasant economy, as producers, reproducers and conservers of family property; but the balance and form of these various roles has varied according to the prevailing modes of appropriation, the demands on peasant production, and the specific relations between appropriators and producers. The condition of the Athenian woman, in an already patriarchal setting, was undoubtedly shaped by the peculiar balance of her functions in the peasant household, the subordination of her continuing role as producer to her roles as reproducer of citizens, and above all as conserver of family property, in a society where peasant strategies of self-preservation were unusually prominent in custom, politics, and law.

The Dynamic Contradictions of the Peasant Regime

The evolution of the democratic polis, then, represents a significant triumph for the Attic peasantry, but it also expresses the incompleteness of that triumph. On the one hand, the Athenian aristocracy was never able to achieve what the Romans, in a roughly similar city-state system, were to accomplish. Athenian landlords were never able to maintain an aristocratic constitution within a civic community uniting landlords and peasants (what Greek conservatives might have regarded as a model 'mixed constitution', perfectly summed up in the Roman formula SPQR). Hence they never managed to amass concentrations of wealth like those of the Roman senatorial class. Disparities of wealth in Athens remained very modest by comparison, and this goes a long way toward explaining the absence of further unrest of the kind faced by Solon. On the other hand, the polis also never became a pure democracy of small producers (if such a thing can be imagined) – even if it may have come as close to it as any other known society in history. Not only was poverty widespread, but the political life of Athens was to the end impelled by the tensions between citizens who had an interest in restoring an aristocratic monopoly of extra-economic powers and those who had an interest in resisting it.

If the community of citizens also acted as an 'association against a subjected producing class' of slaves, as Marx and Engels suggest, this is at best only half the story. This formula disguises the conflict *within* the citizen body – from which the democracy derived its political and cultural dynamism – between citizens for whom the state would serve primarily as a means of appropriation and those for whom it served as a protection from exploitation. Although the political conflicts between democratic and oligarchic factions never coincided neatly with class divisions, these political tensions cannot be understood in abstraction from the divergence of interests which separated those who had a great deal to gain from a reinstatement of a division between rulers and producers and those who had much to lose. (It is significant, incidentally, that in both the major contemporary Marxist studies of ancient history, Anderson's *Passages from Antiquity to Feudalism* and Ste Croix's *Class Struggle in the Ancient Greek World*, there is a sharp disjunction as the analysis passes from a general and theoretical definition of the 'slave mode of production' or the 'slave economy' to an account of specific historical processes and political developments, when slavery recedes and class divisions between appropriating and producing citizens, or 'propertied' and 'unpropertied' classes, take centre stage.) And the same tensions must be invoked to explain the cultural vitality of Athens (about which more in Chapter IV) – not least the oppositional culture which produced some of the most notable achievements of Greek civilization, such as the philosophy of Plato.

If the political victory of the smallholders' regime is a central fact of Athenian history, then, so is its incompleteness and fragility. And here is another paradox. On the one hand, the incompleteness of the peasant regime limited the democracy, not only allowing the survival of an aristocracy but also, even as it restricted the means of appropriation, encouraging the growth of slavery as an alternative source of wealth, and reinforcing the subordination of women. On the other hand, the democracy proved more dynamic in many ways than it might have been had the peasant regime been stronger. The tension between classes was politically and culturally fruitful; and the very imperfection of the smallholders' triumph swelled the ranks of those on the margins of the peasant community. The demos was increasingly composed not only of peasants but also of craftsmen in the growing urban economy, and the land-poor *thetes*, who manned the fleets and became the backbone of Athens' naval power in the heyday of democracy. Many of these citizens still had one foot in the peasant community – especially the *thetes* who worked in the fields as casual or seasonal labourers, or may even have been poor proprietors in need of income supplements – but they also lived outside it. If the democracy was founded in response to peasant aspirations, it was these other elements that formed the core of the 'radical' democracy in the late fifth century BC and figured most prominently in the nightmares of aristocratic thinkers, who now, long after the rural unrest of Solonian times, looked with nostalgia at the sturdy but quiescent Attic peasant.[59]

Democracy and Empire

It could, of course, be argued that the whole contradictory structure of Athenian democracy, with all its anomalies and delicate balances – between landlords and peasants, town and country, farmers and craftsmen – depended for its coherence, and even its survival, on a supporting apparatus external to the polis: the 'empire' whose revenues allowed the democracy to live beyond its productive means and without taxing to the limit the labouring capacities of its citizens. It is undoubtedly true that the empire, at least for a time, sustained the democracy in various ways, direct and indirect. Imperial tributes and other less direct benefits of hegemony made up a substantial portion, even the bulk, of public revenues during a critical part of the fifth century. The empire provided confiscated land for some poor Athenians and work for the thousands of others who rowed its ships or the many who worked in the dockyards. The imperial income, at least in the fifth century, helped to maintain not only the massive building projects which employed Athenians (as well as slaves) in the construction of monuments to the glory and pride of the democracy, but also the unprecedented payments for public service which both admirers and critics of Athenian democracy regarded as its most radically democratic feature. Above all, the naval force maintained largely by imperial tribute (as long as the empire lasted) guaranteed the supply of imported grain, which at the very least helped to sustain a substantial population not engaged in agricultural production without making impossible or unacceptable demands on the surplus labour of Athenian farmers, and in so doing contributed much to the democracy's vitality and political stability.

There are, nevertheless, strict limits to the explanatory power of the

Athenian empire. The most obvious limit is the temporal one. The period of 'empire', even if we include the early days of the anti-Persian league established in 478 BC, covered less than half the duration of the democratic age from Cleisthenes (let alone Solon) to the Macedonian conquest. Even the navy predated and outlived the empire and its sources of revenue (though with considerable difficulty); and if payment for some public duties, notably jury service, may have been introduced (as M.I. Finley maintains) in consequence of this new wealth, not only did such payments survive in the fourth century when the imperial sources dried up, but new and even more radically democratic payments – for attending assemblies – were only later introduced and then increased, at a time when public finances, always in a parlous state, were sorely stretched. We must be careful, too, not to exaggerate the effects of imperial revenues, or indeed of imported grain, in transforming the structure of Athenian production. Neither of these factors permitted Athens to relinquish subsistence strategies in agricultural production or to abandon the objective of self-sufficiency. It may be just as fruitless here as in the case of slavery to proceed by asking whether 'imperialism' was *the* or even *a* 'basic' element of Athenian democracy, and whether 'it caused this or that'. What might be more instructive in the present context is simply to consider how the specific character of the empire was determined by its imbrication with the peasant regime.

Ancient historians have often remarked on the *normality* of war in ancient Greece and Rome. War, it might be said, was simply a continuation of economics by other means; and in both cases 'empire' was the outcome of war. But if the Athenian and Roman empires were, in their respective and very different ways, unique, the same cannot be said of the general tendency to supplement their capacities of production and appropriation by military means. Both Athens and Rome may have been remarkable (though surely not unique) in the frequency of their resort to war; but in all pre-capitalist societies where appropriation is inextricably bound up with 'extra-economic' powers – juridical, political, and military – and where wealth is typically expanded by coercive surplus extraction rather than by enhancing labour-productivity, military activity is always a more or less natural extension of appropriation, whether in the form of booty raids, coercive expropriation of peasants at home, or the exaction of tribute and territorial expansion abroad. Military appropriation can, however, take a variety of forms – and here, both the similarities and the differences between Athens and Rome are revealing.

Athens and Rome (at least at the outset) had in common a 'city-state' form which united landlords and peasants in a single civic community and in a citizens' army. In both cases, peasants formed the original backbone of the army and, again in both cases, military actions were to a greater or lesser extent responsive not just to the requirements of warlords, hero-nobles, or military aristocracies, as in many other states which have resorted to military appropriation, but also to the demands and capacities of peasant-soldiers. It is arguable, too, that in both cases the military drive beyond their own territorial boundaries was conditioned by the restrictions on coercive appropriation at home, imposed by the civic status of the peasantry.

In Athens, however, the peasant regime (as we have seen) was far more restrictive than it was in Rome, where aristocratic rule prevailed. Each of these different regimes imposed its own logic on warfare and on the scope and objectives of imperial expansion. The differences in means and ends can be sharply counterposed by a few simple contrasts – apart from the obvious differences in size, duration, and degrees of control between the vast, long-lasting territorial empire governed by Rome and the relatively small, short-lived, and loose collection of tributary states over which Athens exercised hegemony. Rome's citizens' militia grew into a standing army of long-serving professional soldiers, which became 'the largest and most expensive military force the world had ever seen'.[60] The proposition that the empire was built and maintained by a peasant army must be substantially amended by the qualification that the professionalization of the army which accompanied the growth of empire tended to separate farmer from soldier, at least for long stretches of time (or even absolutely, as there developed 'a growing tendency for the army to recruit from soldiers' families "in the camp", and to form a closed order, cut off from both the local population and the rest of provincial society'[61]). 'Imperial' Athens had no standing army at all and won hegemony in Greece with a military force of citizens who remained firmly tied to their communal roots and whose terms of service were tailored to the agricultural calendar in seasonal campaigns. The Roman army fought for territory and established a huge territorial empire; Athens in this sense never had an empire at all but (once the purely defensive objectives of the alliance led by Athens had been met with the final removal of the Persian threat) deployed its military force primarily to acquire *tribute* rather than territory, often (though not always) sustaining its hegemony by supporting democratic forces in the 'allied' states against their local oligarchies.

Robin Osborne's telling observation that Greek warfare was an adjunct to agriculture can be adapted to illuminate the Athenian empire. Whatever else the Athenians may have achieved with the naval superiority on which their hegemony rested, its principal object was to guarantee the food supply by securing sea-routes for the importation of grain. In this respect, the extension of military power out to sea belonged to the same logic as did the border raids which, as Osborne points out, were the typical Greek mode of supplying agricultural deficiencies. But an extension of this logic on such a scale and in this new domain created economic and political imperatives of its own. Command of the seas, however modest its objectives, was an expensive business, and imperial revenues were substantially devoted to the building and maintenance of ships. Instead of assuming that the Athenian navy grew in order to satisfy an imperial impulse, we might come closer to an understanding of the empire if we reverse the order of causation: the empire grew in order to maintain the naval force.

The contrasts with Rome are striking. There, the territorial impulse did indeed take precedence. Expansion was the object of the imperial exercise; and not only the organization of the army but also the structure of agriculture itself was shaped to the demands of territorial expansion. The army constituted the primary cost of the Empire, and supplying the army – either directly, or indirectly through taxation – became a major factor in determining land use. 'This was exploitation, and in aggregate exceeded anything witnessed previously in the Mediterranean world.'[62] It is true that ordinary soldiers might benefit from the territorial gains which they fought to acquire and protect, when they were granted land as a reward for service; but the principal imperatives to which imperial expansion responded were those of the Roman aristocracy. It was they who amassed huge fortunes from the spoils of the Empire – and it was they who profited at home from the vulnerability of absent peasant-soldiers.

The same aristocratic regime made possible the characteristically Roman mode of imperial administration, without an elaborate bureaucracy, through a vast confederation of local aristocracies united by the Roman 'citizenship'. This expedient – or indeed any means of holding together a massive territorial empire – was simply unavailable to the Athenians. Citizenship, like military service, remained intimately tied to the local community; and the integrity of Athens as a civic community, especially a community based on democratic citizenship, would have been fatally threatened by a violation of its political particularism or a wide territorial extension of citizenship. Where the Roman Empire absorbed and subverted the 'city-state' forms, the Athenian always remained subordinate to the polis. If, then, both Athenian and Roman 'imperialisms' represented continuations of production and appropriation by other means, it was in significantly different ways, which corresponded to their divergent dispositions of relations between producers and appropriators, landlords and peasants.

Athenian Democracy:
A Peasant Culture?

The Greek Concept of Freedom

'The peasant Utopia,' writes Eric Wolf, 'is the free village, untrammelled by tax collectors, labor recruiters, large landowners, officials.'[1] This Utopia does not, apparently, include the peasants' domination of the state or the cities 'which house the centres of control, of the strategic non-agricultural resources of the society':

> Ruled over, but never ruling, they also lack any acquaintance with the operation of the state as a complex machinery, experiencing it only as a 'cold monster'. Against this hostile force, they had learned, even their traditional powerholders provided but a weak shield, even though they were on occasion willing to defend them if it proved to their own interest. Thus, for the peasant, the state is a negative quantity, an evil, to be replaced in short shrift by their own 'home-made' social order. That order, they believe, can run without the state. ...

The peasant Utopia has, of course, never existed. There has never been a peasant community completely free of taxes, rents, fees, tithes or labour services, a 'free village' in which smallholders have had absolute security of tenure and freedom from subjection to a higher authority in the shape of landlord or state. The aspirations of peasants for this kind of independence have, however, made themselves felt in various ways – in peasant rebellions, in political and religious movements, and in cultural traditions.

Many of the most cherished ideals of Athenian culture, and even some of the most exalted notions of Greek philosophy, may owe their origins to the experience and aspirations of the Attic peasantry. If, as

Robin Osborne maintains, Attic smallholders cannot properly be called peasants 'in any strong sense of that word', on the grounds that they were not clearly dominated or exploited by 'outsiders', and that 'there is no evidence at all for their possessing a distinct cultural tradition',[2] it may be because the whole of Athenian culture was so thoroughly imbued with the values of the peasant-citizen that the cultural traditions of the smallholder are not visibly distinct.

While even the most democratic polis was far from a peasant Utopia, the peasant-citizen came as close as any peasant ever has to the freedom described by Wolf, and his deme as close as any peasant community ever has to the ideal of the 'free village' — not as a 'home-made' social order divorced from the state, but precisely as the basic constituent unit of the state through which the peasant for the first time had access to this formerly alien 'negative quantity'. But even short of the democratic polis, the experience of the peasant-citizen even in more limited forms was distinctive enough to produce unprecedented cultural patterns and ideas.

An example of how the aspirations of peasants, the striving for a particular kind of independence, autonomy and self-sufficiency motivated by the particular experience of peasant dependence, might be diffused throughout society and become part of a more general cultural ideal, is suggested by Rodney Hilton's observation that 'it might be said that the concept of the freeman, owing no obligation, not even deference, to an overlord, is one of the most important if intangible legacies of mediaeval peasants to the modern world'.[3] Hilton is surely wrong to credit the mediaeval peasant with inventing the concept of the freeman. A strong case can be made that the credit belongs to the ancient Greeks. As the chorus of Persian elders tells the king's mother in Aeschylus' play *The Persians* (241 ff.), to be an Athenian citizen is to be masterless, a servant to no mortal man. It has often been remarked that the Greek and Roman ideas of freedom, referring both to states and to individuals, have no parallel elsewhere in the ancient world: 'it is impossible,' writes M.I. Finley, 'to translate the word "freedom", *eleutheria* in Greek, *libertas* in Latin, or "free man", into any ancient Near Eastern language, including Hebrew, or into any ancient Far Eastern language either, for that matter.'[4] It seems undeniable that this apparently unprecedented idea was one of the most important cultural legacies of the Graeco–Roman world. But Hilton's comment is suggestive because it locates the impetus for the invention of this far-reaching idea in the experience of the peasant. It is worth considering how the ideals of autonomy and self-sufficiency so central to Greek, and especially Athenian, culture might be traceable to the peasant experience.

The uniqueness of the Greek and Roman concepts is often attributed to the importance of slavery in these societies, on the grounds that the absolute servility of the slave brought out in sharp relief the freedom of the citizen and evoked an unprecedented consciousness of individual liberty. There can be no doubt that the uniquely sharp and dichotomous contrast of freedom and servility in Greek and Roman systems of ideas is in some way related to the inseparable nexus of citizen and slave; but just as the latter itself cannot simply be explained by the proposition that the bondage of the slave produced the freedom of the citizen, neither is it convincing to treat slavery as the condition for the concept of freedom. Nor is it enough to say that the two ideas have been inseparable from the start. While it is no doubt true that the juridical clarity of the servile condition and that of the citizen's freedom defined one another, we should not allow the conceptual unity of this dichotomy in its fully developed juridical form to obscure the possibility that the idea of freedom preceded the unusual expansion of slavery; that it was born of the unique experience of the peasantry in relation to landlord and state; and that, although the idea may have awaited the growth of slavery in order to reach its fullest conceptual clarity, the autonomy of the peasant and its conceptual recognition were preconditions to the juridical definition of the slave. Or, to put it another way, it was not until the peasant was liberated that the concept of slavery could be separated out with any clarity from more general and inclusive notions of servitude. In other civilizations where there existed no concept comparable to the Greek and Roman notions of freedom, there was certainly no lack of servile and dependent conditions, including slavery; what was missing was a stark contrast between servility and freedom. It was only when the whole spectrum of dependence between slavery and freedom was wiped out – a spectrum largely occupied by peasants in various conditions of juridical and political subordination – that the gap widened to permit a dichotomous conceptual distinction.

Jean-Pierre Vernant, in an illuminating comparison of ancient China and Greece, has given the following account of Greek cultural ideals and how they were grounded in the liberation of the peasantry:

In Greece the advancement of the peasantry was a liberation not only from the ancient forms of servitude but from any kind at all. It was brought about by the peasant in the rural demes opposing the land-owning aristocracy who lived in the town and controlled the State. It came about through social antagonisms, conflicts and confrontations which were much more violent than in China where the power of the new States transformed the old social relationships by gradually absorbing them. Through their own efforts the Greek farmers, small peasant owners of a parcel of land, were to confiscate all the ancient privileges of the aristocracy to their advantage, making them 'common property': these included access to legal and political magistracies, the administration of public affairs, control of the army and even of the culture, with its particular modes of thought and feeling and its particular system of values. This widening and democratisation of the aristocratic culture is one of the features that characterises the Greek civilisation. It explains the persistence of a certain ideal of man, and of certain attitudes: the agonistic spirit, the desire always and everywhere to prove oneself the best, the scorn for utilitarian and commercial values, the ethic of generosity exalting the concept of largesse and the gracious giving of gifts, disinterestedness and, finally and above all, a desire for autonomy, non-servitude, coupled with a concept that the human quality of a man depends upon his relation to other men. We should note straight away that it is only within such a society in which the concept of the autonomous individual, free from all servitude, has emerged and been confirmed that the legal concept of the slave can, by contrast, be clearly defined as an individual deprived of all the rights which make a man into a citizen. Greece at one stroke invented both the free citizen and the slave, the status of each being defined in relation to the other. Without free citizens there would be no slaves but instead a hierarchy of degrees of dependence stretching from the top to the bottom of the social scale, a general state of servitude from which even the king, in his relations with the gods or the divine order, is not exempt.[5]

Vernant thus traces the concept of the autonomous individual together with other Greek cultural values to the liberation of the peasantry, their 'confiscation' of ancient aristocratic privileges and the 'democratization' of aristocratic culture. Even his remark that free citizen and slave were together invented 'at one stroke' must be read in the context of an argument that gives clear priority to the historic liberation of the peasantry.

One important qualification must, however, be introduced. Although there is much in Greek culture that can undoubtedly be traced to the diffusion of aristocratic values, appropriated by the demos as it confiscated aristocratic powers and privileges, and although the characterization of peasant liberation as the 'confiscation' of aristocratic privileges is certainly a fruitful way of looking at the evolution of the polis and especially the distinctive nature of Greek democracy, it seems misleading to attribute to aristocratic culture the fierce attachment of Athenians to autonomy and non-servitude. It may be the aristocracy of landed property that most perfectly embodied the ideal of *eleutheria*; but for that very reason the conscious commitment to that ideal is unlikely to have been born out of their own experience. Freedom in this sense was something they could take for granted.

It seems more plausible that the cultural ideal of autonomy emerged out of the opposition between peasant dependence and the experience of liberation. At least, there is no reason to suppose that peasants need instruction by aristocratic culture to generate a desire for freedom from servitude or an appreciation for the value of liberation. This appreciation may not be systematically expressed in juridical or philosophical concepts until it is articulated by members of dominant classes; but the need for such articulation is not likely to arise from the social experience of the aristocracy – except insofar as the aristocratic experience itself is defined in relation to the liberation of the demos. An aristocracy can, out of its own experience, produce a notion of *privilege* and class prerogatives – something akin to the Roman *libertas*, with its connotations of aristocratic class rule – or a challenge to monarchical power, of the kind which emerged out of conflicts between kings and nobles in early modern Europe; but such concepts of freedom do not carry the full charge of autonomy, masterlessness and freedom from servility associated with the assertion of the right to labour for oneself and serve no mortal man.

The concept of *eleutheria* taken out of the context of its changing associations with other ideas – such as *autonomia* (independence, specifically with reference to being governed by one's own laws, in the first instance applied to the autonomous polis), *isonomia* (equality of rights or political equality), and *isegoria* (equality of speech, imperfectly translated as 'freedom of speech') – cannot by itself convey the full meaning attached to the freedom of the Athenian citizen; but its evolution, insofar as we can reconstruct it, is suggestive. In its earliest known occurrences, on Linear B tablets, the adjective *eleutheros* (*ereutero*) and a related verb never refer to the condition of *persons*. Instead, they denote a quality of *commodities* such as linen cloth or thread, apparently referring to something like their exemption from some kind of tax or impost. Scholars have tended to regard this 'fiscal' meaning as 'secondary', implying that there must have been a category of persons which provided an analogy for the application of the concept to inanimate things.[6] It is nevertheless tempting to speculate about the possibility that the fiscal meaning was primary, especially since the word *eleutheros* never appears as a personal status even centuries later, in the writings of Homer and Hesiod, making perhaps its first appearance in that role in the lyric poetry of the seventh century BC. But even if the silence of the texts does not indicate the absence of a category of people designated as *eleutheroi*, it seems likely that the concept had a strongly 'fiscal' content, and that the *eleutheroi* were people who enjoyed a privileged status the principal benefits of which included freedom from tribute, and the right to receive it from others, in opposition to various categories of people bound by various obligations of tribute or labour service.

One of these tributary categories was the *doeros* or *doera*, that is, the *doulos* or *doulē* of the classical language. These were not, however, chattel slaves. They seem to have been in possession of property, living independently in households of their own, but obliged to pay tribute to some official or religious institution. If *eleutheroi* and *douloi* were clearly distinguishable as respectively receivers and givers of tribute, there is nonetheless no need to assume that the two concepts were dichotomously paired like the classical free man and slave, since the status of *doulos* was evidently only one specific condition in a complex spectrum of obligation. For this reason, it may be misleading to insist, as is commonly done, that the two concepts were always definable only in relation to one another. At any rate, since the *douloi* were not slaves, the (putative) *eleutheroi* cannot have been defined in antithesis to slavery.

In the Homeric epics, *eleutheros* appears three times in the formula 'free day' or 'day of freedom' – the opposite is servile (*doulion*) day, or day of servitude – and once as the characteristic of a mixing bowl. These usages remain obscure, but a persuasive interpretation has been offered by Walter Beringer, who suggests that *eleutheros* here 'signifies the condition of belonging to an undefeated and independent group'.[7] There are no *eleutheroi*, but *doulai* (*not* the masculine *douloi*!) do appear, though only twice. We should again not assume that these must be chattel slaves in the classical sense. Servants are never called *douloi* and are always *dmoes* and *dmoai*. *Doulē*, argues Beringer, denotes the concubine, the alien, 'non-belonging' woman whom the aristocrat may not marry and who has no legitimate claims against him, for herself or her bastard children.[8] If, as Beringer argues, the opposition *eleuth-/doul-* refers to the contrast between 'belonging' and 'non-belonging', there is, as he suggests, a sense in which *dmoes*, who (as the word implies) were attached to the aristocratic household, could be said to 'belong' to the privileged community, in contrast to *douloi* whose condition in other respects – the possession of a household, some rights in property – was less servile. But if the *dmoes* 'belonged', it need not follow that they were entitled to be called *eleutheroi*, as long as we give up the probably misleading notion that *eleuth-* and *doul-*, because they were mutually exclusive, also covered all possible relations between freedom and bondage or servility. In particular, we should allow for a distinction between the relation of subject to ruling communities and the relation of personal servant to master. Only later, when chattel slavery becomes the dominant mode of 'non-belonging', do the two conditions merge.

In Homer, then, there is no direct evidence of *eleutheria* as a condition of persons; and in Hesiod, no word of either the root *eleuth-*

or *doul-* appears at all – the slaves, if such they are, are *dmoes*. The temptation is very strong to conclude that the concept did not exist in this form from Mycenaean times to the eighth century. This would not be surprising, since the 'freedom' of the privileged community could be taken for granted, while the obligations of its subjects would need to be specified. The 'freedom' of a dominant group arguably requires no explicit assertion until its dominance is challenged. But whether or not a formal category of this kind existed to designate the ruling community, we can infer from the existing usages an original opposition between a 'free' community, undefeated and privileged, and a subject community standing outside the privileged circle and owing its rulers tribute or service. This opposition would have undergone considerable modification as the ruling and subject communities of Mycenaean times gave way to more individualized relations between aristocratic landlords and subordinate peasants. When *eleutheroi* finally do appear in the texts in human form, in the works of the seventh-century lyric poets and then in legal texts – that is, at a moment when the ruling class is dangerously vulnerable to challenge from below – they appear to be a privileged *class*, an aristocracy.

In this sense, the original application of the word *eleutheros* to a condition of persons may indeed have been aristocratic, as Vernant implies. But at this stage, the concept did not yet have the distinctive connotations which were to make the Greek *eleutheria* so untranslatable in the terms of other ancient societies. If the emphasis was on privilege and exclusivity of rights (much in the same way that 'free' cities in the middle ages were defined by their exclusive corporate privileges[9]), in a concept which still carried the connotation of belonging to a ruling community though it was increasingly an attribute of *individuals*, it did not yet bear the distinctive implications of individual autonomy and masterlessness which were to characterize the freedom of the democratic citizen. Although *eleutheria* would always retain the element of privilege and belonging to an exclusive community, it acquired another dimension once the *angle of vision* changed, when freedom was seen from the vantage point of the *un*privileged, those who needed to be *made* free. In Solon, we see the first explicit evidence of this new perspective, from the viewpoint of the liberator: he *freed* what had been *enslaved* – land and people; the peasants who had served aristocratic landlords were now *eleutheroi* – free from obligations of tribute and service to their aristocratic compatriots.[10]

At this critical moment, and at this angle of vision, *eleutheria* derives its meaning from an opposition not to chattel slavery but to the formerly dependent condition of the peasantry. If the *eleutheria* of the peasants is defined by contrast to their former *douleia*, it is not *douleia* in the sense of chattel slavery, but in the older sense of a 'non-belonging' tributary population. Indeed it is perhaps only now that *doulos* begins to refer unambiguously to the chattel slave, as the spectrum of servile conditions disappears and slaves alone remain in the (literal) condition of *douleia*, as unprivileged outsiders bound to the service of their masters. It is only now that they become, by default, exclusive claimants to the title of *douloi*. On the one hand, *doulos* as a category of persons seems to have predated the category of *eleutheros*, whose 'freedom' could be taken for granted; on the other hand, though slaves existed, *douloi* could not become clearly and exclusively identified with chattel slaves until it was no longer possible for peasants to be *douloi*, that is, when *personal* dependence completely absorbed the ancient division between ruling and subject communities. The sharp dichotomy *eleutheria/douleia* of classical times – and probably the massive growth of slavery itself – presupposed the liberation of the peasantry.

The Greek concept of freedom cannot be adequately defined either as an appropriation of aristocratic privilege nor as the antithesis to chattel slavery, even if each of these definitions contains an element of historical truth. It is the status of the 'multitude' (*to plethos*) in relation to their erstwhile lords, and to those who still aspire to lordship over them, that gives the concept its distinctive emphasis on individual autonomy and masterlessness, the quality which for Aeschylus distinguished Athens so radically from states with *subjects* and no *citizens*. The Athenian citizen is the man who, like Hilton's free man, owes no service or deference to any man. It is only from this vantage point that it makes sense to say, as Aristotle does, that freedom and equality (*eleutheria* and *isonomia*) are the essential characteristics of democracy, as distinct from other types of polis.[11]

Once the democratic meaning of *eleutheria* had firmly established itself, two conceptual strategies were available to opponents of democracy. They could redefine *eleutheria* to exclude *to plethos*, or they could give it – the *eleutheria* of peasants and craftsmen – a pejorative meaning. Both of these strategies were adopted by the great anti-democratic philosophers of classical times. A new aristocratic concept of *eleutheria* was invoked as a way of excluding the demos from the life of true citizenship by defining freedom to exclude the condition of those who must labour for a livelihood. This exclusive conception, however, required a departure from conventional usage. When, for example, Aristotle identifies the *eleutheros* with the gentleman who does not live 'at another's beck and call' because he practises no 'sordid' or 'menial' craft (*Rhet.* 1367a 28–32), and when in his outline of the ideal state in the *Politics* he treats all working farmers, craftsmen and shopkeepers as servile 'conditions' of the polis, whose services make possible the life of true citizenship for the few who are integral 'parts' of the state, he is clearly redefining the dichotomy of freedom and servility as understood by the ordinary Athenian, the peasant or artisan who regarded himself as free. He is also departing from the usage which goes back at least to Solon, who applied the concept both to the land and to the men whom he had freed in his *seisachtheia*, referring to the liberated peasants as *eleutheroi* (fr. 36).

Insofar as there existed in classical Athens a distinctively aristocratic conception of freedom, then, it was in a sense derivative. It is as if aristocratic opponents of democracy responded to the *eleutheria* of the demos by appropriating and narrowing the conception of freedom. For ordinary Athenians, the peasants and craftsmen who constituted the bulk of the citizen body, *eleutheria* meant freedom from subjection to another, whether as a slave or in some other condition of dependence. It was only for those of aristocratic persuasion, who opposed the democracy precisely because it treated peasants and craftsmen as *eleutheroi*, that the notion of servility might be expanded to include anyone who was obliged to labour for a livelihood. For one type of citizen, *eleutheria* meant the freedom *of* labour; for the other, it meant the freedom *from* labour. To conflate these two meanings by tracing the Greek concept of freedom to the 'confiscation' of aristocratic values is perhaps to reproduce the confusion created by Burckhardt when he attributes to the demos an aversion to labour traceable to the anti-banausic attitude of their aristocratic forebears, or when he, like so many others, speaks of the demos' idleness when he means their freedom from servitude. The association of *eleutheria* with a contempt for necessary or even useful labour is an aristocratic accretion, and perhaps the best indication that the aristocratic concept of freedom was largely a negative one – *anti*-banausic – defined against the freedom of the demos. The aristocratic redefinition of freedom was, as it were, a way of raising the stakes.

An alternative way of turning the concept of *eleutheria* against the democracy was to use it as a term of abuse. Given the tendency to associate freedom with democracy in Athenian culture, it might seem inappropriate for an opponent of democracy to treat *eleutheria* as a virtue. Plato's definition of *eleutheria* as *licence* is the most familiar example of this reconceptualization (*Rep.* 557B ff.). Aristotle may also be tending toward this view of democratic freedom as indistinguishable from licence or anarchy when he defines it as 'living as you like' (*Pol.* 1317b). And it is certainly the intention of the pseudo-Xenophontic account of the Athenian constitution, commonly known as the 'Old

Oligarch', to depict democratic freedom as synonymous with licence and indiscipline, so much so, he maintains, that even metics and slaves in Athens lead 'singularly undisciplined' lives (I.11–12).

In fact, as we shall see, there is much else in Athenian culture and philosophy that can be interpreted as a reactive adaptation of concepts which were demotic in inspiration or had acquired a democratic meaning, an attempt to redefine these concepts to deprive them of their democratic implications. In any case, the Greek concept of freedom was neither simply a response to slavery, nor an extension of aristocratic values, but an expression of the peasant experience, sharpened and refined by the interaction of citizens and slaves and by the refraction of peasant values through aristocratic opposition.

The Greek concepts of freedom and autonomy, then, may have their roots in the experience of a free peasantry, a distinctive phenomenon which existed not only in the democracy, where the last vestiges of peasant dependence disappeared with the abolition of debt-bondage and clientship in the reforms of Solon, but perhaps even before those reforms and in any polis in which peasants were not serfs or helots, permanently subjected to an alien ruling community. In fact, it is worth noting the extent to which all three aspects of freedom – the individual freedom of the masterless citizen, the freedom of the citizen community from subjection to a ruler or despot (*despotēs* is the word which describes the master of slaves), and the autonomy of the polis in relation to other states – were conceived in terms of freedom from the necessity to work for another. So, for example, Herodotus (V 78), in his famous explanation of Athenian strength in the Persian Wars, attributes the unique courage and zeal of the Athenians to the fact that, having become a free people by overthrowing the tyrants, they no longer 'worked for a master' but for themselves. And just as the free peasant is one who is not subject to a juridically determined and politically enforced extraction of surplus labour by virtue of a dependent status, so the truly free and autonomous state is one that not only governs itself by its own laws but also owes no tribute to another state.[12] For the Greeks, to be the subject of a king was also to labour for him, perhaps even to be looked upon as part of his *household* (like the tax- and tribute-paying subjects of the 'redistributive' kingdoms?).[13] In an admirable description of a free people, a speech in Euripides's *Suppliants* (429 ff.) counts among the blessings of a free city not only the fact that the rule of law allows equal justice to rich and poor, strong and weak, alike, and that anyone who has something useful to say has the right to speak before the public, but also that here the labours of a free citizen are not wasted, in contrast to despotic states, where one labours simply in order to enrich the tyrant by one's toil.

All these conceptions reflect the close connection which existed in antiquity between political power and the right of appropriation. As in mediaeval Europe, where the peasants' demand for freedom also gave rise to a conception of the freeman who owed nothing to an overlord, the Greek conception of freedom was conditioned by the unity of political and economic power. In the mediaeval case that unity was embodied in the concept of *lordship*, which entailed a juridical status, a political authority, and an economic power all at once and inseparably. And it is significant that, as Hilton points out, the mediaeval peasants' demand for freedom was above all a demand for an end to lordship. It is, however, worth noting that the famous rebel leader, Wat Tyler, expressed the demand for the abolition of lordship by proposing that it be distributed among all men. 'This would mean the liquidation of lordship,' writes Hilton, 'but it is an interesting indication of the power of the notion of lordship that its equal partition rather than its abolition was proposed.'[14] The Greek conception of *citizenship*, which can be regarded as a 'confiscation' or equal distribution of aristocratic powers and privileges, has something in common with this perception of what freedom for the peasant would entail. In both cases, as is typically true in pre-capitalist societies, the traditional power of the aristocracy to appropriate the labour of peasants had been inseparable from a privileged juridical and political status; and in both cases, the freedom of the peasant could be perceived as depending upon his appropriation of that status.

Even the insistence of the Athenians that they were *autochthonous*, children of the soil, living on and from their own land, not the descendants of ancestors who came from other lands (like the Spartan conquerors), seems to imply freedom conceived in these terms. In the dialogue *Menexenus*, Plato(?) puts in the mouth of Socrates a speech which may be intended as a satire on the typically patriotic funeral oration, but which nevertheless expresses ideas and sentiments that were conventional in Athens. A popular theme in such orations was the autochthonous descent of the Athenians. The land of the Athenians, says Socrates, is their true mother, not a stepmother as in other countries; and in contrast to tyrannies and oligarchies, in which some are masters and others slaves, Athenians are all children of one mother, who think it wrong to be another's master or servant. Since, needless to say, Athenians found it perfectly acceptable to own chattel slaves, the reference here is clearly to some other kind of servitude and domination. The contrast with those poleis, notably Sparta, in which an indigenous population laboured for an alien ruling community makes it clear what Socrates has in mind. The autochthony of the Athenians, their natural equality as children of one mother which also compels

them to seek legal equality, means that they are neither alien appropriators like the Spartans, nor subject producers like the helots; and
it is in this sense that they are, as Socrates maintains, 'brought up in
freedom'.

The Athenian Attitude to Labour

If freedom as most Athenians conceived it implied, among other things,
the freedom of labour, in contrast to the freedom *from* labour, and if
the contempt for servility must be distinguished from a disdain for
labour as such, then clearly something more needs to be said about the
very common proposition that one of the principal characteristics of
Athenian culture was a general contempt for labour. We have already
encountered this view in Burckhardt, who attributed the 'decline' of
Athens largely to the fact that a generalization of the 'anti-banausic'
prejudice, its spread to the lower classes, made the demos idle and
indolent. We noted here the tendency to conflate the freedom from
servitude with a shirking of labour as such. Burckhardt's characterization of the Athenian attitude toward labour is not at all
unusual, though it is more common to attribute this alleged contempt to
the association of labour with slavery rather than an appropriation of
aristocratic values by the demos. This argument also figures
prominently in another common proposition about ancient Greece,
namely that the development of technology was impeded by slavery,
not only because of structural constraints imposed by this organization
of labour, but more particularly because the cultural devaluation of
labour by its association with slavery suppressed the incentive to
creative innovation.

All these propositions are open to question. It is, first, impossible
to demonstrate that the contempt for labour undoubtedly felt by
aristocratic critics of the demos was generally shared by the people
themselves, in other words that it was a cultural ideal and not largely an
upper-class prejudice. Insofar as it is possible to reconstruct what the
ordinary Athenian thought about labour, the prevailing attitude was
probably that, while labour is generally hard and often unpleasant, and
while dependent or servile labour is to be shunned, labour can also be a
source of pride. The arts and crafts can be regarded as the foundations
of civilization, and above all, the need to labour for a livelihood, or
even to engage in 'vulgar' and 'menial' occupations, is not morally or
politically disabling, a ground for exclusion from the life of true
citizenship. Such a view of labour, furthermore, would be completely
consistent with a culture stamped by the values of peasants and artisans,

who know the burdens and pains as well as the virtues of labour, and who, while demanding respect for their work, are not inclined to romanticize about the glories of toil. Again, the peasant-citizen accounts for much that cannot be explained by slavery. The same is true of technology in Athens, the development of which, or lack thereof, is – as we shall see – at least in great part explicable by reference to the smallholders' regime which dictated the nature, extent, rhythm and pace of Athenian production, the limits of appropriation, as well as the cultural evaluation of labour and its techniques.

There can be no doubt that Greek opponents of democracy like Plato, Xenophon, and even Aristotle showed a profound contempt for labour and those who were compelled to engage in it. And a similar disdain has figured prominently even in later attacks on Athenian democracy well into the modern age. The difficulty arises when this aristocratic contempt is made to represent the ethos of the Athenian people as a whole, ascribed even to the labourers who were the prime targets of anti-democratic attitudes. The tendency to generalize from these aristocratic attitudes has travelled freely across ideological boundaries and has, as we have seen, played an important role in both conservative and Marxist histories.

There is a tendency among some commentators to lump together the disdain of dependence with a contempt for labour as such, without distinguishing among the very different social attitudes and interests which these views respectively reflect.[15] Such a conflation is justifiable only, if at all, in the case of those Greeks for whom all necessary labour was by definition dependent and servile or those who believed that all labourers ought to be kept in juridically or politically dependent conditions, and particularly that they should be excluded from the rights of citizenship. Such a confusion would not, however, have much to recommend it to the free peasants and artisans who constituted the bulk of the Athenian citizenry. Indeed, the rejection of dependence, far from producing a disdain for labour as such, might create a preference for manual labour as against more 'respectable' occupations and managerial functions in conditions of salaried, and hence dependent, employment. Careful distinctions must, then, be made among the several very different attitudes revealed in Greek sources which may in various ways express a prejorative evaluation of labour and those who engage in it but which do so in very different ways and with very different consequences. The rejection of dependence, the unwillingness to be bound to a master, or the identification of labour with misery and pain, is something very different from the condemnation of labour as corrupting to the soul and the moral worth of the labourer and hence also to his political capacity. These attitudes differ not only in their social origins but in the social and political programmes which they can be used to underwrite.

If a disdain for dependent labour can be regarded as a universal cultural norm in Athens, and if few Athenians were likely to dissent from the view that labour for a livelihood could be arduous and painful, the same universality cannot be attributed to the outright contempt for labour and labourers displayed by Plato or Xenophon. In fact, the attitudes of anti-democrats like Plato, Xenophon, or Aristotle themselves constitute convincing evidence that the prevailing cultural ideal was very different from the one they espoused. Their complaint against the democracy was, after all, that the 'banausic' multitude was in command and that its servile mentality had placed its stamp on the polis. In other words, those who were most vociferous in their expressions of contempt for labour were clearly not *reflecting* but *attacking* the dominant world-view.

The suggestion that the pejorative judgment of labour – as distinct from the disdain for dependence or the failure positively to glorify work – derives from its association with slavery obscures the most important facts about this attitude: that it was a class prejudice more than a universal cultural ideal, and that its principal inspiration was not the existence of slaves but the predominance of labouring *citizens*. The denigration of labour and labourers to be found in Greek literature, while perhaps especially emphatic precisely because of the unusual status enjoyed by free producers in the democracy, is certainly not uniquely characteristic of slave societies but can be found among propertied classes in other times and places, especially at moments when the interests and power of the privileged few have been challenged by classes engaged in the despised activities. Indeed, it is difficult to think of a more common defence of class privilege than the idea that the 'mechanic' multitude, enslaved in body and mind by the vulgar concerns of subsistence, cannot rise above its base preoccupations and, if admitted to the public councils, must bring to them only 'confusion and tumult, or servility and corruption'.[16]

As for how the vulgar multitude itself evaluated labour, we can only reconstruct their attitudes by inference, since, not surprisingly, they left no systematic statements of their views. Apart from the middling farmer, Hesiod, whose experience in Boeotia around 700 BC may tell us little about the world of the peasant or artisan in democratic Athens, we have no direct voice from the demos. In Hesiod, there is certainly no inclination to glorify labour; work for him is a painful necessity. It can safely be assumed that this attitude was widely shared by others of his class, and certainly by the many less prosperous peasants and artisans whose poverty was not likely to encourage a rosy view of the glories of labour. Yet there is nothing that should surprise us in this perception of the world as seen through the somewhat jaundiced eye of a labouring peasant or craftsman, and there is certainly nothing specifically Greek about it. The very word *labour* in English, like the French *travail*, has pain and trouble at its very core.

The fact that the Greeks – like the Romans – had no word for labour as a general social function tells us little about the cultural evaluation of work.[17] A concept of labour which is both specific in its differentiation of social labour from any other physical or mental exertion, and general in its application to all kinds of social labour without distinguishing among specific work activities, is a modern (or at least early modern) idea. Its full development required the transformation of labour-power into a commodity which is exchangeable with other commodities and therefore bears an exchange value that can be abstracted from the specific nature of the activities involved. At any rate, in its earlier usages, the English *labour*, much as the Greek *ponos*, refers, as the Oxford English Dictionary tells us, to all 'exertions of the faculties of the body or mind, esp. when painful or compulsory'. Beyond this very general meaning, which makes no distinction between social labour and any other painful exertion, there is in early English, as in ancient Greek or Latin, no word to convey a general abstract category which unites various kinds of work – especially those having to do with the 'supply of the material wants of the community' (*OED*) – in a single social function. It is only in the seventeenth century that the modern meaning of labour begins to differentiate itself with any clarity from the more diffuse conception of exertion and effort; and it is only then that the word begins to lose 'its habitual association with pain'.[18]

To return, then, to Hesiod, who, if he associates the work of the peasant with trouble and pain, nevertheless also tells us that 'There is no shame in work; shame is in idleness' (*Works and Days*, 311). At least we are offered here some hint of an alternative virtue to hold up against the *arete* of the traditional *agathoi*, the greedy lords in whom we see a very different side of the heroes whose noble deeds are recorded by Homer. It is, however, arguable that Hesiod still regards wealth and the leisure it brings as the condition of true *arete* and is simply enjoining his recalcitrant brother, Perses, to accept his situation, work hard and make the best of things, instead of aspiring to a life of leisure and gentlemanly virtue beyond his means. If this is so, then Hesiod has not in this respect strayed as far as at first appears from the world-view of the lords whom he otherwise so severely castigates; and this may confirm the suggestion that he belonged to a family of *agathoi* fallen on hard times.[19] Such a background may also be reflected in

Hesiod's version of the myth of Prometheus, in which the fire-thief is the author of human misfortune, including the burden of labour. In any case, this account contrasts sharply with later versions of the myth in which Prometheus is the benefactor of humanity, the bringer of those human arts which are the foundations of civilization. In the transformation of this myth, as in other works of Athenian culture, there are signs of a new and different attitude toward the productive arts and those who engage in them.

It should be interjected at this point that it can be profoundly misleading to contrast the Greek refusal to glorify labour with later European attitudes which identify labour with virtue and the Christian calling, if this comparison is meant to imply that the status of manual labour was unambiguously more elevated in early modern Europe than in slave-ridden Greece. The glorification of labour in European culture has always contained a certain ambiguity. The changes in the concept of labour to which we have referred, and the apparently more positive cultural evaluation of work, coincided with the growing and increasingly systematic preoccupation with *productivity*. The problem with the ethic of productivity, as we saw in Fustel's conception of 'wealth acquired by labour', is that it often attributes that admirable quality – and, indeed, labour itself – not to the labourers who produce but to the entrepreneurs who put them to work. Historically, the elevation of 'labour' cannot be easily disentangled from the glorification of bourgeois 'productivity' as against the passive appropriation of parasitical rentier aristocracies; and this means that the virtue of labour is likely to belong not so much to the labourer as to the 'productive' entrepreneur or capitalist who appropriates his labour.

John Locke, the first major political theorist to construct a systematic doctrine on the principle that labour is the foundation of property and that the world belongs to the rational and industrious, vividly illustrates the ambiguities in this 'glorification' of labour in the famous 'turfs' passage from his *Second Treatise of Government*:

> Thus the Grass my Horse has bit; the Turfs my Servant has cut; and the Ore I have digg'd in any place where I have a right to them in common with others, become my *Property*.... The *labour* that was mine, removing them out of the common state they were in, hath *fixed* my *Property* in them. (art. 28)

If the 'turfs my servant has cut' are mine, the product of 'my' labour, to whom does the virtue of labour belong? Whom did God have in mind when he gave the world 'to the use of the Industrious and Rational, (and *Labour* was to be *his Title* to it)'? (art. 34). Surely not the servants and menial labourers whose 'share, being seldom more than a bare subsistence, never allows that body of men, time, or opportunity to raise their thoughts above that. ...'[20] The virtuous, rational man tends to be the man of property who uses his property productively, the 'improver' (who is also likely to be the encloser) of land, for example, in contrast to the parasitic gentleman wasting his substance on conspicuous consumption. For Locke, as for others of his time and persuasion, there was no incompatibility between the glorification of 'labour' and the exclusion of labourers from the ranks of the privileged and enlightened few who belonged to the political nation, the ruling community of propertied classes embodied in Parliament. In comparison to this mode of 'glorifying' labour, what are we to say about the cultural status of labour in democratic Athens, where peasants and artisans (including many whose 'share' was hardly more than a bare subsistence) were full *citizens*?

The conventional evaluation of labour in democratic Athens is suggested by the debate reported in Plato's dialogue, *Protagoras*, in which Socrates and Protagoras discuss the Athenian practice of allowing ordinary craftsmen into the public councils. What is at stake here is nothing less than the moral worth and political capacities of labourers. It makes little difference whether this dialogue records any conversation that actually took place between the philosophers named, or between any other historical individuals. What is important is that it reflects an opposition between two essentially different views of labour which undoubtedly confronted each other in Athens.

In a discussion of whether virtue can be taught (a question that is beyond the scope of this study), Socrates makes the following observation on the Athenian conception of political virtue:

> Now when we meet in the Assembly, then if the State is faced with some building project, I observe that the architects are sent for and consulted about the proposed structures, and when it is a matter of shipbuilding, the naval designers, and so on with everything which the Assembly regards as a subject for learning and teaching. If anyone else tries to give advice, whom they do not consider an expert, however handsome or wealthy or nobly-born he may be, it makes no difference: the members reject him noisily and with contempt, until either he is shouted down and desists, or else he is dragged off or ejected by the police on the orders of the presiding magistrates. That is how they behave over subjects they consider technical. But when it is something to do with the government of the country that is to be debated, the man who gets up to advise them may be a builder or equally well a blacksmith or a shoemaker, a merchant or shipowner, rich or poor, of good family or none. (319B–D, trans. W.K.C. Guthrie)

The immediate object of these remarks is to demonstrate that the Athenians apparently do not regard the political art – or political virtue – as a technical skill that can be taught, or else they would surely not treat it as a universal quality belonging to all citizens, even those who have never been apprenticed to a master of virtue. The implications of Socrates' views – or, at least, Plato's – on this score do not become fully apparent until Plato's later work, especially the *Statesman* and the *Republic*; but the groundwork is being laid here for the view that politics, like other arts, is a specialized skill which should be practised only by those who engage in it exclusively. Ruling, indeed the life of citizenship, cannot be the province of people who engage in other arts; the shoemaker should stick to his last. The 'argument from the arts', which is at the centre of Plato's attack on democracy, joins with his view that a life free from the compulsions of labour and material necessity is a condition for virtue, as vulgar arts and crafts 'mutilate the soul' (*Rep.* 495E).

Protagoras in his reply to Socrates provides the only systematic defence of democracy to survive from classical times, by demonstrating that virtue, while capable of being taught, is also universal, in much the same way that a mother tongue is both learned and universal. This is not the place to discuss all the philosophical implications of this argument. What is important here is Protagoras' conviction that political virtue is necessarily a universal quality, belonging not just to a select few but to 'shoemakers and smiths', that is, to 'banausics' as well as to gentlemen or philosophers. To introduce his argument, he makes use of the Prometheus myth; and here Prometheus is clearly a benefactor, not the instrument of man's fall. Where Hesiod's Prometheus brought an end to the golden age in which the fruits of the earth offered themselves freely to mankind without their labour, Protagoras' hero gave them the gift of practical arts which allowed them to turn the earth's riches to their benefit; and once Zeus had distributed political skills to them universally – on the principle that if the political art were reserved for experts like other specialized arts, no polis could survive – human beings were able to make use of their arts to enjoy civilized life. Where for Hesiod the arts of Prometheus are a token of the fall, for Protagoras they are the symbols of civilization. Where for Hesiod the cycle of human life has regressed from a golden age of leisure to a fallen condition of pain and labour, for Protagoras it has progressed from a state of nature where men lived like beasts to a civilized life marked by the practice of human arts and the universal distribution of political virtue.

It is not surprising that when Plato in the *Statesman* adapts the ancient myth to his own political purposes, he reverts to the version in which the need for labour and the practical arts is the mark of an age bereft of divine guidance, at the bottom of the cosmic cycle. What better way of putting working farmers, craftsmen, and labourers in their place? What better way of invoking divinity in support of his anti-democratic argument, spelled out in this dialogue in painstaking detail, that practitioners of the 'contributory' arts, the arts which supply the daily needs of human life, should have no share in the art of ruling?

Protagoras, a moderate democrat and friend of Pericles, is a much more plausible spokesman for the conventional ideology of Athenian democracy than are aristocratic opponents of democracy like Plato, whose intellectual life was devoted to attacking democratic ideals; Xenophon, who not only argued against democracy but became a Spartan general; or Aristotle, whose Macedonian patron dealt Athenian democracy its death-blow. And Protagoras was certainly not alone among the great figures of Athenian culture to praise the practical arts as the cornerstone of civilized life, or to associate the development of the arts with democracy as the apogee of civilization. Prometheus was also a hero, for example, to Aeschylus, who makes him the embodiment not only of reason and ingenuity, but also of freedom and justice, not only the bringer of fire and arts – farming, carpentry, navigation, writing, mathematics – but also the personification of the Athenian opposition to servitude and arbitrary rule, as he resists the tyranny of Zeus and scorns the servility of the god's messenger, Hermes. Sophocles in the *Antigone* breaks the narrative to sing the praises of the practical arts in much the same terms as Protagoras and Aeschylus, this time, however, as a tribute not to the benefactions of Titans or gods but to the powers of humanity. In all these cases, the productive activities of farming and the handicrafts are accorded a dignity that is in striking contrast to the contempt heaped upon their practitioners by Plato or Xenophon. The attitudes of the great tragedians befit a society in which peasants and artisans were citizens and in which craftsmen proudly signed their work, dispelling the anonymity that so often characterized craftsmen in other ancient civilizations, notably in the Near East where they were treated as nameless dependants or appendages of those for whom they worked.[21]

No doubt the ideology of the old ruling class survived to some extent even among democrats: a certain respect for the rentier class appears, for example, in Demosthenes (though it must be added that he was no ordinary humble Athenian but a wealthy man). Ruling ideologies are always tenacious, and Burckhardt is probably right to the extent that he attributes such contempt for labour as there was to an aristocratic cultural legacy, rather than simply to the institution of slavery. What is important here, however, is that a very different cultural formation had emerged out of the new social realities of the democracy, a set of attitudes and ideals more specific to the democracy and more uniquely its own, no longer simply a cultural legacy from another age nor an aristocratic counter-culture formed in revolt against the prevailing democratic order.

It should also be kept in mind that Athenian conventional values and practice in some respects went far beyond the cultural norms which were to prevail in Europe well into the modern age, and that they even exceeded the visionary demands of all but the most radical of early modern democrats in the extent to which they granted not only moral value but even political rights to labourers. One need only consider in contrast the attitudes of radicals, including at least some seventeenth-century English Levellers who were prepared to concede that even legally free labourers in certain kinds of 'dependent' employment might lose their birthrights by virtue of their dependence.[22] Whatever the Athenians may have thought of labour for another, it was not grounds for exclusion from citizenship; and, indeed, there is even a sense in which their disdain for dependence can be understood, in the historical context of classical antiquity, as an assertion of the dignity of labour against the aristocratic view that work for a livelihood is by its very nature base and servile.

Rulers and Producers: The Philosophical Subversion of Athenian Democracy

There is, however, one sense in which Plato can be read as an expression of democratic ideals – and that is, paradoxically, precisely in his adoption of the ethic of craftsmanship as a means of attacking democracy. His attitude to the arts as normally understood by Athenians is unambiguously revealed in the hierarchy of souls which he outlines in the *Phaedrus*, where artisans and farmers are seventh in a list of nine, superior only to demagogues, sophists, and tyrants in their moral capacity. Yet the analogy of the arts, the concept of *technē*, is the very foundation of his political philosophy. In his doctrine, the ideal of craftsmanship and respect for those who work with their hands is transmuted into an argument for the exclusivity of politics and for a hierarchical division of labour which excludes the possessors of *technē* from the '*technē*' of citizenship. By placing *technē* at the centre of his argument, Plato pays democracy the tribute of turning its ideals against itself, of meeting his enemies on their own ground. And perhaps this is the most eloquent testimony to the tradition of craftsmanship which the Athenians may have been the first to articulate as a cultural ideal.

Plato's transformation of *technē* is not the only instance in which he conducts a political argument in opposition to democracy by redefining concepts so as to turn them against the democratic meanings implicit in conventional usage. In fact, this is arguably the principal strategy of his political philosophy, and its effect is to undermine precisely those principles that most specifically defined the democratic polis. It might even be fair to say that one way of identifying what Athenians regarded as most essential to democracy is to look for the targets of Plato's attacks, those principles whose conventional meaning he most radically redefines.

A dominant theme running throughout Plato's project of redefinition is the principle of division between ruling and producing classes, which he establishes as a challenge to the democratic conception of citizenship expressed in Protagoras' theory of political virtue. Indeed, this division lies at the very heart of his political theory, in his conception of *justice* as elaborated in the *Republic*. Building upon the argument from the arts and the principle of specialization according to which those who engage in the productive and practical arts cannot also master the specialized art of politics, Plato redefines *dikē* so that justice itself becomes synonymous with the principle of specialization, with all its implications for the exclusivity of politics. Justice in the state, as in the soul, is a hierarchical division of labour, and the just state is one in which, as it were, the cobbler sticks to his last. It is difficult to imagine a definition of justice more subversive of *dikē* as it was understood by Athenians in a political order whose operative principle was *isonomia*, the principle of political equality.[23]

The historical importance of the opposition between rulers and producers – and of its subversion by Greek democracy – cannot be overestimated. The separation of administrative and/or military functions on the one hand, and production or specifically agriculture on the other – a separation embodied in the division between state or royal palace and village, between administrators or warriors and the villagers who feed them – was a very widespread principle of social organization in the ancient world. In some cases, especially those ancient 'bureaucratic' kingdoms where royal officials presided over vast public projects – drainage and irrigation, the building and maintenance of canal systems, etc. – which were vital to agricultural production, the ruling society consisted of an administrative hierarchy directly dependent on the king. In others, including perhaps the Mycenaean kingdoms of Bronze Age Greece, the ruling community may have had a more predominantly military character, embodied in an aristocracy of warrior-administrators surrounding the king. This principle of organization is expressed in the opposition between warriors and villagers which is sometimes attributed specifically to Indo-European societies but which has a wider application. It is perhaps reflected in Mycenaean social structure and its complex system of land tenure, which seems to distinguish between men whose tenure derives from their association with palace and king, and those who occupy the common land of the village and belong to a separate world organized by the village commune and its regulation of agricultural life.[24] In a very different form, the division between ruling and producing classes, between a dominant community exercising both political and military functions and a separate community of farmers and villagers, appears as the dominant principle of social organization in Sparta and the poleis of Crete.

This principle of social organization was acknowledged theoretically by the great philosophers of classical Greece and figures prominently in their theories of politics. Aristotle's distinction between the integral 'parts' of the ideal polis and its 'conditions' is based on precisely this division between the governing class – which combines deliberative and military functions – and the producing classes which feed them and provide the 'conditions' of the state's daily life (*Politics* 1328a–1329a). The division between 'conditions' and 'parts' is summed up by the proposition that 'there is nothing joint or common to the means which serve an end and the end which is served by those means – except that the means produce and the end takes over the product' (1328a, trans. E. Barker). In practice this means that 'a state with an ideal constitution – a state which has for its members men who are absolutely just, and not men who are merely just in relation to some particular standard – cannot have its citizens living the life of mechanics or shopkeepers, which is ignoble and inimical to goodness. Nor can it have them engaged in farming: leisure is a necessity, both for growth in goodness and for the pursuit of political activities, (1328b–1329a). It follows that 'the farming population ought by rights to be one of slaves or barbarian serfs' (1329a). Aristotle supports these principles by invoking the historical authority of Egypt and Crete: 'It does not appear to be a new or even a recent discovery in the theory of the state that states ought to be divided into classes, and the military class and the farming class should be separate. Even today this is still the case in Egypt, as it is also in Crete. ....' (1329a–b).

The invocation of Egypt as a model of social organization, particularly with reference to the principle of specialization which divides ruling from producing classes, seems to have been common in Athens. Isocrates in his *Busiris* attributes to Egypt a tripartite structure which divides society into a priestly class, a military class, and a class that engages in the arts and crafts. He also credits the Egyptians with a strict division of labour which enforces the principle of specialization and prohibits changes of occupation; and he suggests that Sparta owes many of its best institutions and practices to the example of Egypt, notably the principle that no citizen fit for military service should engage in any other craft. The *Busiris* may not be a very serious work, but Isocrates is certainly alluding to an important cultural fact about Athens when he refers to certain unnamed philosophers – clearly critics of Athenian democracy – who have gained great reputations for their discussions of political institutions and who prefer the Egyptian form of government to all others, and the government of Sparta insofar as it imitates Egyptian principles of social division and specialization. The example that comes most immediately to mind is Plato.

Indeed it is Plato who elevates the division between ruling and producing classes to a philosophical system. In the *Republic*, the fundamental principle of the polis is the division between, on the one hand, governing and military functions, united in the Guardians, and on the other hand, the productive functions embodied in farmers and craftsmen. The political implications of this division do not, however, exhaust its significance for Plato. It is for him not merely a political axiom that there exists an essential opposition between ruling and producing functions. It is, in an important sense, the first principle of philosophy in general, the key to both ethical and epistemological truths. The tripartite division of the polis into deliberative, military, and productive functions – or, more precisely, the bipartite division into a ruling class which in its different aspects performs both political and military functions, and a subject class that engages in the arts and crafts – parallels the division of the soul into its ruling and subordinate functions; and the hierarchical organization of the soul, which is invoked to justify the organization of the ideal polis by identifying various social classes with those parts of the soul that are said to be dominant in them, defines both the hierarchy of ethical values and the different forms of perception and knowledge. The Platonic theory of knowledge, with its clear opposition between the sensible and intelligible worlds, and the forms of cognition that correspond to them – the sensible indisputably inferior to the intelligible – is all of a piece with his theory of justice as a hierarchical division of labour and his conception of the polis as properly a hierarchical organization of classes in which the ruling class is fed by the ruled.

It has been argued that the radical opposition between the sensible and intelligible worlds is a distinctive characteristic of Greek thought which distinguishes it fundamentally, for example, from the Chinese. Jacques Gernet, in a comparison of Chinese and Greek ideas, draws the following contrast:

Mencius (end of the fourth and beginning of the third centuries) makes a distinction between the mind (the 'heart' or seat of the intelligence) and the senses (the 'ears and eyes'). But we should be quite wrong to interpret this in terms of our own familiar opposition. On close analysis it becomes clear that this distinction rests upon another: that between the productive and the administrative functions. Mencius is simply expressing a dualist hierarchy of complementary grades and values. Indeed the radical opposition so characteristic of Greek thought, between the sensible world and the intelligible, is totally unfamiliar to the Chinese writers before the empire. No doubt they would have rejected it emphatically as artificial.[25]

It is not immediately obvious from Gernet's account where the line of contrast should be drawn between Mencius' distinction and Plato's opposition. If the Chinese thinker's distinction rests upon that between administrative and productive functions, much the same can be said about the relation between the Greek philosopher's epistemological opposition and the division between governing and producing functions. Plato would surely concur with Mencius' remarks to the lapsed Confucian, Ch'en Hsiang, when the two were discussing the qualities of rulers:

Why then should you think ... that someone who is carrying on the government of a kingdom has time also to till the soil? The truth is, that some kinds of business are proper to the great and others to the small. Even supposing each man could unite in himself all the various kinds of skill required in every craft, if he had to make for himself everything that he used, this would merely lead to everyone being completely prostrate with fatigue. True indeed is the saying, 'Some work with their minds, others with their bodies. Those who work with their minds rule, while those who work with their bodies are ruled. Those who are ruled produce food; those who rule are fed.' That this is right is universally recognized everywhere under Heaven.[26]

If there is a fundamental difference between Mencius and Plato, it certainly does not concern the division between those who work with their minds and those who work with their hands, those who are fed and those who feed them, nor the association of these divisions with the separation between rulers and ruled. Nor can it be said that these distinctions are less closely related to Plato's theory of knowledge than they are to Mencius' views on the nature of the 'heart' and the senses. The difference seems to lie in the *complementarity* of the 'complementary grades and values' in Mencius' 'dualist hierarchy' as compared to the stark *opposition* of the grades and values in Plato's epistemological and social hierarchies.

Perhaps the clue to this difference can be found in Mencius' last sentence. If it seemed self-evident to him that these hierarchical principles were 'universally recognized everywhere under Heaven', it was far more difficult for Plato to assume such a consensus, or even to proclaim it for rhetorical purposes. In the context of Athenian democracy, which represented an unprecedented challenge to precisely these 'universal' principles, axioms that in the Chinese setting could be taken for granted had to be asserted *against* the prevailing social order and the cultural values that sustained it. Here, where it was a question of *reimposing* a hierarchical division which had been replaced first by the peasant-citizen and then more completely by the mature democracy, there could be no illusions about the harmonious interdependence of hierarchically ordered grades, the non-antagonistic complementarity of rulers and ruled. Plato's political philosophy illustrates more dramatically than any other masterpiece of Athenian culture the pervasive cultural effects – whether direct or through the medium of opposition – of the unique relation between governing and productive functions, personified in the first instance by the peasant-citizen and brought to fruition by the democracy.

Technological Stagnation?

A reassessment of the attitude toward labour in democratic Athens requires a reconsideration of yet another truism about Athenian culture. It is often said that there was a remarkable lack of technical innovation throughout the Greek and Roman worlds and that this technological 'stagnation' is attributable above all to the predominance of slavery and to the cultural devaluation of labour which resulted from it, hindering the incentive to creative innovation. These propositions need first to be placed in perspective. How slow was technological progress in ancient Greece and Rome, and in comparison to what, or by what standard of 'normal' development? What kind of technological change is in question, and were Greece and Rome backward in respect to all kinds of technological innovation equally? Are we talking about the rate of technical innovation or about the degree to which existing new technologies were utilized? And if generalizations can be made about both Greece and Rome, are they equally true of all times and places in Graeco–Roman antiquity? At least some of these questions must be briefly canvassed before we can ask to what extent and in what ways, if there was something distinctive about the pace and direction of technological development in Greece and Rome, that pace and direction were set by slavery. In other words, before looking for an explanation, we must ask whether there is something remarkable that needs to be explained.

M.I. Finley gives the following overview of technological development in ancient Greece and Rome:

> It is a commonplace that the Greeks and Romans together added little to the world's store of technical knowledge and equipment. The Neolithic and Bronze Ages between them invented or discovered, and then developed, the essential processes of agriculture, metallurgy, pottery, and textile-making. With these the Greeks and Romans built a high civilisation, full of power and intellect and beauty, but they transmitted to their successors few new inventions. The gear and the screw, the rotary mill and the water-mill, the direct screw-press, the fore-and-aft sail, glass-blowing, hollow bronze-casting, concrete, the dioptra for surveying, the torsion catapult, the water-clock and water-organ, automata (mechanical toys) driven by water and wind and steam – this short list is fairly exhaustive, and it adds up to not very much for a great civilisation over fifteen hundred years.
>
> Paradoxically, there was both more and less technical progress in the ancient world than the standard picture reveals. There was more, provided we avoid the mistake of hunting solely for great radical inventions and we also look at developments within the limits of the traditional techniques. There was less – far less – if we avoid the reverse mistake and look not merely for the appearance of an invention, but also for the extent of its employment. Food-processing offers a neat illustration. In the two centuries between 150 BC and AD 50 (in very round numbers) there was continuous improvement in the wine and oil presses used on the Roman *latifundia*. I am not referring to the screw-press, but to such advances as refinements in the shape of the millstones and their cores, by which craftsmen made presses more efficient and more manageable. Somewhere in this same period the water-mill was invented, and this must rank as a radical invention permitting the replacement of muscular power, human or animal, by water power. But for the next three centuries its use was so sporadic that the total effect was very slight.[27]

A few preliminary observations come to mind. There is surely nothing remarkable about the failure to repeat or match technical advances on the scale of the invention or discovery of agriculture and metallurgy. Inventions (if that is the right word) such as these do not happen every day – or, for that matter, every millennium. Indeed, it is difficult to think of any other innovation that quite measures up to the development of agriculture. Few periods in history anywhere have been marked by developments as momentous as these, and we can hardly take such epochal transformations as our standard of normal development. In any case, a development like the emergence of agriculture was very likely a protracted process made up of far less dramatic innovations, spread out over centuries, which disappeared into a single revolutionary outcome.

We might then ask whether technological progress was slow in Greece or Rome in comparison to, say, the millennia that preceded the 'invention' of agriculture; or perhaps we should ask whether Greece and Rome were slow in comparison to other great civilizations like China; or how the advances in productive techniques in Rome between 150 BC and AD 50 compare with Europe in the centuries after the decline of Rome, let us say between the seventh and twelfth centuries, when 'the level of material civilization remained so low that the main point of economic life is to be found in the struggle that man had to wage against natural forces day by day in order to survive'.[28] Measured against these cases, it is not at all clear that there is anything remarkable about the 'stagnation' of Greek and Roman technology. Even the contrast between periods of slow development and those marked by revolutionary change may not tell us very much if moments of spectacular innovation are simply those in which centuries of incremental and cumulative changes come to fruition in one far-reaching transformation.

There is, however, one kind of technological development that must be clearly distinguished from the general history of slow cumulative change interspersed with occasional revolutionary leaps and moments of regression. In early modern Europe, there emerged a completely new dynamic of change, driven by the compulsion for a continuous revolutionizing of the forces of production associated with the evolution of capitalism. It cannot be emphasized enough that this drive for constant technological innovation belongs to the logic of capitalist accumulation and competition and not simply to some natural law of technical progress. If there is some kind of 'natural' tendency toward the progressive development of productive forces, perhaps rooted in a drive inherent in human nature to find ways of curtailing labour – a proposition that is itself debatable – the specific dynamic of technological change in capitalism must be distinguished from it.

It would, therefore, be profoundly misleading to adopt as a standard of normality the rate and direction of technological change in the West since the age of feudalism, and to look for *obstacles* – such as the ideology of slavery – wherever changes of this kind fail to occur. Far too often, implicitly if not always explicitly, the question of technological development in ancient Greece and Rome is distorted by assumptions derived from the capitalist norm – for example, the assumption that human wants are 'infinite' (in the particular sense intended by conventional economic textbooks); that under 'normal' circumstances there is an acquisitiveness in human nature, combined with a compulsion to improve productivity by technological means; and that the absence of a drive for ever-expanding surplus production and capital accumulation is somehow unnatural and needs to be explained by some *obstruction* in the constitution of society. Or else the assumption may be that the 'natural' form of production is universal commodity production, production for exchange value, or even the capitalist mode of production, which is in principle unlimited in its need for surplus; and that there is something abnormal about production that is limited in its objectives, in its need for surplus, or in its compulsion to increase productivity by technical means.

All this is simply to stress that the specificity of technological 'stagnation' in Greece and Rome is by no means self-evident. It is not at all clear that the rate of technological development in Greek and Roman civilization was so remarkably deficient that we must seek an explanation for it in some peculiarity of Greek and Roman society. Nevertheless, granting the uncontroversial premise that technological innovation in ancient Greece and Rome was very far from equalling either the more dramatic moments of the Neolithic and Bronze Ages or the developments associated with the evolution of capitalism, first agrarian and then industrial, let us for the sake of argument examine the characteristics of Graeco–Roman, and more particularly Athenian, civilization that might be regarded as impediments to technical innovation.

First we must be clear about what we mean by technical innovation. What is almost always at issue is the kind of advance that enhances the *productivity* of labour. Discussions of technical progress do not, for example, generally concern innovations whose object is to improve production qualitatively rather than quantitatively, in accordance with, say, aesthetic criteria or standards of durability. On these counts it would, of course, be difficult to question the technical skills of the people who built the Parthenon. In this connection, M.I. Finley introduces a useful clarification of the issues at stake, citing the example of the silver mines in fifth- and fourth-century Athens:

> The sheer craftsmanship of the work in the Athenian mines requires comment because it introduces a necessary distinction into the discussion. There was a precision, a perfection of measurement, and hence an aesthetic quality, about the gallery walls and the steps – to give but two examples – which were never duplicated in antiquity. For parallels one must turn not to other mines, but to the contemporary temples and public buildings of Athens. The quality is psychological, so to speak, not technological. The artisans of fifth- and fourth-century Athens, whether free or slave, had a tradition of craftsmanship which imposed itself even in the most 'unlikely' places, such as the galleries of the silver mines. But this factor must not be confused with technical progress. Nor must increasing mastery of materials, an inevitable corollary of pride and virtuosity. I do not underestimate the

significance of these qualities, or of the quality of the products which they created. Within fairly broad limits, however, limits which the pre-Greek civilisations of the Eastern Mediterranean had already reached, such considerations of quality are irrelevant in an analysis of technological and economic growth. The unmatched beauty of Greek coins, after all, contributed nothing to their function as money. . . .[29]

We shall return to the Athenian tradition of craftsmanship because, however 'irrelevant' such craft skills may be to technical progress and economic development, this cultural tradition tells us a great deal about the social relations and the system of production which determined the rhythm and direction of technical development in Greek and Roman civilization. For the moment, let us consider some of the conditions in which the technical improvement of productivity has occurred – or failed to occur – to see what they suggest about technological development in Greece and Rome.

The first point that needs to be made is that important innovations did occur in Graeco–Roman production, such as those enumerated by Finley, and that they occurred in times and places that belie the simple equation of slavery with technical stagnation. The innovations in food-processing mentioned by Finley, as well as the introduction of the water-mill (whether by original invention or external influence), took place at the very height of the Roman slave latifundia. The fact that the Romans – and, for that matter, their European successors for several centuries thereafter – were slow to recognize the full potential of this innovation and apparently unimaginative in their application of it is not in itself so remarkable. The slow spread of technical innovations may be a rule rather than an exception in the history of technological development in the pre-capitalist world. (China, after all, was equally 'unimaginative' in the application of such technical innovations as the water-mill.[30]) Certainly there is nothing so specific in this that it requires explanation by reference to the uniquely widespread use of slaves in production. The very least that can be said is that the most intensive use of slaves in production, the Roman latifundia, did not prevent, and to some extent encouraged, technical innovations in agricultural production. The effect of slavery on technological progress seems to have depended on the context and the form in which slaves were utilized; and the spectrum of possibilities was fairly broad, up to and including the enhancement, rather than the obstruction, of productive innovation.

The differences between Greece and Rome may illustrate the point. Both Athens and Rome were 'slave societies', but the use of slaves occurred in very different contexts in the two cases. As we have seen, concentrations of property and slave estates on the Roman scale did not exist in Athens; indeed, slavery was probably relatively unimportant in agricultural production. Yet the advances that occurred in Roman agriculture did not occur in Athens. Since it would be difficult to maintain that slavery was more widespread or more important in Athens than in Rome, and since it would be impossible to maintain that Athenians held labour in greater contempt than did Romans, the simple association of technical stagnation with the devaluation of labour by slavery is of limited value here. The critical variable is more likely to lie somewhere in the different patterns of landholding which distinguish the two cases. The crucial consideration probably has to do with the concentration of landed property in Rome and the lack of it in Athens. It is not simply a matter of the size of Roman estates or the extent of the labour-force which worked them – although these factors undoubtedly made possible and encouraged certain kinds of technical innovations. It is also important that the concentration of property in Rome established a sector of agriculture not dominated by the peasantry, and that in Athens such concentration was obstructed by the consolidation of the smallholders' regime. In other words, the critical determinant may be the relation between landlord and peasant. We may find that, whatever specific limits of its own slavery – like any other form of labour – may have placed upon the nature and direction of technical change, at least in Rome it opened up new possibilities by removing large areas of production from the specific constraints of the peasant regime.[31]

It may be informative to examine briefly the conditions in which the water-mill finally did spread in mediaeval Europe. An explanation has been suggested by Pierre Dockès which has the virtue of accounting both for the slowness of the process and for the particular timing of its successful implantation. Building on an argument originally proposed by Marc Bloch – that 'the gradual victory of the water-mill was won ... by force; the lords drove out the hand-mills, destroyed them, and enforced use of the banal water-mill in their stead'[32] – Dockès concludes that

> The spread of the water-mill ... should be seen as a reaction by the lords to the peasants' conquest of rights to their own tenements and reductions of the dues associated with the manorial system. The peasants won these victories in widely scattered and hard-fought contests over a troubled expanse of two centuries, the ninth and the tenth, a crucial phase ... in the class struggle of the peasantry. For the lords to respond as they did a new coalition of the masters (the feudal superstructure that supplanted the Carolingian attempt to rebuild the state) had to be forged. Seigniory in its new form was based on new ways of exploiting the peasantry, such as monopolies, the administration

of justice, taxes connected with the exertion of political power, and Church tithes, rather than on the old dues associated with the tenure of land or corvée labour. These new means of exploitation, and in particular the mills, were introduced and imposed by force. By force and for the profit of the master, at the expense of the peasant and above all the poor peasant. Did the mill ultimately lead to an increase in the total product by dint of saving labour? Perhaps, but that was not why it was introduced! It was above all a way of redistributing income, increasing the surplus that accrued to the masters.[33]

There are several important points contained or implied in this argument. Slavery, as the basis of large production units, had encouraged the initial development of the water-mill, but perhaps at the same time, as a source of cheap and coercible labour, weakened the incentive to further technical development. But if there is one continuous factor that acted as an impediment to the diffusion of the water-mill throughout both the slave-system and the centuries which followed its decline, it is peasant property – first, simply because a technical innovation of this sort required resources incommensurate with ordinary peasant property, and then because techniques associated with large-scale agriculture were available to small producers only when they were collectively organized under the exploitative authority of lords. Hence, for peasant producers, technical innovations on this scale were either impracticable or inseparable from exploitative rents and dues. Thus, the labour-saving qualities of the water-mill did not, by themselves, recommend this innovation to the producers, the peasants, who were to use it. They fought against it long and hard, not simply out of blind conservatism but because in the circumstances its introduction was not to their advantage. As for the lords, their response to this innovation was determined by the complex interaction between the *limits* imposed by peasant tenures upon lordly appropriation, and the *possibilities* made available by new forms of lordly power.

The diffusion and development of the water-mill in the Middle Ages did not, however, signal a major revolution in agricultural technique or mark an era of dynamic technical progress in contrast to the ancient Graeco–Roman world. As in the ancient world, there were spurts of innovation, but on the whole, when looked at in the same epochal perspective applied by Finley to the ancient world, mediaeval Europe was no less characterized by a 'general condition of technical stagnation':[34]

Greater understanding of nature could not come from technical improvements, chiefly because technical improvements were so few. Medieval occupations continued for centuries without appreciable change of method. After the great period of initial development, i.e. after the late eleventh century, the routine of medieval farming in the greater part of Europe became as fixed as the landscape itself. In the history of smithies, the weaving shops, or the potteries, there were occasional periods of innovation, but taking the Middle Ages as a whole technical improvement was very rare and very slow.[35]

And much the same questions have been asked about mediaeval Europe as about ancient Rome, concerning not only the slow rate of innovation but more particularly, the failure to apply technical innovations that were already available. As Robert Brenner writes in his seminal study of economic development in pre-industrial Europe,

> technologies capable of significantly raising agricultural productivity by means of relatively large-scale investments were indeed available in medi-aeval Europe – and they included some of the central components of what was later to constitute the agricultural revolution of the early modern period. What is more, these technologies were actually *used*, on at least some occasions, during the thirteenth and fourteenth century, even in England. The question which needs to be asked, therefore, is why were they not *more widely applied*. The problem in other words was ... the feudal economy's inability to *make use of* the possibilities which existed.[36]

Indeed, it is difficult to think of any well-documented pre-capitalist era anywhere about which, when viewed in grand epochal terms, similar questions could not be asked. In this respect, there seems to be nothing remarkable about the 'technical stagnation' of the Graeco–Roman world or its failure to make widespread use of the technical innovations which it did produce. The period of economic growth that began in early modern Europe, and specifically in England, is distinctive precisely because it broke the pattern of 'stagnation' punctuated by sporadic innovation typical of earlier ages. It was here that for the first time a dynamic of *self-sustaining* economic growth, accompanied by systematic technical innovation, was set in train. The conditions of this radically new dynamic of change are instructive:

> the original breakthrough in Europe to a system of more or less self-sustaining growth was dependent upon a two-sided development of class relations: first, the breakdown of systems of lordly surplus extraction by means of extra-economic compulsion (especially serfdom); secondly, the undermining of peasant possession or the aborting of any trend towards full peasant ownership of land. The consequence of this two-sided development was the rise of a novel social-property system, above all on the land, in which, for the first time, the organizers of production and the direct producers (sometimes the same persons) found it both *necessary* and *possible*

to reproduce themselves through a course of economic action which was, on a system-wide scale, favourable to the continuing development of productive forces. Because in this system the organizers of production and the direct producers were separated from direct, non-market access to their means of reproduction or subsistence (especially from possession of the land), they had no choice, in order to maintain themselves, but to buy and sell on the market. This meant that they were compelled to produce competitively by way of cost-cutting and, therefore, that they had as a rule to attempt to specialize, accumulate and innovate to the greatest extent possible. They were, on the whole, able to succeed in this because the collapse of the system of surplus extraction by extra-economic compulsion, in connection with the separation of the direct producers from their means of subsistence, freed labour power, land and the means of production to be combined (accumulated) in the most profitable manner. In particular, the rise of the landlord/capitalist tenant/wage-labourer system provided the basis for the transformation of agriculture and, in turn, the breakthrough to the ongoing economic development which took place in early modern England. On the other hand, throughout most of the Continent in the same period, the perpetuation, in various forms, of social-property systems characterized by peasant possession and surplus extraction by extra-economic compulsion (the tax/office structure in France, serfdom in eastern Europe), was at the root of continuing agricultural stagnation, involution and ultimately general socio-economic crisis.[37]

Brenner's point is dramatically illustrated by the contrast between England and France during the sixteenth and seventeenth centuries, when the former experienced an agricultural revolution while the latter was going through a particularly stagnant period. The difference can be accounted for by the different relations between landlords and peasants which had evolved in the two cases. In France, although large units of property had emerged which were superficially similar to the large landholdings of England, they were surrounded by a massive and land-hungry peasantry whose small properties were often insufficient even for subsistence. On the one hand, these peasant properties could not themselves sustain highly productive agricultural techniques; and on the other hand, landlords had little incentive to promote technical improvements in productivity since the land-hunger of the peasantry made them susceptible, as tenants, to rent-squeezing methods of surplus appropriation by the landlords. Even larger tenants seem to have been for the most part the dependants of lords, acting more or less as intermediaries between lords and peasants and favouring labour-intensive techniques. In other words, the 'rentier mentality', which is often held responsible for impeding technical improvements, was in these circumstances profitable.[38]

In England, by contrast, the history of relations between landlords and peasants had issued in new relations on the land, notably a drastic decline in the number of landholding peasants; and there existed no 'semi-proletarianized' land-hungry peasantry. Much of the land was controlled by large capitalist tenant-farmers who, as we have seen, were compelled to increase productivity but who could not simply be squeezed for more rents. They increasingly employed wage-labourers and commanded a capital-intensive husbandry which, as long as the farmers were allowed to make a reasonable profit, produced substantial returns for the landlord as well. Any attempt to squeeze these capitalist tenants could simply induce them to curtail investment and ultimately even to give up their leases. In these circumstances, the interests of both landlord and tenant depended upon the accumulation and innovation that permitted the tenant to farm productively and cost-effectively.[39]

It should be emphasized that, although peasant production is compatible with a wide variety of economic systems and forms of surplus extraction (so that it is, for example, misleading to speak of a 'peasant mode of production'), there is an irreducible limit in the structure of peasant production itself. It can perhaps be stated as a general rule that small peasant property is not fertile ground for large-scale technological innovation. There is, in a sense, a logic inherent in the productive unit of the peasant family that is resistant to such innovation. In part, it is simply a matter of property size and the resources available to sustain technological improvements, and the successful small farm with high output may be the one *without* advanced technology; but there are, as we saw in Chapter II, other factors that may work against production beyond the immediate needs of family subsistence. The tendency to underutilize even existing productive techniques and to increase production, when necessary, by intensifying labour rather than by improving labour productivity – or to deal with 'underemployment' by maintaining less costly, labour-intensive techniques – is inherent not only in the limited resources available to the small producer but also perhaps in the organization of the domestic unit of production and the conditions of its maintenance as a unit. As Marshall Sahlins suggests,

> the norm of domestic livelihood tends to be inert. It cannot move above a certain level without testing the capacities of the domestic labor force, either directly or through the technological change required for a higher output. The standard of livelihood does not substantially increase without putting into question the existing family organization.[40]

Thus, unless the domestic unit is forced beyond itself by some external factor, production will tend to be limited in its objectives and in its means. Needless to say, it is difficult to imagine any society in which this inherent logic is not to some extent counteracted by 'external' factors, kinship obligations, the needs of the community, the demands of appropriators in positions of superior power. On the other hand, that logic is never completely overcome until, to use Brenner's words again, 'the direct producers [are] separated from direct, non-market access to their means of reproduction or subsistence' and thus forced to compete in the market simply in order to survive – as happened first in early modern England.

In any case, it is not to be supposed that external demands for surplus production will necessarily, or even normally, be met by increasing labour productivity through the application of technical innovations, rather than by the intensification of labour. Even in the case of pressures exerted by the demands of higher authorities – historically the most important force pushing the peasant family unit beyond the needs of its own subsistence and reproduction – there need be no incentive, even where there is a technical possibility, to overcome the limitations of traditional peasant production. As we have seen, appropriators themselves will have little need or incentive to supply the deficiencies of peasant production by means of investment in the improvement of productive forces if the opportunities for extra-economic pressure are sufficient to make rent-squeezing profitable. At the same time, secure peasant tenures – which, as in the case of France, are not necessarily incompatible with opportunities for profitable rent-squeezing – and the peasant's control of the labour process will limit the *possibility* of replacing such methods with strategies for improving productivity. In general, it is no exaggeration to say that the 'rentier mentality' has been the rule in pre-capitalist societies and has joined with the pressures against innovation inherent in peasant property to inhibit technical progress. If this 'mentality' encourages any kind of technical innovation, it is likely to be the kind that serves as a means of appropriating rent – that is, not as a means of enhancing productivity but as a means of increasing the opportunities of surplus *extraction* – either by strengthening the extra-economic powers of the appropriator, as in the development of military techniques, or by providing a new source of rent, such as the banal mill.

Although in all the societies under discussion land remained the major source of wealth, something must be said about manufacture and the opportunities it afforded for technical progress. For the present purposes, all that needs to be said is that, until there existed a mass market for manufactured goods – something that did not occur until very late in European history, hardly before the eighteenth century, and then only for a limited number of products – manufacture, often the production of luxury goods, would continue to be dominated by considerations of quality rather than quantity; in other words, craft traditions would predominate over labour productivity. The limitations on the need or incentive for technical innovations inherent in this kind of production would, of course, have been reinforced by the small scale of production. The independent craftsman would be affected by the same deficiency of resources as the peasant, and perhaps some of the same organizational requirements, especially where the family remained the basic unit of production. The more independent the craftsman and the less subject to external demands for surplus production, the more resistant he might be to innovations designed to increase productivity – and perhaps also the more inclined to remain proudly wedded to the traditions of his craft. But even in cases where many craftsmen were united under the control of a single surplus-extracting master – as was the case in some workshops of ancient Athens – the traditional methods of craftsmanship predominated, even where the craftsmen were slaves. In this sense, the prevailing 'psychology' was that of free craftsmen, not slaves, while the 'mentality' of the master tended to be that of a rentier.

All these 'inhibiting' factors – the control of substantial areas of production by peasants, the structure of wealth as rentier property, hence a 'mentality' that was (to quote Finley) 'acquisitive but not productive', and the predominance of craft production in the absence of a mass market for manufactured goods – operated in ancient Greece and Rome.[41] Together they would be enough to account for the – unremarkable – degree of 'technical stagnation'. Slavery certainly added limitations of its own – for example, as Max Weber once suggested, given the instability of economic conditions and slave prices, the owner had to keep his slave property easily divisible and to organize production in such a way as to permit the rapid disposal of slaves whenever the need arose, a fact which militated against a cooperative division of labour in production;[42] and the availability of slaves as a cheap and coercible labour force would have acted as an additional incentive to strategies of labour-intensification instead of investment in the improvement of labour-productivity by technical means. But slavery at least in Rome, as we have seen, also had the effect of liberating a significant part of the economy from the limitations of peasant production and in parts of the Empire was the basis of the large-scale property which permitted the application of technical innovations precluded by peasant agriculture. So there is little evidence to suggest that the net effect of slavery was to aggravate the 'stagnation' inherent in any pre-capitalist economy.

In fact, if there was anything in ancient Graeco–Roman civilization that created more than the usual pre-capitalist limitations on technical progress – and it is perhaps only in the case of Greece that a claim to an 'abnormal' lack of innovations in productivity might be plausible – then it was arguably the position of *free* producers, not that of slaves, which determined it. In Athens, in particular, the smallholders' regime, the predominance of peasants in agricultural production and their relative freedom from external compulsions to surplus production, was certainly an overriding factor in determining the pace and rhythm of technical change. The status of the craftsman-citizen certainly enhanced the importance of traditions of craftsmanship, the 'psychology' of pride and virtuosity to which Finley refers, in contrast to the very different impulses of 'technological and economic growth'. And, again, the political incentives to village settlement, subsistence strategies and self-sufficiency might also have discouraged advances in surplus-production.[43] If this is so, then the technical stagnation of democratic Athens, far from being determined by a contempt for labour associated with slavery, was on the contrary a corollary of the uniquely high and respectable status of Athenian producers.

The Cultural Vitality of Athens: A Contradiction Between 'Base' and 'Superstructure'?

If it is misleading to ascribe a pathological degree of backwardness or stagnation to Athenian technological development, would it still be correct to say that there was an extraordinary disparity between the relative simplicity of technology and the sophistication of culture in Athens? It is certainly true that, with a technological base easily matched and often surpassed by other civilizations, Athens left a cultural legacy whose richness has seldom been equalled. With productive capabilities hardly superior to many impoverished peasant societies, Athens sustained an intellectual and artistic life whose fruits are with us still. Does this signal a contradiction between 'base' and 'superstructure' which requires some special explanation, and is that explanation to be found in slavery, or perhaps in the Athenian empire?

There is, first, something wrong with the premise of these questions. What, after all, is the 'correct' fit between technology and intellectual productivity? How do we quantify culture in a way that allows us to measure its commensurability with productive techniques? Two things we can say with reasonable confidence about the material base and its cultural superstructure. First, it is just as impossible to produce cultural artifacts as it is to produce food or shelter without techniques and materials appropriate to them, and art-forms rise and fall as new technologies become available. For that matter, there is a world of intellectual activity unavailable to a society without the techniques of literacy. Secondly, a flourishing intellectual culture presupposes a substantial degree of freedom from material exigencies, and productive capacities that allow some people to live on what others produce. It is, tautologically, the case that Athens had technological means adequate to her material culture; and it is self-evidently true that the material base was sufficient to sustain a non-producing class of cultural specialists. In what sense, then, was Athenian culture incommensurate with its material base? Or is it simply that slavery – and/or the empire, at least for a short time (but what about before and after?) – permitted a degree or distribution of leisure not normally available to societies at this technological level?

There is no meaningful sense in which Athenian culture can be said to have outstripped its material capabilities. If there is an incommensurability, it is in comparision with other cultures with comparable or superior technologies (let us take, say, mediaeval Europe). But if Athenian culture does indeed stand out, it cannot be said that the level of Athenian culture corresponds to some exceptional degree of material wealth or leisure enjoyed by the citizens of Athens. The fortunes and comforts even of Athenian privileged classes were modest by comparison to many others; and there is in any case little evidence in history that the rate or quality of culture increases in simple and direct proportion to the magnitude of wealth and leisure. Again, the most that can be said is that Athens possessed the necessary material conditions for an active cultural life – as have many other civilizations without producing comparable results.

Perhaps we are simply asking the wrong question. It may be that what we are looking for is not *necessary* but *sufficient* conditions; not the limits of technical possibility but an active impulse to cultural creativity. What was it in the social arrangements of Athens that impelled Athenian cultural development toward the outer limits of its material capacities? And if there was something in those arrangements which discouraged the technical improvement of material productivity, did that same thing encourage cultural development? If, for example, the smallholders' regime helps to account for technological 'stagnation', can it do the same for cultural vitality?

Let us start with the advent of literacy, retracing our steps to Mycenaean times in search of those roots. We have noted that one remarkable consequence of the mysterious cataclysm which destroyed Mycenaean civilization was the apparent disappearance of writing from Greece. What is equally remarkable is that when writing reappears in the evidence (the first datable evidence of the new writing occurs on pottery from 750–700 BC, while the Homeric epics are the first substantial record of Greek literacy available to us) it is very different both in form and in function from its Mycenaean predecessor. The Mycenaean script, though clearly Greek, was like other ancient scripts a syllabary, with all the limitations of this form; and it was apparently used only for bureaucratic purposes, the state records and inventories which have come down to us in Linear B inscriptions. The Greek writing of the eighth century is an alphabet, capable of flexibly and unambiguously recording all human speech, in a form easily accessible to ordinary human minds and memories;[44] and the Homeric epics, followed by an unbroken tradition of literary, scientific, and philosophical invention, testify to a completely new cultural function for Greek writing.

It might be tempting to attribute this cultural explosion to the simple contingency that it was the Greeks who happened to invent the alphabet by modifying the Phoenician script (often called an alphabet, but perhaps more precisely an 'unvocalized syllabary'[45]) and thereby opened up all the technical possibilities of this flexible form. There are even those who would argue that the whole subsequent development of Greek society, including the evolution of democracy, was determined by this one technical innovation.[46] But apart from the fact, yet again, that technical *possibilities* are far from absolute necessities, it is difficult to accept this degree of contingency or to hang so much cultural weight on this one single thread. There is no doubt that the alphabet created new and rich possibilities, but we may still want to ask not only why the Greeks made such full use of them (the underutilization of technical capacities has, as we have seen, been as much a rule as an exception in history) but why they seem to have experienced the need for them in ways which other cultures (like the Phoenicians themselves?) did not.

It may not be an idle question to ask whether the Greeks had an unusual need which could be met neither by any type of script sufficient for every other advanced civilization nor by the age-old oral tradition. The state-forms of Bronze Age Greece, like those of many other civilizations, made do quite well with a syllabary script capable of recording its political and economic transactions; while the oral tradition had sufficed many cultures as a means of storing and transmitting communal knowledge, values and memories. Archaic Greeks apparently needed something else – and what they got not only made possible new intellectual forms but eventually made the Greeks perhaps the first *literate* society, that is, the first to go beyond a 'craft-literacy' confined to professional scribes, to a widespread use of writing for a wide variety of purposes, in what has been called the 'democratization' of writing.[47]

In light of the controversies surrounding Greek literacy, however, it probably needs to be emphasized that the transformation of Greek culture is remarkable even if we attach less significance to the technical innovations of the alphabet. There has been debate concerning the novelty of the Greek alphabet and the extent to which it represents a radical innovation upon the Phoenician script. Indeed, even the disappearance of writing from Greece for the whole period between the last known use of Linear B and the first known appearance of the Greek alphabet in the eighth century has been questioned, or at least there has been disagreement about the late dating of the alphabet and of Greek literacy. The most radical argument in favour of an early introduction of the alphabet into the Aegean, and an earlier Greek literacy, has been made by Martin Bernal, who argues in his provocative book, *Black Athena: The Afroasiatic Roots of Classical Civilization* that the impulse both to exaggerate the novelty of the Greek alphabet and to insist on the late arrival of literacy in Greece is rooted in an essentially racist denial of the Eastern, African and Semitic origins of Greek culture.[48]

The predominant view (whose merits, or lack of them, do not depend on their provenance or on their association with ideologies like racism) that there was a sharp and long break between the two forms of Greek writing is persuasive not just because no examples of Greek writing from the intervening period had survived, but because the two scripts are so entirely different, with no blurring of the lines between them and no evidence of coexistence.[49] As for the conceptual importance of the vowels introduced into the Greek alphabet, at the very least there can be little doubt of the greater flexibility and the avoidance of ambiguity made possible by the new Greek script in comparison with any other known form of ancient writing. Nevertheless, although the present argument proceeds on the assumption that there was a hiatus (of whatever duration) between the bureaucratic literacy of the Mycenaean kingdoms and the very different kind of literacy which emerged in archaic Greece, as well as the assumption that the Greek alphabet represented a significant innovation, there is a sense in which neither of these assumptions matters very much.

Maybe some Greeks throughout the dark age knew that writing existed, and some may have been familiar with one or another script. Since there is no interest here in proving or disproving 'non-European' influences on the development of Greece, or in denying the importance of Phoenician culture, there is no a priori reason to deny the possibility that the alphabet existed in Greece before its appearance in the evidence. (For that matter, there is no incompatibility between recognizing continuities and influences and acknowledging radical changes and differences – the occurrence of change within continuity seems a normal way for history to proceed.) What is more important – as so often in the question of technological development – is the use and application of technical innovations, the transformation of possibilities into actualities.

So the argument being advanced here still stands, whether or not we accept the evidence for a late introduction of the alphabet. Whenever the alphabet was invented, it seems reasonably clear that from the eighth century onwards the Greeks were becoming literate in unprecedented ways and degrees. In fact, if the alphabet actually existed long before (assuming, of course, that it is right to call the Semitic scripts alphabets and by definition to deny the innovative development of the new Greek script – which in a sense begs the question), it becomes even more necessary to explain its radically new applications and diffusion in the archaic and classical periods, and to explain them as a response to new social and cultural needs. Indeed this is particularly true if the Greek modification of the Phoenician script was so minor that its absence elsewhere cannot possibly account for the social and cultural differences between Greece and other possessors of the 'alphabet'. Even if we acknowledge that the diffusion of literacy in Greece may itself argue for an earlier introduction of the alphabet, on the grounds that such developments could not have happened overnight, it still remains to be explained how and why they took place in that time and place and nowhere else, not even in those places where the 'alphabet' existed earlier.

The Homeric epics themselves provide a clue. These remarkable works represent a historic meeting of the oral tradition with the new form of writing. They mark a transition not only in the technical capacities of the culture, but also in its social needs. The poems are backward looking both in the sense that they record an oral discourse in the process of its supersession, but also in the sense that they depict a social order at the moment of its passing. The idealized society of Homer's hero-nobles, unchallenged in their dominance, is being overtaken by an order in which they are increasingly 'a threatened or even "besieged" minority', no longer able to take for granted the obedient respect of their subordinates.[50] And as the ruling society of the Homeric *basilees* gives way to a beleaguered dominant class, the traditional mode of transmitting cultural knowledge and values becomes inadequate. At a time when the ruling society is itself subject to challenge, its values can no longer be accepted as universal cultural norms. It is no longer enough to sing of lordly exploits or to hold up the example of heroes as cultural ideals.[51] A challenge to the dominant culture requires new methods of storage, transmission, and – crucially – debate, not only to stabilize and substantiate the ephemeral culture of a 'besieged' ruling class but to negotiate transactions between challenge and defence.

Here the contrast between Homer and Hesiod is particularly telling. A near if not exact contemporary of Homer, Hesiod apparently still sees himself as part of the bardic tradition, but he represents a very different social phenomenon and the content of his work is accordingly different. He is a 'middling' farmer and a self-assertive individual, not an elusive personality like the traditional bard (there is still debate about whether 'Homer' even represents a single person) who sings the praises of aristocratic patrons, but a self-acknowledged author, the first to give his own name, and describing the conditions of people like himself. There is no idealization of a passing order in his *Works and Days.* Amid farming information and moral advice, it is one long poetic grumble about the lot of hard-working farmers and the injustices inflicted on them by greedy *basilees.* For the first time, he records a challenge to the dominant world-view.

The critical moment in Hesiod's poem occurs in his complaint against the 'crooked' judgments of the *basilees,* who use their juridical prerogatives to exploit their unprivileged compatriots. Hesiod here invokes a principle unprecedented in any historical record available to us. At the right hand of Zeus, he warns the 'gift-eating' lords, there sits the goddess Dikē, watching and judging them; and they will get their come-uppance for all their crooked judgments. It is true, of course, that Hesiod leaves to the gods the punishment of crooked lords, and he is far from advocating rebellion. Nevertheless, his grumbling quietism should not obscure the significance of what he has done. Possibly for the first time, he has asserted a principle of *justice* (*dikē*) apart from and opposed to the jurisdiction of the dominant class, a standard against which their actions can be judged and indicted.[52]

The significance of this innovation can be judged by comparing Hesiod's usage to Homer's. The word *dikē* appears in Homer several times, but hardly in its abstract ethical meaning. With the exception of one or two ambiguous or 'transitional' instances where the word has some moral connotations, the general meaning is simply 'the *way* of things', their given nature or customary behaviour. It is even possible to speak of a dog's *dikē,* for example its customary mode of fawning on its master. There is here little conception of *justice* as an ethical norm against which all actions, and most particularly the actions of ruling authorities, can be judged. There is only a customary, natural, and unchallenged *way* of things.

Between Homer and Hesiod, then, there is the huge conceptual and social chasm between a ruling society whose values and judgments pass for universal norms, and a divided community in which there is acknowledged conflict over social norms and even over the authority of those who seek to impose them. If the former could enshrine its values in oral epic poems in the form of heroic patterns and examples, the latter requires a different discourse to conduct and record the conflict over values and authority. The use of writing to deal with this new dispensation covers a wide range of functions. The need for written laws is only the beginning, perhaps first to reassert and give a new authority to aristocratic dominance (as in the laws of Drakon), and eventually to protect the demos from tyranny and oligarchic rule. The intellectual process of adjustment to this new terrain of conflict, and the use of writing for increasingly complex and abstract debates over principles, comes to fruition in the philosophical discourse of the fifth century BC, the 'Golden Age' of the democracy in Athens, a momentous cultural invention sparked off by the debate on the origin and legitimacy of social and moral norms.

No other ancient civilization produced anything comparable to these developments, and it is difficult to avoid the conclusion, reached by many commentators, that the unique cultural vitality of Greece is somehow related to the unique social and political experience of the polis, and especially the democracy, with its unparalleled climate of debate in juries and assemblies. Historians have often observed that the pride in their own accomplishments, the exploits of men and not gods, especially after the victory over Persia, inspired Athenians to new cultural heights, in literature, art and architecture and in the replacement of myth and legend by the invention of 'history', as monuments to their own self-confidence and glory. But it needs to be emphasized that the process of intellectual adjustment began before the 'Golden Age' of the democracy, as did the challenge to dominant authority. The development of the polis as a distinctive ordering of relations between ruling and subordinate classes – in the first instance, landlords and peasants – from the beginning went hand-in-hand with revolutions in cultural forms, including the transformation of writing itself and proceeding from new literary genres through cosmological speculations and historical writing to the advent of philosophy.

It is, of course, impossible to say that the culture of democratic Athens, the climax of these cultural developments, was the product of the smallholders' regime in the sense that Athenian poets and philosophers were peasants, or even craftsmen. It is true that little is known about the social origins of many Greek cultural figures, and there was no shortage of rumours, often undoubtedly scurrilous, about the humble origins of this or that celebrity, from Protagoras to Euripides. Nevertheless, examples of this humble cultural type have been rare throughout history, and might be expected to be even more so in a society which, for all its revolutionary advances in literacy, was still in transition from an oral culture. What we have come to know as the height of 'classical' culture may in fact derive its distinctive characteristics from its transitional character, as Eric Havelock has argued, at an unrepeatable moment in the development of this society as it passed from the oral tradition to literacy.[53] The literature and philosophy of this classical period – the formulaic tropes of Aeschylus' tragedies, the dialogue form of philosophy, even the slow acceptance of *prose* which was not fully established until the fourth century – still bear the marks of the oral tradition; and there are other signs that Athenians had not yet settled comfortably into their literate condition. For example, not until well into the fourth century BC, after the lawlessness of the Thirty Tyrants in 404–403 BC had made the restored democracy obsessively concerned with the rule of *written* law, was written evidence accorded the legitimacy of oral witness in the courts.[54] If writing was not yet firmly established as the most privileged mode of self-expression, it would not be surprising if the cultural aspirations of ordinary Athenians failed to encompass literary ambitions, even in the absence of practical obstacles to their fulfilment. The small producers of Athens were its cultural mainspring in a different sense – not least, of course, in their own craft-productions, to which we have already referred, or in their demands as audiences for Athenian drama and comedy, but above all in the challenge which they represented to aristocratic dominance. And here we may find a clue to the cultural dominance of Athens in relation to other Greek states. Athens was neither the first polis to experience an intellectual explosion, nor was it the only democracy. But in its unique disposition of relations between landlord and peasant, appropriator and producer, town and country, village and state, it may indeed have been the most literally democratic.

The evolution of Athenian philosophy will illustrate the point. The novelty of Greek philosophy as a mode of argumentation about moral, social and political principles cannot be exaggerated, nor should we underestimate the difficulty of its implantation. It was preceded not only by generations of poetic adjustments to changing values, but also by scientific and cosmological theories which sought in nature some principle of order and permanency in a world increasingly beset by movement and flux. Not until the firm establishment of Athenian democracy was the same kind of rational and systematic discourse applied explicitly to the social world itself, to its moral principles and political institutions. But if this cultural development was long in coming, it had a progenitor in the controversy over justice implicit in the poetry of Hesiod. Hesiod's opposition to the crooked judgments of the lords impelled him to seek a principle of right outside his immediate social world to invoke against the values of the dominant class. Implicit in this search were the questions which preoccupied the fifth-century thinkers and specifically the so-called Sophists who pioneered the Western philosophical tradition by opening up for systematic debate such issues as the foundations of moral principles.

The bad reputation inflicted on this loose collection of thinkers, principally by the writings of Plato, should not detract from their importance as expressions of Athenian cultural vitality, nor from the ground-breaking ideas which at least some of them produced. With no common doctrine and little to unite them except that they were paid teachers (something which Plato particularly held against them from his disdainful aristocratic vantage point) together they bespeak the intellectual liveliness of democratic Athens. Typically they were foreigners drawn to this exciting city and its growing demand for education. But their most significant testimony to the cultural ferment of that time and place is the kinds of things they were inquiring and teaching about.

It is as if one can trace the evolution of democracy in the development of Greek philosophy, from the early natural philosophers and their search for absolute and universal truths in nature and the cosmic order, to Protagoras, the first important and probably the greatest Sophist, for whom, in the absence of absolute knowledge, in a world of flux and uncertainty, man must be the 'measure of all things'. His pedagogical project was truly a curriculum for the democracy: not an education for the attainment of philosophical wisdom but one designed, as Plato has him say in the dialogue *Protagoras*, 'to make good citizens' (318e). Nevertheless, for all that he disclaims philosophical intentions, his project – and that of the Sophists who came after him, even those whose objectives never went beyond the teaching of rhetorical techniques – raised new questions which were to set the agenda of philosophy. When the systematic quest for absolute truth was revived in the philosophy of Plato, it was no longer only a question of physical nature and cosmology but also of virtue and justice in man and the state.

Do ethical values such as justice exist by nature or by convention? If by nature, what kind of nature? And if by convention, are they legitimate or not? These questions were thrown up by political life in the democracy, and arguments about them were deployed both for and against the prevailing political order. But whatever the answers to these questions, and whatever political side they served, the questions themselves, and the Sophists who asked them, even when they were of oligarchic persuasion were very much a democratic phenomenon. The very fact that social values were subjected to systematic analysis and debate, becoming a subject for *philosophy*, reflected social conditions which, though they existed in embryo in any polis where traditional authority was subject to challenge, were most fully developed in the Athenian democracy. Challenges by the demos to traditional authority, the practices of public deliberation and law-making, brought to fruition the flux of social values set in train by the evolution of the polis, and the felt need for a discourse to deal with the grounds of ethical and political principles which could no longer be taken for granted. Even the form of this discourse owed much to the procedures of democracy, the dialectic of the law court, the lawyer's rhetorical principle that there are 'two sides' to every question, and the worship of 'holy Persuasion', the essence of the polis which – as Aeschylus tells us in the *Oresteia* – replaced both the tribal law of blood vengeance and the dominance of aristocratic jurisdiction.

In this sense, even Plato, the severest critic of Athenian democracy, was a quintessential creature of the democracy. Greek philosophy, and with it the foundations of the Western philosophical tradition, are often credited to his invention – and no doubt with some justice; but he was dealing with questions raised by the Sophists and, like them, he was responding to the exigencies of the times. He devoted much of his life to countering the view enunciated by Protagoras that ethical and political values, though no less binding for lacking a foundation in some universal transcendental standard, are conventions, the common currency of civilized life, in a world where 'man is the measure of all things'. In opposition to this view and in place of the cultural universals embodied in the heroic example of the Homeric epics, Plato looked for philosophic universals grounded in a transcendent cosmic order, reviving the old cosmological search for first principles but this time applied also to the social world. The discourse of philosophy replaced the epic poem as a conduit of wisdom and values.

Plato sought a universal and permanent order underlying the world of experience and flux; he looked for a universal principle of justice and the good to set against the conventions of popular morality; he elaborated a principle of hierarchy to challenge democratic aspirations to equality, and a theory of justice diametrically opposed to the democratic concept of *dike*; he used the analogy of the practical arts to exclude their practitioners from the specialized 'art' of politics; he hoped to restore the age-old division between rulers and producers, developing a theory of knowledge and a concept of the soul which corresponded to it. Virtually all the philosophical problems he confronted were questions raised by the new social order. Plato was anything but a peasant or craftsman; but it is difficult to imagine his invention of philosophy without the provocation offered by peasant-citizens and all their 'banausic' compatriots, whose very political existence challenged eternal verities, the truths and values 'universally recognized everywhere under Heaven' – at least, almost everywhere.

Textual Evidence Concerning Slavery

The textual evidence most commonly cited to demonstrate either that slaves were used in agriculture or, more generally, that slaveownership was widespread throughout Athenian society, extending far down the social scale, is fairly sparse and can be canvassed rather briefly. Apart from Xenophon's *Oeconomicus*, the following passages are often mentioned: on agricultural slavery, various passages from Aristophanes' *Plutus*, especially 26–29 and 1105; his *Peace* 1138–9, 1146–8 (Ste Croix adds *Plutus* 510–21 and *Ecclesiazusae* 651); Ps.-Demosthenes XLVII 52–3 and LIII 6 and Dem. LV 31–2, 35; Lysias VII 16–17, 43, to which Jameson adds VII 11; on widespread slavery in general, Lysias V 5 and XXIV 6.

Let us look first at Aristophanes. It hardly needs to be said that great caution is required in using him as a witness to historical reality, since comic distortion and exaggeration are his stock in trade. A writer who can turn Socrates into the leading sophist, or a man of substance like the democratic leader, Cleon, into a simple tanner or even a slave, must be read with a very critical eye. It is important to note, for example, that one of Aristophanes' principal literary devices is to replace the tragic hero of Greek drama with often vulgar common folk, especially peasants; and although much can no doubt be gleaned from his comedies about Athenian social values and practices, he does not seem to be particularly scrupulous about portraying his demotic heroes in realistic terms. When a simple peasant becomes the comic Athenian Everyman, he may also acquire traits characteristic of the community he represents but not necessarily specific or appropriate to his class; and slaves were certainly an essential fact of Athenian life, even if not the life of a poor Attic peasant. The possibility should also be considered that, if Aristophanes was writing from the standpoint of a fairly wealthy citizen, he would be even more likely to take slave-ownership for granted as a basic condition of life. (See K.J. Dover, *Greek Popular Morality in the Time of Plato and Aristotle* (Oxford: Basil Blackwell, 1974), pp. 35 ff. for a discussion of Aristophanes' 'upper-class standpoint'. The book is full of useful insights on tragedy, comedy, and oratory as historical evidence.) Thus, even if we discount the fact that the slave is a stock-character in Attic comedy, it is difficult to know what to make of Chremylus in the *Plutus*, an apparently modest farmer who seems to have several slaves (26, 29, 1105). The same questions would apply to Trygaeus in the *Peace*.

Two other passages from Aristophanes' plays, cited by Ste Croix in support of his argument, raise more questions than they answer. In *Plutus* 507–21, a dialogue occurs between Chremylus and Poverty. The farmer suggests that Plutus should eliminate poverty by distributing wealth more equally. Poverty replies that if wealth were more equally distributed and everyone could afford a life of leisure, no one would work. Who would practise the various crafts and trades or plough the soil? Chremylus' answer is that slaves would do the work; and in reply to Poverty's question about where these slaves would be obtained, the farmer says they would be bought. Poverty expresses doubt that any merchant would traffic in slaves if he could have money without engaging in such business, and concludes that Chremylus' life would be harder than it is now. Not only would he have to labour himself but he would be unable to obtain the products of other men's crafts since poverty would no longer compel craftsmen to work. The contrast suggested here between the real world, where peasants and craftsmen toil, and the ideal, where slaves would do their work, need not imply that the toiling peasant or craftsman in reality had no slave to work by his side; but it hardly serves to prove that in the real Attic world peasants normally employed slaves.

The passage from *Eccles.* (651) cited by Ste Croix inspires even more doubts about the extent of slaveownership among small farmers. Here, Praxagora proposes a utopia in which property would be held in common and farm work would be done by slaves. Again, this is a fictional situation which is explicitly contrasted to the reality in which one man has vast acres while another has too little land even to be buried in, and one man has many slaves while another has not a single one (592–3).

The most that can be said about such texts is that they indicate that slavery was taken for granted and people generally *aspired* to own slaves; but this is quite different from demonstrating that all, most, or even many Athenians owned them – any more than the aspiration to be rich so characteristic of American culture proves that most Americans are wealthy. The utopian visions which Aristophanes attributes to Chremylus and Praxagora seem, on the contrary, to mean that what was a reality for the prosperous landowner was merely a dream for the ordinary peasant.

It may be significant that the modest but slaveowning peasant appears in Athenian literature largely as a comic turn. At any rate, there is little textual evidence apart from Aristophanes to indicate the widespread use of slaves in agriculture. The passages from Demosthenes and/or Ps.-Dem., cited by both Jameson and Ste Croix, are rather limited in their application. Ps.-Dem. XLVII 52–3 refers to a farm – the speaker's home estate – on which there are household servants (*oiketai*). We are not told that these servants work in the fields, though we may perhaps infer that they do, since they are apparently occupied somewhere away from the main house at the moment described in the speech. In any case, their master, a trierarch, is clearly among the wealthier landowners of Attica. So all this passage tells us is that a wealthy Athenian landowner had household slaves on his home estate, where he would have a substantial household to maintain and where he could personally supervise his slaves. This is something that no one would question, not even an historian (like A.H.M. Jones) inclined to the most conservative estimates of the number and distribution of slaves in classical Athens. Such a text tells us nothing about the use of slaves on less wealthy farms, or about slaves on farms owned by wealthier landlords apart from their home estates, or indeed about the use of slaves in agricultural labour in general.

Ps.-Dem. LIII 6 mentions three household slaves – again *oiketai* – who have run away from a farm. Again it is apparently the home farm of the citizen in question, and again we are told nothing about what the servants do. (In another passage [21] reference is made to two other slaves who sometimes hire themselves out as farm labourers for wages, especially for harvesting.) The identity of their master, Nikostratos, is not certain; but his accuser, his neighbour and formerly intimate friend, Apollodoros, is himself very wealthy, a trierarch and son of Pasion, the ex-slave banker who was reputed to be the richest man in Athens. The intimate association between Nikostratos and Apollodoros may indicate that the former too was a wealthy man (at least before his alleged misfortunes), and other evidence suggests that he was. The text refers to his brother Arethousios, and Davies in *Athenian Propertied Families* (Oxford: Clarendon Press, 1971, p. 481 n.1) concludes that the latter is the Arethousios Aristoleō Pēlēx who bought a part share of the lease of the Piraeus theatre. This passage, then, tells us nothing more than does the first about the extent of agricultural slavery in classical Athens.

To these examples of slaves on farms, Jameson adds three passages, all from the same speech by Lysias: VII 11, 16–17, 43. The slaves in this case again belong to a rich man, and again the nature of their services is unclear. 16–17 and 43, which do refer to slaves, do not specify their duties; the inference that they are farm labourers is apparently based on the speaker's argument that he is hardly likely to have committed the crime with which he is charged (digging up a sacred olive stump which had allegedly been on his property) in front of slaves (hence outdoors on the farm) who could use their knowledge of his crime against him. Passage 11, which refers to cultivators or people engaged in agricultural work, says nothing about slaves at all. The *ergazomenoi* of this passage are people to whom the land has been leased in the past; and the *ergazomenos* one or two sentences later could be either the landowner himself – since he speaks of farming the land himself (*geōrgō*) after the previous tenants (or sharecroppers?) – or anyone employed by him, not necessarily a slave.

Dem. LV 31–2 is the only passage among those cited from the *Orators* which may concern a farmer of modest means with a slave who seems to perform such outdoor tasks as the building of walls on his master's farm (which may or may not imply that he regularly does farm labour). The owner speaks of himself in passing as a man of small property (35); but nothing is known about him, not even his name. In particular, we do not know how small his 'small property' was; and it must be noted that he is the defendant in the case and subject to a penalty, so that it is in his interest to downplay his wealth.

It should be said, too, that all evidence concerning the conditions of 'rich' and 'poor' Athenians – including their possession of slaves – must be considered critically in the light of the misleading ways in which Athenians themselves often spoke of poverty and wealth. As Davies has pointed out (*Athenian Propertied Families*, xxi n.2), the antithesis *penēs/plousios* was often little more than a rhetorical device. For example, at least for rhetorical purposes anyone who was not rich – indeed even very rich – might be treated as *penēs* or *aporos*. Thus, Dem. XVIII 102–108, defending his Trierarchical Law, refers only to the richest 300 citizens as *plousioi* – that is, only those at the top of the trierarchic register – while the rest of the 1200 richest citizens are called men of moderate or small means and even *penētes* or *aporoi* (102, 108; cf. Davies xxi n. 5). Perhaps we should have second thoughts, then, when Aristophanes' farmer, Chremylus, describes himself as *penēs* or when Demosthenes' client calls himself a man of small property.

Other commentators too have stressed the fact that *penia* did not for the Greeks mean poverty as we understand it. (See, for example, A.R. Hands, *Charities and Social Aid in Greece and Rome*, London: Thames and Hudson, 1968, pp. 62 ff.; and W. den Boer, *Private Morality in*

Greece and Rome: Some Historical Aspects, Leiden: Brill, 1979, pp. 151 ff.) Not only was *penia* distinguished from indigence, *ptōcheia*, but it often applied to all those who were unable to live the life of a gentleman, that is, a leisured and independent life free of the necessity to work. The *penētes* would therefore include a great many prosperous farmers and owners of businesses who were obliged to take an active hand in the work of their enterprises, however many people they may have employed. By this standard, the vast majority of the Athenian citizenry would be *penētes*, since only the largest properties could ensure the completely leisured life of a passive rentier whose 'work' – if any – was purely supervisory, like that of the great landed gentleman. Sometimes the word could be used in a political sense, so that *penētes* could be synonymous with the *dēmos*, as against the exclusive *oligoi* (den Boer, p. 152). Demosthenes' very broad use of the term in XVIII 102–108 may not be typical – unless we assume that only the 300 wealthiest citizens of Athens could live the life of a true gentleman; but there can be little doubt that 'poverty' as conceived by the Greeks could cover a very wide spectrum of material conditions.

Rhetorical distortions may also affect another scrap of evidence sometimes cited as proof that ownership of slaves was all but universal in Athens. In a legal case where the testimony of slaves is at issue, the speaker remarks that the matter is of common concern because those directly involved in the case are not alone in owning slaves. 'The rest', or 'everyone else' (as the translation usually goes), has slaves (Lysias V 5). Apart from the sweeping vagueness and ambiguity of the phrase ἀλλὰ καὶ τοῖς ἄλλοις ἅπασιν, one or two other points must be noted about this passage. The object of this statement, as A.H.M. Jones reminds us, is to convince the jury that it is a matter of public concern not to encourage slaves to inform against their masters (*Athenian Democracy*, Oxford: Basil Blackwell, 1957, p. 12); so this may be another typical case of rhetorical licence. We cannot be sure precisely how great an exaggeration it would have been to say that everyone in Athens owned slaves, but that it would have been a great exaggeration we can be reasonably certain.

It is also worth considering (without making too much of it, since the evidence is open to varying interpretations) a point made by K.J. Dover in his assessment of Athenian orators as witnesses to popular values in general. Their evidence, he suggests, must be critically evaluated in light of certain characteristics of the juries they were addressing. In particular, he concludes that 'either the majority of the jurors addressed by the fourth-century orators were fairly prosperous – not rich, for it was possible to exploit their dislike of the really rich ...; or, if they did not belong to the prosperous class, they liked to be treated as if they did, and were willing, at least while performing the role of jurors, to adopt the values of that class' (*Greek Popular Morality* p. 34). Dover leans toward the view that the first of these possibilities is more likely, that juries were increasingly manned by prosperous citizens, and that, especially given the rates of pay for jury duty, the poor became less and less inclined to serve as the century progressed. It is possible, then, that Lysias' sweeping generalization about the universality of slavery (if, in fact, this is what the phrase in question means) reflects the disproportionate prosperity of his listeners, or at least their inclination to be treated as men of substance.

One final, and especially problematic, bit of evidence deserves mention. Lysias XXIV is sometimes cited as if it demonstrated that 'an Athenian had to be decidedly poor not to have a slave' (Michael Jameson, 'Agriculture and Slavery in Classical Athens', *CJ* 73 (1977), p. 122). See also M.I. Finley, *Economy and Society in Ancient Greece* (London: Chatto and Windus, 1981), pp. 97–8. Although the speech says nothing about agricultural slavery, it is worth examining because it is often cited as evidence that slaveownership was virtually universal in Athens, and, at least in some cases (e.g., Jameson), as if this applied to poor farmers as well as craftsmen. In this speech, a nameless invalid defends himself against a charge that he is not entitled to a pension for the disabled. He remarks that he has no children as yet (οὔπω) to take care of him, nor has he yet acquired a slave to take over his work (6). This text, if it provides positive evidence of anything, testifies only to the existence of a tradesman *without* a slave to help in his work, but it could conceivably be used as evidence of widespread slavery if we stress the οὔπω, suggesting that a poor tradesman could expect some day to own a slave. There are, however, a great many problems in this speech, not the least of which is a general lack of verisimilitude. Let us, nevertheless, try to take it seriously for a moment.

First, the text tells us little about how many citizens there are like this slaveless tradesman, or how far up the social scale his slaveless condition goes. This is particularly so because the degree of his own poverty is open to question. He suggests that his accuser has described him as a man of wealth (5, 9), using the word *euporia*, which is usually reserved for the very wealthiest (Davies, *Athenian Propertied Families*, p. xxi). While this is without doubt a gross rhetorical exaggeration, it seems unlikely that anyone would dare to level such a public charge against him if his own description of his poverty were not equally exaggerated. (Cf. Davies xxi n. 4. Davies also notes the fact that this man could even afford the services of Lysias, whose clients were generally wealthy.) One other scrap of evidence may be significant in determining this citizen's status. He remarks (25) that during the regime of the Thirty Tyrants, he went into voluntary exile even though he was free to live without fear as a citizen with the Thirty. If he was free to live with the Thirty *as a citizen*, does this mean that he had been selected as one of the 3000, the minority who were named by the Thirty as privileged citizens while so many others were expelled from the city? And does this then mean that he was a man of sufficient substance to be regarded as a worthy and reliable citizen of the oligarchy? Even if some poor men may have stayed behind (someone presumably had to provide goods and services), they would not have been among the 3000 with citizen rights.

The speech is riddled with such anomalies, and they lend support to the view that the text is not authentic. It has been argued, on the grounds of its poor argumentation and complete lack of verisimilitude, that this text represents a school exercise – probably by a not very bright student of Lysias (Louis Roussel, *(Pseudo) Lysias (L'Invalide)* [1966]). Roussel goes through the speech paragraph by paragraph, identifying its many absurdities. He shows that it combines poor imitations of Lysias' other speeches with simple nonsense. For example, the opening lines echo those of Lysias XVI, where Mantitheus expresses his gratitude to his accusers for giving him an opportunity to render an account of his life. A rhetorical device which sounds impressive in the mouth of a rich and prominent young man undergoing public scrutiny before taking office becomes a little absurd in the mouth of a poor and obscure invalid, argues Roussel. The statement about the invalid's self-exile during the regime of the Thirty is simply a repetition of a theme common to several of Lysias' speeches (including the defence of Mantitheus). Paragraphs 5–6, in which the critical passage about slavery occurs, Roussel calls 'particularly calamitous' (10), pointing to the absurdity of the invalid's statement that as yet he has no children to take care of him. The οὔπω – which for Jameson is so suggestive in reference to slavery, indicating that such a poor tradesman could expect to own a slave – becomes a little ludicrous in the case of his expectation of children, given his repeated references to his advanced age and general infirmity and the fact that, as Roussel argues, he would have to wait about seventeen years for the projected child to assume the desired role.

Furthermore, if, like Jameson, and despite the decades intervening between Lysias and Aristotle, we take Aristotle's *Constitution of Athens* as our evidence concerning the conditions of eligibility for such a pension, our confusion about the invalid's circumstances simply grows. Aristotle writes:

... there is a law which orders that those whose property is less than three minae and who are so completely disabled that they cannot do any work shall, after having been examined by the Council, receive two obols daily for their support from the public funds (49.4, trans. Von Fritz).

We may leave aside the discrepancy between Aristotle's two obols and the one obol of the speech (13, 26) – which may indicate that the pension was raised later in the fourth century, or that the speechwriter was mistaken, or that Aristotle was wrong (though other references to a two-obol pension exist: see P.J. Rhodes, *A Commentary on the Aristotelian* Athenaion Politeia, Oxford: Clarendon Press, 1981, p. 570); but if we assume, as Jameson seems to do, that the conditions of eligibility were the same in Lysias' time, what are we to make of the condition that recipients must be completely unable to do any work? This is clearly not true of our invalid, according to his own testimony, and was even less so when he first received the pension as a young man (7–8).

In any case, there are a great many anomalies, both stylistic and substantive, in this problematic text. Instead of trying to make convoluted sense out of all these discrepancies, it would be easier to accept that the speech is inauthentic (not simply in the attribution of authorship but in its substance), as Roussel and others have done, or else to read it as an elaborate joke by Lysias himself. This possibility has also been suggested. (See M.D. Reeve's review of Roussel's pamphlet, *CR* 18 [1968] 235–6, for a brief summary of various views on this speech.)

It would not, moreover, be very convincing to argue that, authentic or not, the text at least indicates what Athenians regarded as possible and plausible. There are simply too many anomalies and contradictions in the invalid's circumstances to provide useful clues. In the end, we do not really know what social type is being described here, let alone whether or not this particular citizen actually existed.

In any case, again, none of this has much to do with agricultural slavery.

Some Considerations on the Evidence for Tenancy

Tenancy is in general an elusive category of land tenure. In the absence of a clear dichotomy between property and propertylessness, and with the wide spectrum of conditional possession which seems to characterize pre-capitalist societies, the range and stringency of conditions can be extremely varied. The notion of 'tenancy', suggesting possession of land on condition of paying a rent to the owner, can be misleading when it must cover such a broad range of tenures and relations between 'owner' and 'tenant'. It can be made to include everything from the leasing of a large estate for a fixed rent by a wealthy proprietor to the exiguous and exploitative arrangements of sharecropping. It can, furthermore, be very misleading to expect all of these varied conditions to have equal weight in documentary evidence – for example, to look for written leases as evidence of their existence.

Thus the shortage of leases in the Athenian evidence is sometimes cited as an indication that tenancy was rare, or that the incidence of tenancy increased in the fourth century BC, simply because that is the period from which leases have survived. Such conclusions, first, ignore the obvious point that private contracts may just have disappeared (see J.W. Jones, *The Law and Legal Theory of the Greeks*, Oxford: Clarendon Press, 1956). They also overlook the important fact that written agreements, or indeed any written record of legal transactions, were rare before the middle of the fourth century, since verbal agreements in front of witnesses were still regarded as more reliable than the written word in this society not yet completely at home in its relatively new and unprecedented literacy (see above, p. 169, and Richard Garner, *Law and Society in Classical Athens*, London: Croom Helm, 1987, pp. 137–8). But at least equally significant is the failure to appreciate the enormous differences among the various conditions of tenancy and the varying degrees of legal protection and mutuality which they would entail. The legal protections available to a wealthy lessee renting a large estate are likely to be very much greater and more formal than those afforded to the impoverished sharecropper or 'tenant-at-will', whose legal rights, if any, would be very limited. To put it another way, the differences here may be those between a kind of *locum* landlord, himself the employer of labour, and an exploited labourer whose access to the basic conditions of subsistence depends on transferring surplus to the landowner – in a sense, a paid labourer who differs from other employees simply in the form of payment, consisting of the proportion of his product which the landlord allows him to keep. In the first case, we might expect a written lease – although even here not necessarily – which by its very existence acknowledges mutual rights and obligations. In the second, we should not be surprised to find no lease, no legal acknowledgement of mutuality.

Agricultural leases surviving from classical Attica paint what is clearly a very partial picture. Typically, they represent the leasing of public or institutional land, properties belonging to cult, deme, or phratry. In Robin Osborne's *Classical Landscape with Figures: The Ancient Greek City and its Countryside* (London: George Philip, 1987, pp. 42–3) there is a table of classical and hellenistic agricultural leases, with their provisions. There are eleven leases from Attica listed for the whole period (the list is not exhaustive but includes all those cases for which there is adequate information to be usefully tabulated), in which the leasing bodies are as follows: three cult, seven deme, and one phratry. The leasing periods range from ten years to 'all time', four of them for ten years, four for all time, one for thirty years, one for forty, and two not given. The size of each property is apparently unknown. It is possible that written leases were most commonly reserved for transactions of this official kind.

In all such cases – as the length of the leases suggests – the lessee, as agent of the leasing institution, would undoubtedly have had a relationship to the land, a security of tenure and a control of its management, substantially different from those of the tenants mentioned, for example, in Lysias VII (esp. 4 and 9–11), which suggests another kind of tenancy arrangement altogether, between private individuals and probably without written leases. This legal speech, which has nothing to do with a dispute between landlord and tenant, as background to the case at hand (a wealthy landowner has been charged with illegally digging up the stump of a sacred olive tree alleged to have been on his land) records the history of the plot of land in question. It passed through a series of lettings before the owner – who suggests (24) that he owns several such plots – took it over to farm for himself (apparently with the help of slaves – if the opaque references to slaves here permit this inference – as might be expected on the land of a wealthy man which he 'farms' himself). Of the four successive tenants, one held the land for two years, another two for one year each, and the last for three years. Each tenant is named, and one is identified as a freedman. The words used to describe the arrangements are variants of the root *misthos-* (as in 'let out to' or 'hired by'), and in one case *eirgasato* ('worked by') the tenant.

The picture we get is of a very wealthy landlord (he is a trierarch) who owns several small and scattered properties and who adopts what was probably a typical expedient for employing labour to work a plot of land on which he does not live and work himself: farming it out, probably to men of modest means, in exchange for a rent. The arrangement is treated as completely unremarkable, as if this were the most natural way to dispose of agricultural land. It is clear that the previous owner had also let out the land (4). There is no reason to suppose that a written lease was regarded as necessary in such circumstances, any more than in the case of agricultural labourers 'contracted' to do a particular job of work. (Some indication of how informal leasing arrangements in general may have been is provided by a dispute recorded in ps.-Demosthenes XLVIII 44–5, in which there is a controversy over whether a certain house was rented or owned.) It may not be legitimate to infer from this series of short lets that the tenants had little security and remained in possession of the land entirely at the whim of the landlord, but it would not be at all unusual in the history of tenancy if this were so; in any case, the contrast with the duration of the written institutional leases is significant.

We would also not expect to see disputes between landlords and tenants of this kind appearing in the courts. (Rental arrangements, treated as sources of income in much the same way as interest-bearing loans or wage-earning slaves contracted out, if they appear in the legal records at all, are more likely to figure – rather one-sidedly – in property inventories listing the assets of a wealthy man. See, for example, Isaeus, *On the Estate of Hagnias*, 42.) The evidence in the case of Lysias VII, which may be the most important available to us if only because it seems to treat letting as a common and routine practice, is character- istically fortuitous, emerging from a legal case in which tenancy arrange- ments are not at issue.

There is, at the very least, no warrant for concluding that the letting out of land was uncommon. The most that we can say is that, in the (unremarkable) absence of written leases, we know very little about the letting out of private land. There certainly exists evidence testifying to tenancy arrangements of various kinds: from the substitute landlord of the major institutional leases; to the more formal and secure forms of private leasing – notably the leasing of land to be held in trust for orphaned minor heirs until they reached majority (I am told that Robin Osborne, in an as yet unpublished work, argues on demographic grounds that there were substantial numbers of such leases), to (perhaps) the tenant-manager of Xenophon's *Oeconomicus*, to the modest tenant-farmers of Lysias VII. But we can say little about the frequency or importance of such arrangements, except by inference and by judging the evidence in context. One thing is certain: the evidence which does exist can only mislead if we come to it with mistaken expectations and particularly if we fail to recognize the existence of tenancy relations which represent not a means of possessing property, with its attendant legally protected rights, but a means of employing labour, not a transfer of land but a contracting of work.

Notes

Chapter I

1. M.I. Finley, *Ancient Slavery and Modern Ideology* (London: Chatto and Windus, 1980), p. 20.

2. Charles de Secondat, Baron de Montesquieu, *The Spirit of the Laws*, trans. Thomas Nugent (New York: Hafner, 1949), p. 235.

3. Ibid., p. 46. On the number of slaves, see p. 21 note e. Montesquieu is here relying, like many other writers of the eighteenth and nineteenth centuries, on the figures given by Athenaeus, according to whom Demetrius of Phalerum numbered slaves at 400,000 in the late fourth century BC. This figure is now generally regarded as vastly inflated. As we shall see in the next chapter, even the highest estimates proposed by scholars today come nowhere near this figure. Estimates now tend to range between a somewhat implausibly low 20,000 to a perhaps excessively high 110,000; and a frequently cited maximum for peak periods is 60–80,000.

4. Ibid., p. 38 and note z.

5. Ibid., p. 46.

6. G.W.F. Hegel, *The Philosophy of History*, trans. J. Sibree (New York: P.F. Collier and Son, 1912), p. 332.

7. Ibid., p. 336.

8. James Harrington, 'The Commonwealth of Oceana' in *The Political Works of James Harrington*, ed. J.G.A. Pocock (Cambridge: Cambridge University Press, 1977), pp. 259–60. For a discussion of attitudes to Sparta throughout European history, see Elizabeth Rawson, *The Spartan Tradition in European Thought* (Oxford: Clarendon Press, 1969); on Harrington (and his preference for 'the leadership of the nobility and gentry'), pp. 190–95.

9. Adam Ferguson, *An Essay on the History of Civil Society*, ed. Duncan Forbes (Edinburgh: Edinburgh University Press Paperbacks, 1978), p. 185.

10. Ibid., p. 187.

11. Adam Smith, *The Wealth of Nations*, eds R.H. Campbell and A.S. Skinner (Oxford: Clarendon Press, 1976), vol. 2, p. 684. See also, *Lectures on Jurisprudence*, eds. R.L. Meek, D.D. Raphael, and P.G. Stein (Indianapolis: Liberty *Classics*, 1982), p. 411.

12. Ferguson, pp. 184–5.

13. See M.I. Finley, *Ancient Slavery and Modern Ideology*, Chapter 1, for a brief account of the evolution of the modern interest in slavery.

14. Frank M. Turner, *The Greek Heritage in Victorian Britain* (New Haven and London: Yale University Press, 1981), p. 192.

15. Ibid., p. 194.
16. See A.D. Momigliano, 'George Grote and the Study of Greek History' in *Studies in Historiography* (London: Weidenfeld and Nicolson, Weidenfeld Goldbacks, 1969), esp. pp. 64–5, on the neglect of Greek history on the Continent. This article also contains some illuminating remarks on Gillies and Mitford.
17. William Mitford, *The History of Greece* (London: T. Cadell and W. Davies, 1814), IV 342.
18. Ibid., V 131.
19. Ibid., IV 354–9.
20. Ibid., V 7–8.
21. Ibid., V 34–5.
22. Ibid., V 16.
23. Ibid., V 38–9.
24. Turner, p. 204.
25. Ibid., pp. 208–9.
26. Ibid., p. 204.
27. Momigliano, p. 65.
28. Turner, p. 248.
29. August Boeckh, *The Public Economy of Athens* (1842), pp. 611–14.
30. Ibid., pp. 226–7.
31. Ibid., p. 217.
32. Ibid., p. 119.
33. Ibid., p. 117.
34. Ibid., p. 45.
35. Jacob Burckhardt, *Griechische Kulturgeschichte*, ed. Rudolf Marx (Leipzig: Alfred Kroner Verlag, 1929), pp. 258–9.
36. Ibid., I 221.
37. Ibid., I 232.
38. Ibid., I 254–5.
39. Ibid., III 109.
40. Ibid., III 55.
41. Ibid., III 65–6.
42. Ibid., III 128–30.
43. Ibid., III 209.
44. Ibid., III 182.
45. Ibid.
46. Ibid., III 130.
47. Ibid., III 206.
48. Ibid., III 91.
49. Numa Denis Fustel de Coulanges, 'Le colonat romain' in *Recherches sur quelques problèmes d'histoire* (Paris: 1885), p. 3, quoted in Finley, *Ancient Slavery and Modern Ideology*, p. 67.
50. Fustel de Coulanges, *The Ancient City* (Garden City: Doubleday Anchor, n.d.), p. 11.
51. Nicole Loraux and Pierre Vidal-Naquet, 'La formation de l'Athènes bourgeoise: Essai d'historiographie 1750–1850' in *Classical Influences on Western Thought: A.D. 1650–1870*, ed. R.R. Bolgar (Cambridge: Cambridge University Press, 1979), p. 170.
52. Fustel, *The Ancient City*, p. 67.
53. Ibid., pp. 60–61.
54. Ibid., p. 224.
55. Ibid., p. 251.
56. Ibid., p. 259.
57. Ibid., p. 264.
58. Ibid., p. 273.
59. Ibid., pp. 324–5.
60. Ibid., pp. 318–19.
61. Ibid., p. 325.

62. Ibid., p. 328.
63. Ibid., p. 337.
64. Ibid.
65. Ibid., pp. 337-8.
66. Ibid., p. 338.
67. Ibid., p. 340.
68. Ibid., p. 340, n. 8.
69. Ibid., pp. 334-6.
70. M.I. Finley, 'Was Greek Civilisation Based on Slave Labour?' in *Economy and Society in Ancient Greece* (London: Chatto and Windus, 1981), p. 111.
71. Finley, *Ancient Slavery and Modern Ideology*, pp. 11ff.
72. Finley, 'Was Greek Civilisation ...?', p. 111.
73. Frederick Engels, *Anti-Dühring* (London: Lawrence and Wishart, 1969), p. 213.
74. Ibid., pp. 413-14.
75. Engels, *The Origin of the Family, Private Property, and the State* (London: Lawrence and Wishart, 1972), pp. 180-81. Here is the clearest example of Engels' tendency to exaggerate the importance of 'commerce and industry', his inflation of the slave 'manufactories', and his repetition of Smith's argument concerning the competition between free craftsmen and slaves. In this passage he also takes for granted an impossibly high estimate of slaves in Athens, suggesting that there were 365,000 slaves, or 18 slaves to every male adult citizen.
76. Ibid., p. 231.
77. Benjamin Farrington, *The Civilisation of Greece and Rome* (London: Victor Gollancz, Left Book Club Edition, 1938), p. 47.
78. Ibid., p. 91.
79. G.E.M. de Ste Croix, *The Class Struggle in the Ancient Greek World* (Ithaca: Cornell University Press, and London: Duckworth, 1981), p. 52.
80. Ibid.
81. Perry Anderson, *Passages from Antiquity to Feudalism* (London: New Left Books, 1974), pp. 18-52.
82. Hannah Arendt, *The Human Condition* (Garden City: Doubleday Anchor, 1959), pp. 73 and 323 n.7.
83. Arendt, *On Revolution* (New York: Viking Press, 1965), p. 136.
84. Finley, 'Was Greek Civilisation ...?', p. 112.

Chapter II

1. This chapter, which deals with especially contentious issues and spells out at length many of the premises on which the other chapters are based, contains more detailed discussions of evidence than the others; but I have relegated some of the more laborious discussions to the two Appendices.

2. A.H.M. Jones, *Athenian Democracy* (Oxford: Basil Blackwell, 1957), pp. 76-9; A.W. Gomme, *The Population of Athens* (Oxford: Basil Blackwell, 1933). Gomme's figures have come under criticism in recent years, especially as the field of historical demography in general has made great advances. For example, on the basis of recent scholarship in this field, M.H. Hansen has questioned one of Gomme's fundamental assumptions, namely that peace and prosperity *must* lead to a rapid growth of population; that hence the population of Athens in the fourth century BC, after the devastations of war and the plague in the previous century, could not have been static; and that the figures for the late fourth century must therefore be higher than those proposed, for instance, by Jones. M.H. Hansen, 'Demographic Reflections on the Number of Athenian Citizens 451-309 BC,' *American Journal of Ancient History*, 7:2 (1982). (Hansen had already, in an earlier article, cast doubt on Gomme's figures for the fifth century.) It must, however, be emphasized that my object in what follows is not to engage in this

demographic debate but rather to examine the best case that can be made for agricultural slavery by proceeding from a generous estimate of the ratio of slaves to citizens, such as that proposed by Gomme.

3. S. Lauffer, *Die Bergwerksslaven von Laureion* (Mainz: Akademie der Wissenschaft und Literatur, 1955–6), II 904–16. See also Robin Osborne, *Demos: The Discovery of Classical Attika* (Cambridge: Cambridge University Press, 1985), pp. 111 and 242 n. 2, where other estimates are cited, one by C. Conophagos (1980), who suggests that 11,000 slaves were employed in the mines, and another recent calculation by H. Kalcyk (1982), suggesting that there were 54,100 slaves per year in the fifth century and 22,100 in the fourth. (Osborne appears to have corrected a mistake in addition in one of Kalcyk's tables.)

4. Diog. Laert. V 11–16 and 69–74.

5. Diog. Laert. III 41–3.

6. For example, M.I. Finley, *Economy and Society in Ancient Greece* (London: Chatto and Windus, 1981), p. 102.

7. See below, pp. 70–71.

8. The evidence in this paragraph is drawn from the following passages in Demosthenes (and ps.-Dem.): XXI 156; XXVII 46; XXIX 25, 38, 56; XXX 35; XXXIII 8–13, 18; XXXIV 8, 28–9, 41; XXXV 33; XXXVI 14, 28–30, 45; XXXVII 4, 22–6, 28–9, 40–44, 50; XL 14–15; XL 51; XLI 8, 22; XLV 28, 61, 71; XLVI 21; XLVII 4ff., 35–40, 47, 51–3, 55–60; XLVIII 12–14, 18, 28, 35; XLIX 22–4, 31, 35, 51–3; LII 22; LIII 20–23; LIV 4, 9; LV 31–2; LVIII 305; LIX 18ff., 33–5, 42, 46, 120. In my rough calculation of occupations suggested by these passages, I have, of course, kept in mind that some of them refer to the same slaves more than once. And I have left out other references to slaves which were too vague about their functions.

9. See Osborne, *Demos*, chapter 6, for a discussion of the silver mines, how and by whom they were operated.

10. For some arguments suggesting that agricultural slavery was relatively insignificant in Athens, or even that the role of Athenian slavery in general has been exaggerated, see Chester G. Starr, 'An Overdose of Slavery', *JEH* 18 (1958) 17–32; A.H.M. Jones, *Athenian Democracy*, (Oxford: Basil Blackwell, 1957) pp. 10–20; Victor Ehrenberg, *The People of Aristophanes* (New York: Schocken Books, 1962), p. 80 and Chapter VII, especially pp. 181–2. (Ehrenberg's case is a bit ambiguous, since, while maintaining that farming was the least important occupation of slaves, he nevertheless takes for granted that slaveownership was very widespread even among small farmers.) See also Gert Audring, 'Grenzen der Konzentration von Grundeigentum in Attika während des 4. Jh. v. u. Z.', *Klio* 56 (1974) 445–6; and Lea M. Gluskina, 'Zur Spezifik der klassischen griechischen Polis im Zusammenhang mit dem Problem ihrer Krise', *Klio* 57 (1975) 415–31. Audring stresses the restrictions of the peasant economy in Attica, arguing that it was limited essentially to family labour and noting the limited degree of specialization, division of labour, and production for the market. He also notes the disadvantages of slave-labour even for wealthier landowners, especially in the light of the fact that they often owned their properties in smaller, scattered holdings (p. 454). Gluskina, too, argues that conditions for large-scale slave utilization were not favourable, because large properties were as a rule very parcellized (p. 417).

For arguments in favour of the importance of agricultural slavery, see especially, Michael H. Jameson, 'Agriculture and Slavery in Classical Athens', *CJ* 73(1977) 122–41; G.E.M. de Ste Croix, *The Class Struggle in the Ancient Greek World* (London: Duckworth, and Ithaca: Cornell University Press, 1981). These two works will be discussed extensively in what follows. M.I. Finley is sometimes cited as a proponent of this view, but, while he stresses the importance of slavery in all aspects of Athenian life, in fact he claims only that slaves constituted the *permanent* work force 'in all Greek or Roman establishments larger than the family unit'. (See *Ancient Slavery and Modern Ideology* (London: Chatto and Windus, 1980, p. 81). The emphasis on '*permanent*' is Finley's.) This leaves room not only for a large number of smallholders – who constituted the bulk of Athenian proprietors – working their land with family labour and without slaves, but also for many wealthy proprietors who held their land in separate smallholdings and could have let their farms to tenants who worked them, like other peasants, with family labour alone. It also allows for substantial casual wage-labour on properties of various sizes.

11. Ste Croix, p. 138.

12. M.I. Finley, *The World of Odysseus*, rev. edn (New York: Viking Press, 1965), p. 49.

13. Walter Beringer, '"Servile Status" in the Sources for Early Greek History', *Historia* 31 (1982), pp. 13–32. In these early cases, slaves were often women and were relatively unimportant in production.

14. Ste Croix, p. 138.

15. Robin Osborne has argued that, although Xenophon's *Oeconomicus* is one of remarkably few ancient Greek texts to deal with the countryside, 'the practical value of this discussion is almost nil'. Not only does it concern a very rich man, with advice that is 'no help at all to the poor farmer in his specific situation, for whom it does not even supply a rule of thumb', but also because Xenophon's purpose is moral rather than technical: 'Because Xenophon wants to play down the technical aspects of farming, he fails totally to describe the very real problems of all farmers in Attica, problems faced even by the exceptionally well-off landowner.' *Classical Landscape with Figures: The Ancient Greek City and its Countryside* (London: George Philip, 1987), p. 18. But even if we give Xenophon the benefit of the doubt and assume that he is telling us something about real, if exceptionally wealthy, Attic farmers, his message is, as we shall see, far from unambiguous on the question of slavery.

16. There are, however, some ambiguities even here. See p. 75 ff. for a discussion of the passages in the *Oeconomicus* concerning bailiffs.

17. See M.I. Finley, *Economy and Society* p. 98, for a discussion of the complexities in the usage of this word and others having to do with slavery.

18. See *LSJ* (*Greek–English Lexicon*) and M.I. Finley, *The World of Odysseus*, pp. 54–5, 109–10. Finley discusses the Homeric *therapōn*, neither a slave nor a serf but a retainer, who, though subordinate to the head of the household or chieftain, might occupy a very high position.

19. See p. 176 for a case in which *ergazomenoi* are clearly neither slaves nor labourers but tenants. This kind of flexible usage of words referring to cultivators of various kinds should be kept in mind when we consider the question of tenancy and sharecropping.

20. Michael Jameson refers to these linguistic ambiguities but argues that 'If we have trouble in identifying "agricultural slaves" in Athens it may be in part because they are everywhere' (p. 137). This may be true, but then the texts cannot be used to *prove* that they 'are everywhere'.

21. Aristotle in the *Politics* makes a distinction between the 'conditions' and the 'parts' of a polis in his discussion of the ideal polis. The latter are the full members or citizens, the former, 'which are necessary for the existence of the whole' without being part of it, include those engaged in production and in supplying the basic goods and services for the community – farmers, craftsmen, shopkeepers (1328a–1329a). Elsewhere, he refers in particular to the servile and menial status of craftsmen and labourers, who should never be citizens because they perform menial duties and differ from slaves only in that they perform these menial duties for the community while slaves perform them for individuals (1277a–1278a).

22. STRANGER. There remains the class of slaves and servants in general, and here I prophesy that we shall find those who set up claims against the king for the very fabric of his art, just as the spinners and carders and the rest of whom we spoke advanced claims against the weavers a while ago. All the others, whom we called contingent causes, have been removed along with the works we just mentioned and have been separated from the activity of the king and the statesman. ...

The bought servants, acquired by purchase, whom we can without question call slaves. They make no claim to any share in the kingly art.

YOUNG SOCRATES. Certainly not.

STR. How about those free men (ἐλεύθεροι) who put themselves voluntarily in the position of servants of those whom we mentioned before? I mean the men who carry about and distribute among one another the productions of husbandry and the other arts, whether in the domestic market-places or by travelling from city to city by land or sea, exchanging money for wages or money for money, the men whom we call brokers, merchants, shipmasters, and peddlers; do they lay any claim to statesmanship?

Y. SOC. Possibly to commercial statesmanship.

STR. But certainly we shall never find labourers and hired men, whom we see only too glad to serve anybody, claiming a share in the kingly art.

Y. SOC. Certainly not.

STR. But there are people who perform services (διακονοῦ'ντες) of another kind for us. How about them?

Y. SOC. What services and what men do you mean?

STR. The class of heralds and those who become by long service (ὑπηρετήσαντες) skilled as clerks and other clever men who perform various services in connexion with public offices. What shall we call them?

Y. SOC. What you called the others, servants (ὑπηρέται); not themselves rulers in the states.

Hyperetes is the word for 'servant' which Aristotle uses when he defines the slave (*doulos*) as a servant in the sphere of action (*praxis*) rather than in the sphere of production (*poiesis*) – a passage which, incidentally, is significant because it seems to take for granted that the typical slave is the domestic servant, not one who engages in production (*Politics* 1254a): ὁ δὲ βίος πρᾶξις, οὐ ποίησις, ἐστίν · διὸ καὶ ὁ δοῦλος ὑπηρέτης τῶν πρὸς τὴν πρᾶξιν.

23. See, for example, Jones, pp. 12–17, 76–9.

24. Jameson, p. 125.

25. Ibid., p. 140.

26. Ibid., p. 136. Jameson cites a few bits of positive textual evidence from Old Comedy and the orators which are discussed in Appendix I together with other literary evidence often cited on the question of slavery in Athens.

27. Jameson, p. 140.

28. For an account of early Greek agriculture much more detailed, closely argued, and supported by evidence than Jameson's, see Chester G. Starr, *The Economic and Social Growth of Early Greece, 800–500 BC* (New York: Oxford University Press, 1977). Starr deals with precisely the period of expansion which is most critical to Jameson's argument, and not only questions any rapid or dramatic demographic growth but deals with the problem of pressures for increased production (a great deal more systematically than Jameson) without assuming a need for agricultural slavery. See especially Chapters II and VII. Hansen's arguments (in the article cited in n. 2 above) against assumptions of rapid population growth apply here too, and he castigates those who 'on very slight evidence, are willing to accept an annual increase of a closed population in archaic Attica amounting to 4% per annum, which is more than for Mexico in the 20th century AD'. (p. 175) He considers the likelihood of such an 'incredible increase' against the background of demographic findings for early modern Europe, which show very slow population increases before the eighteenth century, even in periods of peace and prosperity. It should be added that estimates of agricultural productivity for the ancient world are notoriously difficult and have ranged very widely, though there has been a recent tendency toward more optimistic estimates. See, for example, Osborne, *Classical Landscape*, pp. 44–7. Again, however, I have tried to construct an argument which does not depend on proving or disproving any of Jameson's quantitative assumptions (explicit or implicit), either about population figures or about productivity. Instead, I shall concentrate on his central claim that the *citizenship* of the farmer necessitated the widespread employment of slave labour in agriculture.

29. Osborne discusses some of the difficulties in the argument which associates 'strategies of intensification' with the widespread use of slaves in agriculture, concluding that 'the use of slaves seems to be ruled out in just those circumstances (small property owners at the agricultural crises) which it was invoked to explain'. *Demos*, p. 143. He goes on to discuss other alternatives to slavery, suggesting that hired or family labour were

perhaps not the only alternatives to slavery, and proposing 'non-monetary agreements' with neighbours as a likely option.

30. Jameson, p. 130.

31. Ibid., p. 131.

32. See Eric Wolf, *Peasants* (Englewood Cliffs, N.J.: Prentice-Hall, 1966), Chapter III.

33. Osborne, *Demos*, p. 142. In Osborne's more recent book, *Classical Landscape*, he is less hesitant to call Athenian farmers 'peasants', and indeed stresses the 'peasant basis' of Greek society in general – which is, in fact, the theme of the book.

34. See, for example, M.I. Finley, *The Ancient Economy*, (Berkeley: University of California Press, 1973), p. 105.

35. Wolf, pp. 3–4, 9–10. The term 'surplus' is used here in a particular sense which perhaps requires some explanation. In purely technical terms, one could speak of 'surplus labour' to describe any labour above what is needed to provide 'the minimum required to sustain life …, the daily intake of food calories required to balance the expenditures of energy a man incurs in his daily output of labor' (Wolf, 4), plus what is required to maintain and replace the supplies and equipment necessary for the production of that caloric minimum – to repair or replace instruments, feed livestock, maintain buildings, fences, fields, etc. Such 'purely technical' terms are, of course, affected by cultural factors, changing technologies and expectations. For the purposes of the present argument, however, the critical issue does not concern the precise measure of biological needs, cultural necessities, or the cost of the 'replacement fund'; nor are we primarily concerned with how much of the producer's 'surplus' is produced voluntarily in order to enhance his or her own comfort or affluence. The essential issue here is the disposition and distribution of goods and services between primary producers and others not engaged in the production process. When society 'is no longer based on the equivalent and direct exchanges of goods and services between one group and another' (Wolf, 3), when in particular the goods and services of some groups are appropriated by others whose claims rest on a position of dominance, a distinction emerges between what the primary producers produce for their own and their families' use and maintenance (whether directly or through the medium of exchange), and what they produce for others without equivalent exchange. The question of 'surplus production' then has to do with the form and extent of the labour performed by primary producers for non-labouring appropriators. More particularly, the issue is the *compulsory* labour performed by the primary producer in order to meet the demands of a dominant appropriator. The point at issue, then, is the nature and extent of any external social compulsions which may determine the nature and extent of the producer's labour beyond what is required for self-maintenance and the continuance of the family unit. (See Wolf, pp. 2–10 for a more detailed discussion of some of these points.)

36. See Robert Brenner, 'The Agrarian Roots of European Capitalism', in *The Brenner Debate: Agrarian Class Structure and Economic Development in Pre-Industrial Europe* (Cambridge: Cambridge University Press, 1985), pp. 223–4, for a particularly lucid statement of this principle.

37. Finley, *Ancient Economy*, pp. 95–6. The Athenians, again, generally avoided direct and regular taxation on the property or persons of citizens. Metics paid a head-tax, the *metoikion*, while propertied citizens were occasionally obliged to pay a war tax, the *eisphora*, from which 'roughly everyone below the hoplite status' was exempt (M.I. Finley, *Economy and Society*, p. 90). There were also a substantial number of indirect levies, such as harbour taxes, taxes on property transactions or for operating mines; but these too would have fallen more heavily on the rich, as would taxes on property owned outside one's own deme. A substantial portion of public revenues came from the liturgies, by which individual wealthy citizens took responsibility for certain public functions, including entertainments and the maintenance of ships. Thus, the burden on poorer citizens was exceptionally light. It is worth noting that, as Finley has pointed out, there is no evidence that taxation, so often the object of grievance for the poor in other times and places, ever figured among the complaints of the Athenian demos. By contrast, the burden borne by the rich seems to have been a major theme in anti-democratic grievances.

38. Keith Hopkins, *Conquerors and Slaves* (Cambridge: Cambridge University Press, 1978), p. 24.
39. Ibid., p. 25.
40. P.A. Brunt, *Social Conflicts in the Roman Republic* (London: Chatto and Windus, 1971), pp. 40–41. For a sketch of just how enormous and unfettered Roman fortunes were – for example, in comparison to early modern England – see Richard Duncan-Jones, *The Economy of the Roman Empire* (Cambridge: Cambridge University Press, 2nd edn, 1982), esp. pp. 4–5.
41. Finley, *Ancient Slavery*, pp. 83–5 and 166 n. 42.
42. Ibid., pp. 83–4.
43. Hopkins, p. 9.
44. See n. 10 above.
45. Osborne, *Classical Landscape*, pp. 13, 138–9, 144. Just as military campaigns 'tended to concentrate on the slack period of the late spring', that is, just before the grain harvest which took place between late May and early July (pp. 13–14), so too did building projects tend to be concentrated in slack agricultural periods, since construction 'relied heavily on casual labour' and 'could only make headway when there was no prior call on that labour' (p. 15. Osborne provides a table showing the correlation between the Greek agricultural year and the Greek construction year). The seasonal character of warfare applied even to the Peloponnesian War; and it is worth noting that 'the longest invasion of Athenian territory (Attica) in the first phase of the war was forty days ...' (p. 13).
46. Ibid., p. 161.
47. Finley, *Ancient Economy*, p. 96.
48. See, for example, Marshall Sahlins, *Stone Age Economics* (London: Tavistock, 1974), Chapters 1–3, for a discussion of the 'domestic mode of production', its internal dynamics and limits and the 'structure of underproduction'.
49. See, for example, Finley, *Ancient Economy*, p. 106, where he describes the implications of 5- to 6-acre holdings.
50. Stephen B. Brush, 'The Myth of the Idle Peasant: Employment in a Subsistence Economy', in Rhoda Halperin and James Dow, eds., *Peasant Livelihood* (New York: St. Martin's Press, 1977), p. 62.
51. It has been argued – though not uncontroversially – that, especially in the fourth century BC, a substantial part of the average assembly and jury consisted of more prosperous citizens, and that this was particularly true of juries, since the pay of three obols a day was insufficient to keep a family and far less than could be earned even by casual unskilled labour (A.H.M. Jones, *Athenian Democracy*, pp. 35–7, 109–10). See also K.J. Dover, who makes a similar argument about attendance at juries, in *Greek Popular Morality in the Time of Plato and Aristotle* (Oxford: Basil Blackwell, 1974), pp. 34–5. Both Jones and Dover base their arguments not only on the rates of pay but on the content and language of speeches and on what may be inferred about the nature of the audience being addressed.
52. Osborne, *Classical Landscape*, pp. 36, 102, 104, 130.
53. Ste Croix, p. 506. It is not clear that this endorsement of Jameson's views on the use of slaves by peasants is compatible with Ste Croix's often repeated observation that the bulk of Athenian small producers stood outside the system of exploitation and seldom went beyond family labour. (See, for example, pp. 33 and 52–3.) In fact, where Jameson would undoubtedly regard Athens as a 'slave society' precisely on the grounds that slavery was so widespread throughout the social spectrum, Ste Croix generally argues almost the reverse: the system of exploitation, the form in which surplus is extracted from producers, and not the form in which production itself takes place, is the essential characteristic of any society. Athens can, therefore, be regarded as a slave society *despite* the fact that free producers had such a large share in production, precisely because free producers can be set aside as having little part in the system of exploitation.
54. Ste Croix, p. 144.
55. Ibid., p. 40.
56. Ibid., p. 53.

57. Ibid., p. 40. Ste Croix, incidentally, gives little indication here that the evidence concerning slave prices drawn from the Attic stelai is severely limited.

58. For a different evaluation of slavery, its costs, etc., see Hopkins, pp. 10, 108–11. Occasionally, Ste Croix does seem to acknowledge the problems that accompany slavery, though without pursuing the implications for his basic argument. See, for example, p. 241, where he suggests that in Roman Italy the need for supervision may have 'partly discounted' the profitability of slavery, in contrast to leasing. As we shall see, this observation does not affect Ste Croix's assessment of the advantages of slavery in relation to leasing when he makes his case for agricultural slavery in Greece.

59. On the rarity of 'slave societies', see Finley, *Ancient Slavery*, p. 67 and Hopkins, pp. 99–100. Hopkins, for example, suggests that there have been only five 'well established' cases throughout history: classical Athens, Roman Italy, the West Indian islands, Brazil, and the southern states of the USA.

60. Finley, *Ancient Slavery*, p. 77.

61. See Appendix I, for a discussion of the other texts cited by Ste Croix et al.

62. καὶ ἀνδραπόδων πλέον ἢ δύο μυριάδες ηὐτομολήκεσαν, καὶ τούτων πολὺ μέρος χειροτέχναι. In Ste Croix's version, this passage suggests that 'the greater part' were *cheirotechnai*, but as he points out, according to most manuscripts the passage seems to read 'a great part' (πολὺ μέρος) rather than 'the greater part' (τὸ πολὺ μέρος), though the argument here is not affected' by this alternative reading (p. 506).

63. See, for example, Alison Burford, *Craftsmen in Greek and Roman Society* (London: Thames and Hudson, 1972): 'The term "craftsman" is here used of every skilled worker whose labours contributed to the manufacture of objects in durable materials, and who depended on the exercise of his craft for a living. Defined thus, the miner, the bronze-nailmaker, the goldsmith, the jeweller, the quarrymason, the sculptor, the architect, the tanner, … the shipwright, the joiner and inlayer, the potter, the figurine-maker, the vase-painter, the mosaic-layer, the catapult-builder and the glass-blower are all equally deserving of consideration. … In Greek, *technē*, and in Latin, *ars*, were used indiscriminately of painting and cobbling alike, just as *technitēs, cheirotechnēs* or *dēmiourgos*, the *faber* or *artifex*, could be either a sculptor or a miner, a quarryman or an architect' (pp. 13–14). See also p. 73, where Burford discusses the skills involved in mining, and pp. 176–7, where she refers to the epitaphs and dedications by which miners left evidence of their craftsman's pride, including the following statement in the remarkable epitaph of Atotas the miner, apparently a Paphlagonian slave claiming royal descent: 'No one rivalled me in skill [*technē*].' The concept of *technē* itself is discussed in Chapter VI. See also R.J. Hopper, *Trade and Industry in Classical Greece* (London: Thames and Hudson, 1979), Chapter VII, especially 134, where Hopper mentions a dedication apparently referring to the 'skill' of mining.

As for Ste Croix's suggestion that these skilled slaves were more likely to have been agricultural slaves, it must be stressed that *cheirotechnēs* commonly referred specifically to handicraftsmen or artisans (*LSJ*) as distinct from agricultural workers. For an example of such a usage, see Plato, *Republic* 547d, where he recommends that the guardians abstain from farming and handicrafts: γεωργιῶν ἀπέχεσθαι τὸ προπολεμοῦν αὐτῆς καὶ χειροτεχνιῶν.

64. Ste Croix, p. 506.

65. Jameson, p. 136.

66. Ste Croix, p. 505.

67. Ibid., p. 181.

68. The word *thēs*, which referred to a member of the lowest 'class' in the Solonian system of classification according to property, was also used to refer to hired men. It has been estimated that *thētes* constituted about 66 per cent of the citizen population in the early fifth century BC and about 57 per cent in 322 BC (Jones pp. 8, 76–81). Jones bases the figure for 322 on Antipater's ruling which disfranchised 12,000 citizens (out of 21,000) who did not meet his property qualification. There is no way of knowing how many of these people actually worked as casual wage-labourers, but that some were forced to do so is clear. For an argument which goes further than Jones, and probably too far, claiming that the 12,000 disfranchised citizens – that is, the majority of the citizen body –

represented those who had insufficient property for an independent life and would therefore have been compelled to work as day-labourers, see E. Ruschenbusch, *Athenische Innenpolitik im 5. Jahrhundert v. Chr.* (1979) pp. 133-52, especially pp. 147-9.

69. Ste Croix certainly would not argue that the aristocratic contempt for ordinary craftsmen displayed by Xenophon (e.g. *Oeconomicus* VI 5-7) tells us very much about the number of citizens who actually worked as craftsmen in Athens.

70. Ste Croix, p. 505.

71. Ibid., e.g. p. 186.

72. Ibid., pp. 179-82.

73. Ibid., p. 181.

74. Ibid., p. 576 n. 16.

75. Ibid., p. 505.

76. Jameson also points out that the harvester is the typical hired man (p. 131), and that 'One may suspect hired labour was considerably more common than our sources show' (p. 132). Even Ste Croix at one point concedes: 'I do not wish to deny that hired labour, especially at peak periods of agricultural activity, may have been more important than our surviving evidence suggests' (p. 593 n. 59).

77. Ste Croix, p. 505.

78. Ibid., p. 172.

79. Ibid., p. 241.

80. Ibid., p. 172.

81. See Osborne, *Demos*, pp. 62-3, and *Classical Landscape*, pp. 38-9. In the latter, Osborne describes the fragmentation of farmland as a 'privilege', which allowed the farmer with several scattered holdings to avoid some of the risks of Attic farming, notably the danger of having all his crops wiped out in any given year. Fragmented holdings were, he argues, 'yet one more way in which the rich could not only maintain but increase their advantage over the less well off' (p. 38).

82. See Appendix II below for a discussion of some of the difficulties in the evidence on tenancy.

83. R.H. Hilton, *The English Peasantry in the Later Middle Ages* (Oxford: Clarendon Press, 1975), p. 25.

84. Sir Thomas Smith, *De Republica Anglorum*, ed. Mary Dewar (Cambridge: Cambridge University Press, 1982), p. 74.

85. See A.R.W. Harrison, *The Law of Athens* (Oxford: Clarendon Press, 1968), vol. 1, pp. 200-205; Douglas M. MacDowell, *The Law in Classical Athens* (London: Thames and Hudson, 1978), pp. 133 ff; J.W. Jones, *The Law and Legal Theory of the Greeks* (Oxford: Clarendon Press, 1956), pp. 201 ff.

86. Ste Croix, p. 182.

87. Gert Audring has argued (though it is not entirely clear on what evidence) that the free manager at the beginning of the *Oeconomicus* represents not so much an Athenian reality as a proposal by Xenophon, a possible solution for propertied citizens impoverished by the war, in 'Über den Gutsverwalter (*epitropos*) in der attischen Landwirtschaft des 5. und des 4. Jh. v.u.Z.', *Klio* 55 (1973) 114-15. He does, however, suggest that in the fourth century the slave-bailiff may have been increasingly replaced by free tenants, and that the literature after Xenophon displays less interest in slave-bailiffs. He also cites another historian who places more emphasis than he does himself on tenants and free managers (113): H. Bolkestein, in *Economic Life in Greece's Golden Age*, new edn. (1958), p. 29, writes, '... there were plenty of them [landowners] who left the cultivation of their ground either to tenants or to men whom we call working-managers (*epitropoi*) who might be slaves or free men'. On leasing to free men – poor citizens, freedmen, and metics – see also Gluskina (n. 2 above) p. 417.

88. Finley, *Ancient Slavery*, p. 90.

89. See J.K. Davies, *Athenian Propertied Families* (Oxford: Clarendon Press, 1971), pp. 265-8.

90. See K.D. White, *Roman Farming* (London: Thames and Hudson, 1970), pp. 370-76, for a discussion of certain considerations affecting the desirability of slave-run estates.

91. Ἔστιν ἄρα, ἔφη ὁ Σωκράτης, τὴν τέχνην ταύτην ἐπισταμένῳ, καὶ εἰ μὴ αὐτὸς τύχοι χρήματα ἔχων, τὸν ἄλλου οἶκον οἰκονομοῦντα ὥσπερ καὶ οἰκοδομοῦντα μισθοφορεῖν;
Νὴ Δία καὶ πολύν γε μισθόν, ἔφη ὁ Κριτόβουλος, φέροιτ᾽ ἄν, εἰ δύναιτο οἶκον παραλαβὼν τελεῖν τε ὅσα δεῖ καὶ περιουσίαν ποιῶν αὔξειν τὸν οἶκον.

92. Ste Croix points out that *misthos* can mean both 'pay' in a broad sense and 'rent'. Although the distinction between the *misthōtos* and the *misthōtēs* is often that between a hired man and a rent-payer or tenant, Ste Croix suggests that it can also refer to something like the difference between a wage-labourer who hires out his labour power for unskilled or partly skilled work, and the 'contractor' who undertakes a specific task, virtually always skilled or requiring possession of special equipment and probably slaves (p. 189).

93. MacDowell, pp. 140–41.

94. See K.D. White, pp. 388–9, for a catalogue of the 'systems of management' to be found in the Roman evidence, including both management by slaves and various kinds of tenancy, sharecropping, or leasing.

95. See Osborne, *Demos*, pp. 144–6, for a discussion of evidence suggesting non-monetary cooperation between neighbours, as well as kin, in agricultural labour.

96. See V.N. Andreyev, 'Some Aspects of Agrarian Conditions in Attica in the Fifth to Third Centuries BC', *Eirene* 12 (1974) pp. 5–46; and Audring, 'Grenzen...' (n.10 above) for some indications of the persistence of these conditions. Andreyev discusses the distribution of land in Attica, arguing that there was a 'rather numerous' class of peasant proprietors owning from about 3.6 to 5.3 hectares of land, which he estimates was approximately the amount needed to maintain a family. He stresses the stability of this peasant property and questions the extent of upheavals and dispossessions at the end of the fifth century BC and in the fourth. Audring also notes the stability (and stagnation) of the peasant economy, the limits it imposed on land-concentration, and the consequent restrictions on slave-utilization.

Chapter III

1. For a brief discussion of this point, see Oswyn Murray, *Early Greece* (Glasgow: Fontana, 1980), pp. 226–8.

2. M.I. Finley, *Ancient Slavery and Modern Ideology* (London: Chatto and Windus, 1980), pp. 89–90.

3. For a characterization of Athens as a 'regime of smallholders', see Anthony Snodgrass, *Archaic Greece: The Age of Experiment* (Berkeley: University of California Press, 1980), p. 37.

4. Karl Polanyi, *The Great Transformation* (Boston: Beacon Press, 1957), pp. 51–2.

5. M.I. Finley, *Economy and Society in Ancient Greece* (Chatto and Windus, 1981), p. 210. On the organization of the Mycenaean states, see also John Chadwick, *The Mycenaean World* (Cambridge: Cambridge University Press, 1976), pp. 69–83; M.I. Finley, *Early Greece: The Bronze and Archaic Ages* (London: Chatto and Windus, 1970), pp. 38–9, 54–6; Emily Vermeule, *Greece in the Bronze Age* (Chicago and London: University of Chicago Press, 1972), Chapters VI and VIII; R.F. Willetts, *Ancient Crete: A Social History* (London: Routledge and Kegan Paul, and Toronto: University of Toronto Press, 1965), pp. 42–7.

6. Snodgrass, p. 90.

7. Ibid., p. 90.

8. Ibid., p. 93.

9. Willetts, p. 51.

10. Finley, *Economy and Society*, p. 217. I shall not reiterate the arguments made repeatedly by Finley and others concerning the epics as a historical source. I accept that, while the poems represent an amalgam of legends, cultural memories, and the author(s)' own contemporary experience, the social and political structures they describe bear no

resemblance to the Mycenaean civilization which purports to be their setting, telling us more about 'Homeric' society, or something closer to the bard's own time.

11. Ibid.

12. See, for example, Murray, pp. 40–41. My argument, incidentally, is consistent with the view that kingship was not a typical feature of the early Greek polis and that there was no general transition from monarchy to aristocracy in the eighth century BC of the kind traditionally taken for granted in histories of early Greece. It is possible, even likely, that with the destruction of the Mycenaean states, monarchy was effectively destroyed in the emerging poleis and replaced by aristocracies constituted by the *basilees*, the local leaders who had begun as lesser officials or local magistrates in the Mycenaean states and eventually became a landed aristocracy. A persuasive (if somewhat overstated?) case for this kind of development is made by Robert Drews in *Basileus: The Evidence for Kingship in Geometric Greece* (New Haven and London: Yale University Press, 1983). There is no need to assume a simple continuity of personnel or of dynasties in the sense that the aristocratic families of archaic Greece were all direct descendants of the Mycenaean *basilees*. If there was a continuity of the kind being suggested here, it is conceivable that, while the original claimants to aristocratic status owed their position and their property to such direct descent, the important continuity is in the property regime itself, allowing changes and increases in personnel.

13. Finley writes, in *The World of Odysseus*, rev. edn (New York: Viking Press, 1965): 'A deep horizontal cleavage marked the world of the Homeric poems. Above the line were the *aristoi*, literally the "best people", the hereditary nobles who held most of the wealth and all the power, in peace as in war. Below were all the others, for whom there was no collective technical term, the multitude. The gap between the two was rarely crossed, except by the inevitable accidents of wars and raids' (p. 49). Murray suggests that there may have been a time when the aristocracy was physically separated from the multitude (p. 48). A particularly useful discussion of the relationship between aristocracy and multitude, which illuminates the possible continuities between Mycenaean and 'Homeric' societies, occurs in Walter Beringer's 'Freedom, Family, and Citizenship in Early Greece', in *The Craft of the Ancient Historian: Essays in Honor of Chester G. Starr*, ed. John W. Eadie and Josiah Ober (University Press of America, 1985), pp. 48–52. Beringer, who speaks of 'apartheid' in the relations between the ruling group and the multitude (pp. 48 and 52), departs from both Murray and Finley in suggesting that there may indeed have been a kind of dependent peasantry, subject to the 'landowning or land-managing families' which constituted 'a supraregional Establishment providing the personnel for all public offices, whether priestly, military, or political-administrative and legislative-judiciary' (p. 51). Whether or not the Attic peasantry was 'dependent' in the sense of serfdom or helotage, it is misleading to speak – as both Finley and Murray do – of a 'free peasantry', without giving sufficient attention to the implications of the relationship between ruling and subject communities which is at least implicit in their own accounts.

14. Beringer, p. 53.

15. There seems to be widespread agreement on the late arrival of coinage, especially in Athens; on the impossibility of attributing a reform of coinage to Solon; and on the limitations this would have placed on the possibilities of 'debt'. See Antony Andrewes, *Greek Society* (Harmondsworth: Penguin Books, 1971) p. 116; Murray, pp. 181–3; Snodgrass, p. 134; Chester G. Starr, *The Economic and Social Growth of Early Greece: 800–500 BC* (New York: Oxford University Press, 1977), pp. 108–17; and P.J. Rhodes, *A Commentary on the Aristotelian Athenaion Politeia* (Oxford: Clarendon Press, 1981), p. 126. This does not mean that some form of coinage did not exist earlier in some parts of Greece to be used for certain limited purposes. The point is that, as Snodgrass emphasizes, we must be careful not to exaggerate the economic applications or overestimate its commercial uses by drawing upon modern analogies.

16. Andrewes, p. 115.

17. Andrewes, p. 117; Rhodes, p. 94; Murray, p. 183.

18. Murray, pp. 181–2.

19. Cf. Rhodes, p. 95: 'The question, who owned the land worked by the

ἐκτήμοροι, is apt to be discussed in anachronistic terms. In a community which has no written laws, and little or no writing of any kind, ownership as a legal concept can hardly exist. X farms the land bounded by the stream, the wood and the land farmed by Y, and his ancestors farmed it before him: this, together with his neighbours' knowledge of it, is his title to the land. It will have been a similar fact of common knowledge that a sixth of the produce of X's land was due to the local lord, and that if X defaulted the lord would dispose of X and his land as he saw fit. The land "belonged" to X in the sense that as long as he paid his μορτή no one could challenge his claim to it; it "belonged" to X's whole family in the sense that if X died while in occupation of it the land would pass to his sons; but it also "belonged" to the lord in the sense that the μορτή was due to him and if it was not paid he could enslave X and take over the land.'

20. Murray, pp. 183–4.

21. Robin Osborne, *Classical Landscape with Figures: The Ancient Greek City and its Countryside* (London: George Philip, 1987), p. 94.

22. On the subject of aristocratic factionalism as the principal object of Solon's reforms, see Chester Starr, *Individual and Community: The Rise of the Polis 800–500 BC* (New York: Oxford University Press, 1986), pp. 77–80: 'If one turns ... to Solon's own poetry, the only evidence which can lead the historian to speak with confidence, one finds primarily testimony to the dangers of aristocratic factionalism. At one point he comments that "a polis is destroyed of great men," and in a long fragment (3) he grieves over the unrighteous minds of the leaders of the demos who produce civil strife. Aristocratic divisiveness, that is, may have had considerable weight in leading the more sober members of the community to feel that reform was necessary' (pp. 77–8). Starr goes on to comment that Solon was unsuccessful in this respect and that 'within a decade Athenian aristocrats were again wrangling over tenure of the archonship and power in the state. The result was the tyranny of Pisistratus. ....' (p. 80).

23. It is in this connection that we might be inclined to recall Isocrates' pretty tale about the 'sharing' of property in the good old days.

24. The tyrannies have long been a subject of dispute, since Aristotle first created the impression that they represented a conflict between the demos (led by tyrants) and the aristocracy. Although this interpretation is not incompatible with a view of the tyrants as themselves aristocrats, it may have contributed to certain misconceptions about them, such as those often associated with the myth of 'l'Athènes bourgeoise', where they are likely to appear as some kind of bourgeois *nouveaux riches*. Although little is known about the social origins of some tyrants, it is more common nowadays to regard them as typically aristocrats, arising at a time of change in the nature of aristocratic power. For a particularly judicious account of this phenomenon, which connects the rise of the tyrants with 'rural alterations', see Starr, *Individual and Community*, pp. 80–86.

25. Chester Starr, in *The Economic and Social Growth of Early Greece, 800–500 BC* (New York: Oxford University Press, 1977), suggests that these loans may have been made necessary by the limitations placed on private borrowing by Solon's reforms. At any rate, these state loans were offset by a tax on agricultural production of 5 or 10 per cent (p. 186).

26. Robin Osborne, *Demos: The Discovery of Classical Attika* (Cambridge: Cambridge University Press, 1985), p. 189.

27. See Osborne, *Classical Landscape*, pp. 128–32, for a comparison of Athens, with its unique relations between town and country, village and state, and other Greek democracies with different settlement patterns and different relations between the countryside and the political centre – notably Thasos, where 'the democratic town virtually ignored the people of the countryside' (p. 132).

28. Osborne, *Demos*, esp. Chapter 2. Another recent and exhaustive study of the Attic demes, David Whitehead's *The Demes of Attica: 508/7 – ca. 250 BC* (Princeton: Princeton University Press, 1986), while it takes issue with Osborne on certain points, is in agreement on those points that are of major concern to us here: the settlement pattern (Whitehead, p. 9 n. 27); the association of the demes with existing villages (about which more in a moment); and, in Whitehead's own words, on 'most of the broader aspects of the deme/polis relationship' (p. xv).

29.Osborne, *Demos*, p. 41.

30. Georges Duby, *Rural Economy and Country Life in the Medieval West*, trans. Cynthia Postan (Columbia SC: University of South Carolina Press, 1976), pp. 5–6.

31. M.M. Postan, *The Medieval Economy and Society: An Economic History of Britain in the Middle Ages* (Harmondsworth: Penguin Books, 1975), pp. 123–4.

32. See above, p. 55.

33. Teodor Shanin, 'Peasantry as a Political Factor', in *Peasants and Peasant Societies*, ed. T. Shanin (Harmondsworth: Penguin Books, 1971), p. 244.

34. See Osborne, esp. Chapters 2–4, 7 and 9.

35. On the relationship between demes and pre-existing villages, the size of demes, etc., see Osborne, pp. 42–5. Both Osborne and Whitehead (pp. 23–30) emphasize the 'natural' character of the deme system, its 'organic' growth out of traditional village life, questioning the extent to which even *city* demes were artificially created and stressing that the *asty* itself grew out of a collection of villages (Whitehead, pp. 25–7). Whitehead suggests, too, (following Wesley Thompson) that the establishment of the deme network by Cleisthenes may not have been the outcome of an elaborate cartographic survey to fix territorial boundaries but may have been simply the 'natural' result of an ordinance that every man must register in his home village, leaving it to the people concerned to determine which centre was the appropriate one (pp. 29–30). See also Antony Andrewes, 'Cleisthenes' Reform Bill', *Classical Quarterly* 27 (1977), pp. 241–8. One cannot help but note here the contrast between the Attic system of registration in a village for the purpose of claiming the rights of citizenship, and village-registration in other societies where the reward of registration was the obligation to pay tax to a central authority. Whitehead also concludes that, although the evidence is sparse, the likelihood is that people generally tended to remain in their ancestral demes (pp. 353–7). Osborne, too, stresses that citizens generally retained strong links with their ancestral demes (Chapter 3, and p. 225 n. 90).

36. Osborne, *Demos*, p. 189.

37. Osborne suggests that the rich, who might own property in the *asty* as well as in the countryside, 'saw the whole polis as their field of activity, while those less well-off were also less mobile' (*Demos*, p. 87).

38. Ibid., pp. 84–5.

39. Ibid., p. 91.

40. Ibid., p. 184.

41. Finley, *The Ancient Economy* (Berkeley and Los Angeles: University of California Press, 1973), p. 131.

42. See ibid., p. 123.

43. Ibid., p. 133.

44. S.C. Humphreys, *Anthropology and the Greeks* (London: Routledge and Kegan Paul, 1978), p. 131.

45. Ibid., p. 133. The argument that no clear division of interest existed between country-folk and town-dwellers runs counter to the view that an opposition between the interests of Athens and the Piraeus, on the one hand, and the Attic *chōra*, on the other, was reflected in different attitudes toward war during the Peloponnesian War, when the city population is supposed to have been more inclined to war. This opposition, however, must be put in perspective. As R.J. Hopper has argued, 'Such a division between the interests of Attica, and the interests of Athens and the Piraeus, did arise when, at the beginning of the Peloponnesian War, the inhabitants of Attica were withdrawn within the walls as a matter of strategy, and a divided attitude to the war seemed to arise. ... It would probably be wrong to accept too readily the idea of such a clear division, one to a considerable extent based on political ideas' *Trade and Industry in Classical Greece* (London: Thames and Hudson, 1979), p. 148. Hopper goes on to emphasize the difficulty of drawing a line between town and country, especially when farmers seem to have lived in country towns and villages, or in the city itself and its immediate surroundings, rather than scattered throughout the countryside. 'One is reminded,' he concludes, 'of those curious fragments of *rus in urbe* which in Athens today exist mixed up with the suburbs, and even the industrial suburbs (they are, for example, found on the line of the ancient Long Walls, between Athens and the Piraeus, not far from the electric railway and the

main road to the Piraeus). There was no clear or profound dividing line between townsman and countryman, non-cultivator and cultivator, even in spirit and interest.' (p. 152)

46. Osborne, *Demos*, p. 185.

47. Ibid., p. 183.

48. Humphreys, p. 134.

49. Osborne, in *Classical Landscape*, points out that 'Archaeology knows no markets in the whole territory of Athens outside Athens itself, the port of the Peiraieus, and Sounion.' (p. 108) 'As long as the political organization made it unattractive to leave the villages, the agrarian structure remained wedded to subsistence strategies. Although the Peiraieus offered a new concept in exchange, it is notable that markets are one facility that the large villages of Attica do not pride themselves on possessing. ... The villages had "agoras", but these seem rarely to have been more than political meeting places. ... The services developed in the countryside are more manifestations of the independence of the local community than means of integrating that community with a wider exchange network. Theatres, gymnasia, religious buildings and forts are the monumental additions to the villages during the classical period, conspicuously displaying civic pride and self-sufficiency.' (p. 130) 'What is distinct about the Greek city is best revealed by the contrast between that city and the cities of the Roman, mediaeval, and early modern periods. The Greek city is not just a town, it cannot be divorced from its countryside. By the Roman period, this was no longer true even in Greece itself. By the later Roman era the countryside ran itself almost independently of the town: village markets obviated the need for travel to the town to exchange goods; men thought of themselves as from a village rather than from a city and recorded villages as their places of origin; village and city politics had little or nothing to do with each other. The later Roman city foreshadows the enclosed mediaeval city of which Pirenne has written, "Once outside the gates and the moat we are in another world, or more exactly, in the domain of another law".' (pp. 193–4)

50. See ibid., pp. 22 and 108–10. Osborne remarks on the 'limited place' of luxury goods even in the properties of wealthy landowners, despite their role as prestige items for the urban rich. It would probably be safe to assume, too, that items such as clothing (which does seem to figure prominently in the wealth of rich Athenians like Alcibiades) were typically produced by domestic servants. Fine pottery, one luxury item produced for the market of which there is ample evidence, turns out, according to Osborne, to have been of 'trivial economic importance' (p. 109).

51. It has been suggested that Greek civilization was the first in which slaves *could* be used in primary production, because unlike other ancient civilizations, it did not require the kind of close cooperation and communal solidarity demanded by the public works projects, notably control of the water supply and irrigation systems, which were the basis of agriculture in 'Oriental' societies. See A.D. Winspear, *The Genesis of Plato's Thought* (Montreal: Harvest House, 1974), pp. 14 ff. Winspear argues that in such societies, 'everyone who took part in the process of primary production, namely agriculture, must be a member of the communal society, alert and responsive to its sanctions. The whole system of control of the water supply, its use as needed for cultivation, was much too delicate to be entrusted to slave labour.' (p. 14) Whatever merits this argument may have, it fails to take into account the other side of the coin. A corollary of the uniquely Greek pattern of agricultural property and production, without the elaborate communal projects or the large-scale production of the river valleys, was the eventual development of the smallholders' regime which placed its own limits on the nature and scale of agricultural exploitation.

52. See Finley, *Ancient Economy*, Chapter V, esp. pp. 138–41, for a discussion of the limits on production for the market, the 'inelasticity' of the citizen-peasants as a market for urban production, and the generally 'negligible' contribution of manufactures to the 'ancient economy', even in those cities, like Athens, where external trade played a relatively significant role (though not nearly as significant as the exponents of a 'bourgeois Athens' have been prone to suggest).

53. Willetts, pp. 99–101.

54. Duby, pp. 220–21.

55. Cf. Oswyn Murray, *Early Greece*, p. 169. Murray points out that the subordination of Spartan women to the male ethos is dramatically illustrated by marriage customs: for example, a man could 'lend' his wife to another on the suggestion of either man involved, 'showing the dominance of the relation between the two men'; the marriage ceremony involved a ritual seizure of the woman, who had her head shaved and was required to dress as a man while she awaited the bridegroom; and so on.

56. See, for example, Monique Saliou, 'The Processes of Women's Subordination in Primitive and Archaic Greece', in S. Coontz and P. Henderson, eds, *Women's Work, Men's Property: The Origins of Gender and Class* (London: Verso Books, 1986), pp. 169–206. Although this is an illuminating discussion of cultural and ideological developments, the underlying account of Greek history must be approached with a certain caution – among other things, because there may be a little too much of 'l'Athènes bourgeoise' in the chronology, describing archaic Greece as a period during which the development of trade and urbanization produced a class of tradesmen to rival the aristocracy, giving rise to tyranny, etc. (p. 173). See also J.P. Gould, 'Law, Custom, and Myth: Aspects of the Social Position of Women in Classical Athens', *JHS* 100 (1980), pp. 38–59. The position of women in Athenian society, as expressed in laws, mythology, and the attitudes of men, is here described as ambiguous, subjecting them to complete dependence while regarding them with 'obsessive fear and revulsion' (p. 55), perhaps in recognition of their power, especially in the transmission of inheritance. A general treatment of the condition of Greek women can be found in Sarah Pomeroy, *Goddesses, Whores, Wives, and Slaves: Women in Classical Antiquity* (New York: Schocken Books, 1975).

57. On the peasant household as 'both an economic unit and a home', see Eric Wolf, *Peasants* (Englewood Cliffs, N.J.: Prentice-Hall, 1966), p. 13.

58. G.E.M. de Ste Croix, *The Class Struggle in the Ancient Greek World* (London: Duckworth, and Ithaca: Cornell University Press, 1981), p. 102.

59. Aristotle, for example, although he would exclude even working farmers from citizenship in his ideal state, makes middling farmers the backbone of his 'best practicable polis' in the *Politics* – though the principal virtue of such farmers seems to be their limited capacity to participate in politics. Their preoccupation with earning a livelihood leaves them little leisure for regular assemblies, and infrequent assemblies are all to the good for Aristotle, as for others of oligarchic persuasion. Cf. L.B. Carter, *The Quiet Athenian* (Oxford: Clarendon Press, 1986), esp. Chapter 4. Carter, in his illuminating discussion of the varieties of 'quietism' which affected Athenian political life, is perhaps too neglectful of the *village* and its importance in Athenian politics, particularly for the peasant farmer, which Robin Osborne has so persuasively demonstrated in his two important books. Neither of these books had appeared when Carter presented the doctoral dissertation (1982) on which his book is based.

60. Chester Starr, *The Roman Empire, 27BC–AD476: A Study in Survival* (New York and Oxford: Oxford University Press, 1982), p. 4.

61. Peter Garnsey and Richard Saller, *The Roman Empire: Economy, Society and Culture* (London: Duckworth, 1987), p. 194.

62. Ibid., p. 56.

Chapter IV

1. Eric Wolf, 'On Peasant Rebellions', in T. Shanin, ed., *Peasants and Peasant Societies* (Harmondsworth: Penguin Books, 1971), p. 272.

2. Robin Osborne, *Demos: The Discovery of Classical Attika* (Cambridge: Cambridge University Press, 1985), p. 142. In his more recent book, *Classical Landscape with Figures: The Ancient Greek City and its Countryside* (London: George Philip, 1987), Osborne writes of the 'concealment of agriculture', remarking on the paradox that 'On the

one hand the productive countryside was of fundamental importance. On the other the arts and literature of Classical Greece largely ignore it.' (p. 16) The book as a whole is devoted to demonstrating how completely the social life of Greek cities was determined by the countryside and 'the peasant basis of society' (p. 13). And nowhere was this more true than in Athens, with its 'radical recognition of the countryside as integral to the political machine of the city'. (p. 130). In other words, the 'peasant basis of society', and a peasant 'culture', may have been invisible because they were ubiquitous.

3. Rodney Hilton, *Bond Men Made Free: Medieval Peasant Movements and the English Rising of 1381* (London: Temple Smith, 1973), p. 235.

4. M.I. Finley, *The Ancient Economy* (Berkeley and Los Angeles: University of California Press, 1973), p. 28.

5. Jean-Pierre Vernant, *Myth and Society in Ancient Greece* (Sussex: Harvester Press, and New Jersey: Humanities Press, 1980), trans. Janet Lloyd, pp. 81–2.

6. Cf. Walter Beringer, 'Freedom, Family, and Citizenship in Early Greece', *The Craft of the Ancient Historian: Essays in Honor of Chester G. Starr*, ed. John W. Eadie and Josiah Ober (University Press of America, 1985), p. 42.

7. Ibid., p. 46. This interpretation may be supported by the etymology which has been proposed for *eleutheros*, tracing it to the Indo-European root *leudho- (the same root as for the German *Leute*), from which e-leutho-s > eleutheros (on the analogy, for example, of fovos > foveros), producing 'of or belonging to the people'.

8. Ibid., pp. 48–9.

9. Cf. ibid, p. 41.

10. See ibid., pp. 51–2, where it is suggested that there is nothing metaphorical or imprecise about Aristotle's usage of the verb *douleuein* in the *Constitution of Athens* to describe the condition of the peasants liberated by Solon, as long as we understand that words of the root *doul-* referred not to chattel slavery but to 'non-belongingness', 'rightlessness', and 'subjectedness'.

11. *Politics* 1291b, 1310a, 1317a–b.

12. It is worth noting that in Rome, too, 'the relation between king and people is considered to be analogous to the relation between master and slaves. Consequently monarchy is called dominatio; and subjection to monarchy servitus.' Ch. Wirszubski, *Libertas as a Political Idea at Rome During the Late Republic and Early Principate* (Cambridge: Cambridge University Press, 1950), p. 5. On similar principles, a *populus liber*, an autonomous people or state, is opposed to a *populus stipendiarius*, a people subject to tribute (ibid., p. 4).

13. See, for example, the following passage from Didymus' commentary on the *Philippics* of Demosthenes, in which Philochorus is quoted as saying (about the Athenian rejection of a peace proposal in 392/1. '[But] the Athenians did not accept it because there had been written in it that the Greeks who in Asia were living should all in the king's household be accounted members.' Phillip Harding, ed. and trans., *Translated Documents from Greece and Rome, Vol. 2: From the End of the Peloponnesian War to the Battle of Ipsius* (Cambridge: Cambridge University Press, 1985), p. 37.

14. Hilton, p. 225.

15. See, for example, M.I. Finley, 'Technical Innovation and Economic Progress in the Ancient World', in *Economy and Society in Ancient Greece* (London: Chatto and Windus, 1981), p. 194: 'The pejorative judgments of ancient writers about labour, and specifically about the labour of the artisan, and of anyone who works *for* another, are too continuous, numerous, and unanimous, too wrapped up in discussions of every aspect of ancient life, to be dismissed as empty rhetoric.'

16. See above, p. 8, for the full quotation from Adam Ferguson.

17. For arguments that attach a great deal of significance to this conceptual lack, see Finley, *Ancient Economy*, p. 81; J.-P. Vernant, *Mythe et pensée chez les Grecs* (Paris: Maspero, 1974) II, pp. 16 ff; and M.M. Austin and P. Vidal-Naquet, *Economic and Social History of Ancient Greece: An Introduction* (London: B.T. Batsford, 1977), p. 14. Vernant, who elaborates this argument in greater detail than the others, remarks on the absence in Greek of a term which is both specific and general (pp. 17–18) – specific in the sense that it does not refer comprehensively to 'toutes les activités qui exigent un effort

pénible, pas seulement aux tâches productrices de valeurs socialement utiles' (p. 16); and general in the sense that it covers a variety of activities without distinguishing among their specific objects or practices.

18. Raymond Williams, *Keywords* (Glasgow: Fontana, 1976), p. 146. Williams writes: 'From C17, except in the special use for childbirth, *labour* gradually lost its habitual association with pain, though the general and applied senses of difficulty were still strong. The sense of *labour* as a general social activity came through more clearly, and with a more distinct sense of abstraction.'

19. See A.W.H. Adkins, *Moral Values and Political Behaviour in Ancient Greece* (London: Chatto and Windus, 1972), pp. 24 ff.

20. John Locke, *Some Considerations on the Lowering of Interest* in *Works*, 9th edn (London: Longmans et al., IV, 71. For a discussion of the 'turfs' passage, see Neal Wood, *John Locke and Agrarian Capitalism* (Berkeley: University of California Press, 1984), pp. 62 and 86–8. Locke's views are examined in the context of the 'productive' mentality associated with agricultural 'improvement' and the development of agrarian capitalism.

21. See Alison Burford, *Craftsmen in Greek and Roman Society* (London: Thames and Hudson, 1972), p. 212. Burford regards this assumption of personal responsibility for the craftsman's work as 'symptomatic of the new sense of individualism which manifested itself during the seventh century BC, and which from then on was one of the characteristics which distinguished the Greeks most sharply from the peoples of the ancient Near East.... During the seventh century BC craftsmen had ceased to be anonymous; never again in antiquity did there occur so momentous an alteration in their status or in their thinking on the subject.' This new status did not guarantee the elevation of craftsmen to the status of full citizens; and even in democracy, craftsmen who were metics or slaves were excluded. At the same time, the recognition of craftsmen as self-active individuals was surely a necessary condition of their citizenship, and citizenship, in turn, could only enhance the status of craftsmen as free and responsible, rather than servile and dependent, individuals.

22. For example, all three versions of the 'Agreement of the People' exclude some categories of 'dependent' workers (there is no question here of slaves) from the franchise, and at least one excludes all wage-earners explicitly. All three exclude 'servants', a very large category in early modern England. An important recent study suggests that 'In early modern England, the word had a doubly broadened set of meanings. The first, specific use was to denote all those who worked for one master, and were maintained by that master. ... The second early modern meaning of "servant" extended still further to include all those who worked for others. Used in this general sense, "servant" comprised both servants, in the specific sense of the word, and day-labourers.' Ann Kussmaul, *Servants in Husbandry in Early Modern England* (Cambridge: Cambridge University Press, 1981), pp. 5–6. Either of these usages would have accounted for a substantial portion of free Englishmen (not to mention women), who would have been excluded from the Leveller franchise.

23. For an illuminating discussion of *isonomia* and its association with the development of Athenian democracy, see Martin Ostwald, *Nomos and the Beginnings of the Athenian Democracy* (Oxford: Clarendon Press, 1969), especially pp. 137–60. Ostwald suggests that *isonomia* may have been the slogan with which Cleisthenes won over the common people, the principle that most precisely defines his reforms which created 'a balanced form of government by giving all citizens equally the right to participate in the political life of the state and by eliminating the political monopoly which birth and wealth had enjoyed so far' (p. 154). It is also worth considering Ostwald's persuasive argument that Cleisthenes' reforms may have been the occasion for the replacement of *thesmos* by *nomos* as the principal term for statutory law in Athens. This linguistic change, which may have been the result of a deliberate act by Cleisthenes himself, is significant, argues Ostwald, because it marks a transformation in the conception of law from something 'imposed upon a people by a lawgiver legislating for it' to 'the expression of what the people as a whole regard as a valid and binding norm' (p. 55). 'If ἰσονομία literally means "equality of νόμος", that is if the term signifies that what is regarded as valid and binding is so regarded by and for all classes of society, no moment

in Athenian history seems to be more appropriate for the substitution of νόμος for θεσμός than the period immediately preceding and immediately following the reforms of Cleisthenes', which 'recognized as νόμος for the people what had previously been νόμος for the nobility only, namely, the making of important political decisions' (p. 159). 'And if the Cleisthenean reforms do indeed provide the background for the change from θεσμός to νόμος, it explains also why, in preference to other possible terms for "statute", the Athenians adopted νόμος, the most democratic word for "law" in any language' (p. 160).

It might be added that a redefinition of *nomos* is another important aspect of Plato's philosophical project, and that the conception of law outlined especially in the *Statesman* and the *Laws* has much more in common with *thesmos*, the law as imposed from above, than with *nomos* as a democratic concept referring only to norms which the people themselves have 'ratified and acknowledged to be valid and binding' (Ostwald, p. 55).

24. For this characterization of the Mycenaean palace-civilization (which relies heavily on L.R. Palmer), its relation to other Indo-European societies, and the distinctions between these cases and the riverine 'hydraulic' kingdoms of the ancient Near East, see Jean-Pierre Vernant, *Les origines de la pensée grecque*, 3rd edn (Presses Universitaires de France, 1975), Chapter 2, esp. pp. 19–22 and 26–7.

25. Jacques Gernet, 'Social History and the Evolution of Ideas in China and Greece from the Sixth to the Second Centuries BC' (this article consists of two parallel essays by Gernet and Jean-Pierre Vernant) in Vernant, *Myth and Society in Ancient Greece*, p. 76.

26. Mencius, in Arthur Waley, *Three Ways of Thought in Ancient China* (Garden City: Doubleday Anchor, n.d.), p. 140.

27. M.I. Finley, 'Technical Innovation and Economic Progress in the Ancient World', in *Economy and Society in Ancient Greece* (London: Chatto and Windus, 1981), p. 176.

28. Georges Duby, *The Growth of the European Economy: Warriors and Peasants from the Seventh to the Twelfth Century* (Ithaca: Cornell University Press, 1974), p. 5.

29. Finley, 'Technical Innovation ...', pp. 177–8. It is interesting to note, incidentally, that 'the technology available to the ancient Greeks that was used in extracting stone and metals was basically identical to that which continued to be employed until the nineteenth century and the introduction of explosives' (Osborne, *Classical Landscape*, p. 75).

30. See Lynn White Jr, *Medieval Technology and Social Change* (Oxford: Oxford University Press, 1962), p. 82.

31. It should be stressed immediately, and kept in mind in what follows, that to speak of the 'constraints' of the peasant regime is not to succumb to the misconception that 'farming to be successful must be capital-intensive', a notion recently attacked in connection with a discussion of agricultural productivity in the Roman Empire: Peter Garnsey and Richard Saller, *The Roman Empire: Economy, Society and Culture* (London: Duckworth, 1987), p. 77. As Garnsey and Saller point out, 'A sophisticated technology is not in fact required to work much of the land in the Mediterranean basin. Heavy machinery is unnecessary and sometimes harmful in semi-arid and arid zones, as is being painfully discovered at the present time in regions as far apart as south Italy, Portugal and the Middle East. On a tiny property a hoe or mattock may be sufficient for the purpose in hand. ...' A distinction must certainly be made (p. 52) between expanded *output* and higher *productivity* (through capital investment and economies of scale). But if successful farming and the achievement of maximum output, especially on a small peasant holding, may actually be *impeded* by sophisticated technology, we are even more entitled to speak of 'constraints', without any misconceived assumptions about the irrationality of peasant conservatism.

32. Pierre Dockès, *Medieval Slavery and Liberation*, trans. Arthur Goldhammer (London: Methuen, 1982), p. 176.

33. Ibid., p. 181.

34. M.M. Postan, 'Why Was Science Backward in the Middle Ages?' in *Essays on Medieval Agriculture and General Problems of the Medieval Economy* (Cambridge: Cambridge University Press, 1973), p. 85.

35. Ibid., pp. 83–4.

36. Robert Brenner, 'The Agrarian Roots of European Capitalism', in *The Brenner*

Debate: Agrarian Class Structure and Economic Development in Pre-Industrial Europe, ed. T.H. Aston and C.H.E. Philpin (Cambridge: Cambridge University Press, 1985), p. 233.

37. Ibid., pp. 214-15.
38. Ibid., pp. 313-14.
39. Ibid., pp. 314-15.
40. Marshall Sahlins, *Stone Age Economics* (London: Tavistock Publications, 1974), p. 87.
41. See M.I. Finley, 'Technical Innovation and Economic Progress in the Ancient World', p. 188, on the predominance of the 'rentier psychology' in the ancient world as a factor inhibiting technical innovation; and *Ancient Economy*, p. 144, for some observations on the 'acquisitive but not productive' mentality.
42. Max Weber, *Agrarverhältnisse im Altertum* in *Gesammelte Aufsätze zur Sozial und Wirtschaftsgeschichte* (Tübingen: Verlag von J.C.B. Mohr [Paul Siebeck], 1924), p. 144; translated as *The Agrarian Sociology of Ancient Civilizations* (London: Verso, 1988).
43. Osborne suggests other ways in which 'social requirements' constrained technological resources, showing how the mutually reinforcing adherence to local resources and the strength of local feeling associated with the political importance of the deme placed limits on technical innovation in building projects, for example, as the use of local labour gave 'little scope or incentive for technological developments' (*Demos*, pp. 108-10).
44. See Eric Havelock, *The Literate Revolution in Greece and Its Cultural Consequences* (Princeton: Princeton University Press, 1982), passim., esp. Chapter 4.
45. Havelock. p. 66.
46. See, for example, Jack Goody and Ian Watt, 'The Consequences of Literacy', in ed. Jack Goody, *Literacy in Traditional Societies* (Cambridge: Cambridge University Press, 1968).
47. Havelock, passim, e.g. p. 83; Murray, pp. 95-6.
48. Martin Bernal, *Black Athena: The Afroasiatic Roots of Classical Civilization* (London: Free Association Books, 1987), pp. 34-5, 86-7, 393-9, 427-33.
49. See, for example, Anthony Snodgrass, *Archaic Greece*, Berkeley and Los Angeles: University of California Press, 1980), pp. 78-84.
50. Beringer, p. 50.
51. Cf. Werner Jaeger, *Paedeia*, 2nd edn (New York: Oxford University Press, 1945), vol. 1, p. 34.
52. Finley credits Hesiod with expressing a wholly new conception of freedom, as in *Works and Days* he 'presumed freely to criticize his betters'. 'Between Slavery and Freedom', in *Economy and Society*, p. 129. Similarly, argues Finley, a new attitude toward the gods is reflected in another work attributed to Hesiod, the *Theogony* (though as Finley says, the important thing is not whether the attribution is correct but that the two works are approximately contemporary), departing radically from the religious doctrines of the Near East in which 'man was created for the sole and specific purposes of serving the gods'. In Hesiod, there already appears a tendency to grant autonomy to human interests and to describe gods and the universe in relation to them.
53. Havelock, e.g., pp. 9-11, 144-9.
54. Richard Garner, in *Law and Society in Classical Athens* (London: Croom Helm, 1987), speaks of 'the traditional distrust in writing' which was only gradually overcome in the course of the fourth century BC, and of the 'marginal position of writing' which was still, paradoxically, reflected in early Greek literature, where 'devious writings' and 'dangerous documents' appear as dramatic themes – messengers bearing orders for their own death, fatal forged notes, etc. In classical Athens, he writes, 'written agreements were apparently rare until the mid-fourth century and are simply not referred to in early speeches, even when the cases turn on points of fact in matters of finance, marriage and adoption. As a result, the indispensable proof for contracts and agreements was not written evidence but rather witnesses.' (p. 137)

Index

Note: page numbers with *n* refer to footnotes

Printed in the United States
by Baker & Taylor Publisher Services